Temptation in Eden

Lucas Cranach's *Adam and Eve*

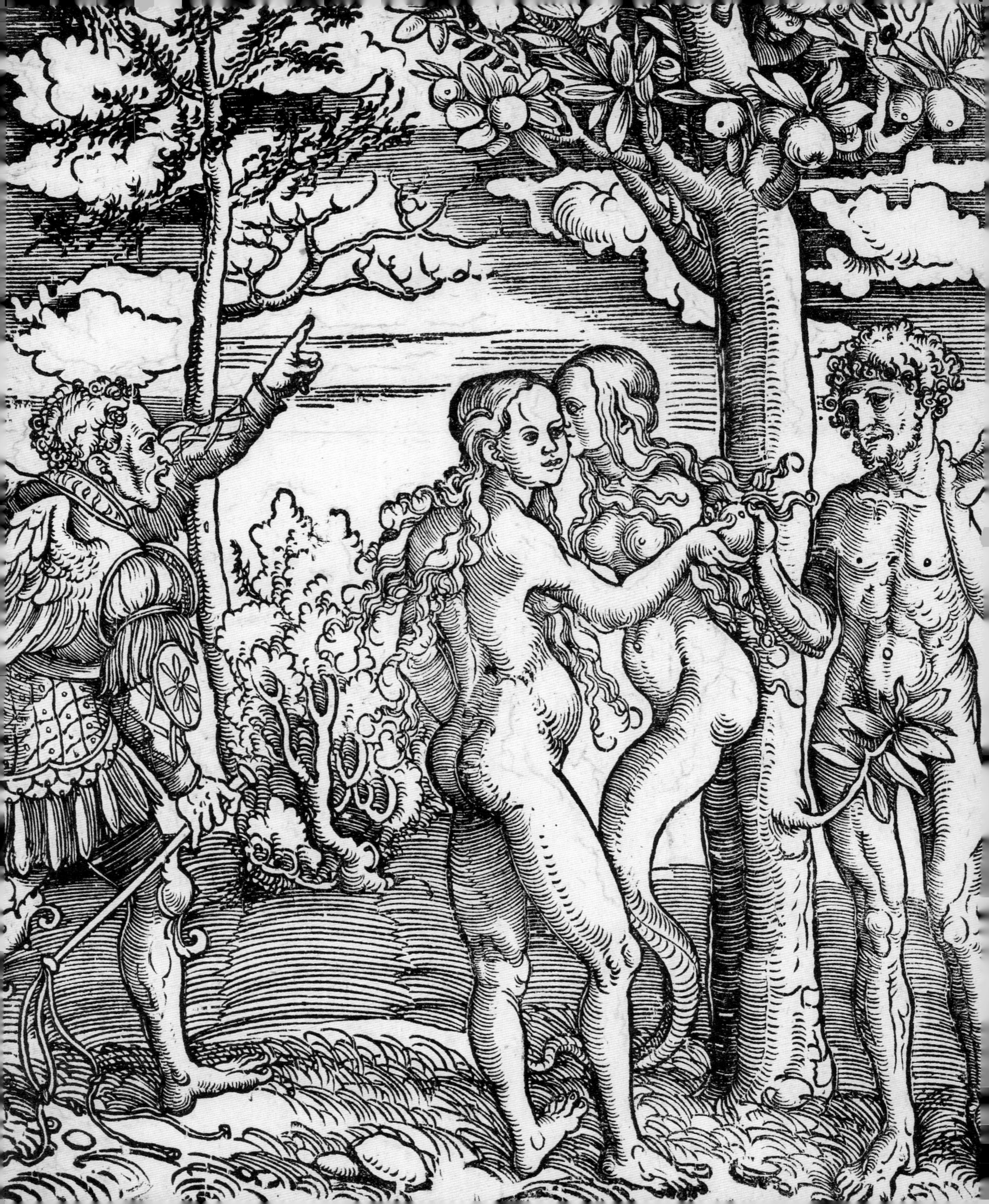

Temptation in Eden

Lucas Cranach's *Adam and Eve*

Edited by Caroline Campbell

CONTRIBUTIONS BY

Stephanie Buck, Caroline Campbell,
Susan Foister, Gunnar Heydenreich
& Anne Woollett

Courtauld Institute of Art Gallery
IN ASSOCIATION WITH
PAUL HOLBERTON PUBLISHING
LONDON

First published 2007 to accompany the exhibition
Temptation in Eden: Lucas Cranach's Adam and Eve
at the Courtauld Institute of Art Gallery
Somerset House, London, 21 June 2007–23 September 2007

This exhibition is supported by Apax Partners, Columbia Foundation, The Doris Pacey Charitable Foundation, The German Embassy London (H.E. the Ambassador Wolfgang Ischinger), Mr & Mrs Hughes Lepic, The Kilfinan Trust and The Mallinckrodt Foundation.

The Courtauld Institute of Art Gallery is supported with funds from the Arts and Humanities Research Council (AHRC).

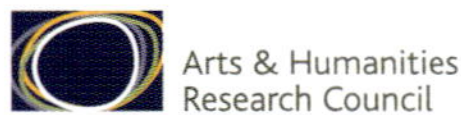

ISBN 9781903470541 HB
ISBN 9781903470565 PB

British Library Cataloguing in Publication Data
A catalogue record for this book is available from the British Library

Produced by Paul Holberton publishing,
89 Borough High Street, London SE1 1NL
www.paul-holberton.net

Designed by Philip Lewis

Origination and printing by Graphic Studio, Bussolengo, Verona, Italy

COVER IMAGE: Detail, Lucas Cranach, *Adam and Eve*, cat. 1
BACK COVER: Lucas Cranach, *A Dead Hind*, cat. 6

Contents

Foreword

I am delighted that the Courtauld Institute of Art Gallery is holding this wonderful exhibition of German Renaissance art. It was with great pleasure that I accepted the invitation to become Patron of the Lucas Cranach Supporters' Circle, whose generosity has made this outstanding exhibition possible.

Temptation in Eden: Lucas Cranach's Adam and Eve brings together for the very first time some of Lucas Cranach's most mature works, illuminating their extraordinary unity of vision and execution. This magical exhibition provides us with a key to the world of this exquisite artist, and highlights his special place in the history of European art.

I hope that these marvellous paintings, drawings and prints inspire further interest in Cranach, one of the greatest German painters of the sixteenth century. May this unique exhibition give joy to a great many people!

WOLFGANG ISCHINGER
German Ambassador to the Court of St James's

Director's Foreword

By any account Lucas Cranach the Elder is among the greatest artistic figures of sixteenth-century Germany. However, despite the best efforts of recent generations of scholars, Cranach remains under-appreciated outside Germany, and *Temptation in Eden: Lucas Cranach's Adam and Eve* is the first exhibition devoted to him in England. It seeks to understand the qualities which made Cranach so famous in his lifetime, and which still entrance modern viewers. Being an expeditious painter did not exclude him from being a very talented one. He was able to invent new pictorial narratives and iconographies, indebted to the innovative intellectual developments of Protestant theology and humanism, as well as to revitalise well-established genres including traditional biblical subjects. These aspects of Cranach's artistic personality are well represented in the Courtauld Institute's *Adam and Eve*, the focus of this exhibition. Dating from 1526, this painting is a very fine example of the mature style which Cranach perfected in Wittenberg, reflecting the inspiration he derived from involvement in the life of the Saxon court, the civic élite, and the city's university. In Eve's temptation of Adam Cranach found a subject ideally suited to his outstanding gifts as a portrayer of landscape, animals and the female nude, and to which neither Protestant nor Catholic theologians could object.

Uniquely in Britain the Courtauld encompasses specialist research and teaching, a gallery and a conservation department, each of international stature. This exhibition is the product of collaboration between staff from all these areas of the Courtauld's activity. Professor Joseph Koerner provided much good advice to Caroline Campbell, Schroder Foundation Curator of Paintings, who devised the project. She has subsequently been joined as curator of the exhibition by Stephanie Buck, our recently appointed Curator of Drawings. *Temptation in Eden* is profoundly indebted to the pioneering work of the Conservation and Technology Department in the development of technical art history, and in particular the late Caroline Villers, to whose memory this exhibition is dedicated. The two co-curators have worked extensively with members of this department (in particular Graeme Barraclough, the Gallery's Paintings Conservator, Robert Bruce-Gardner, Clare Richardson and Kate Stonor), who undertook a new examination of Cranach's *Adam and Eve* in preparation for the exhibition.

Exhibitions cannot happen without generous support, and it is with pleasure that I acknowledge the much-appreciated assistance of the exhibition sponsors: Apax Partners, the Columbia Foundation, The Doris Pacey Charitable Foundation, The German Embassy London (H.E. the Ambassador Wolfgang Ischinger), The Kilfinan Trust, Mr & Mrs Hughes Lepic and The Mallinckrodt Foundation. I would also like to thank the German Ambassador, His Excellency Wolfgang Ischinger, for kindly agreeing to be Patron of the Lucas Cranach Supporters' Circle.

DR DEBORAH SWALLOW
Märit Rausing Director, Courtauld Institute of Art

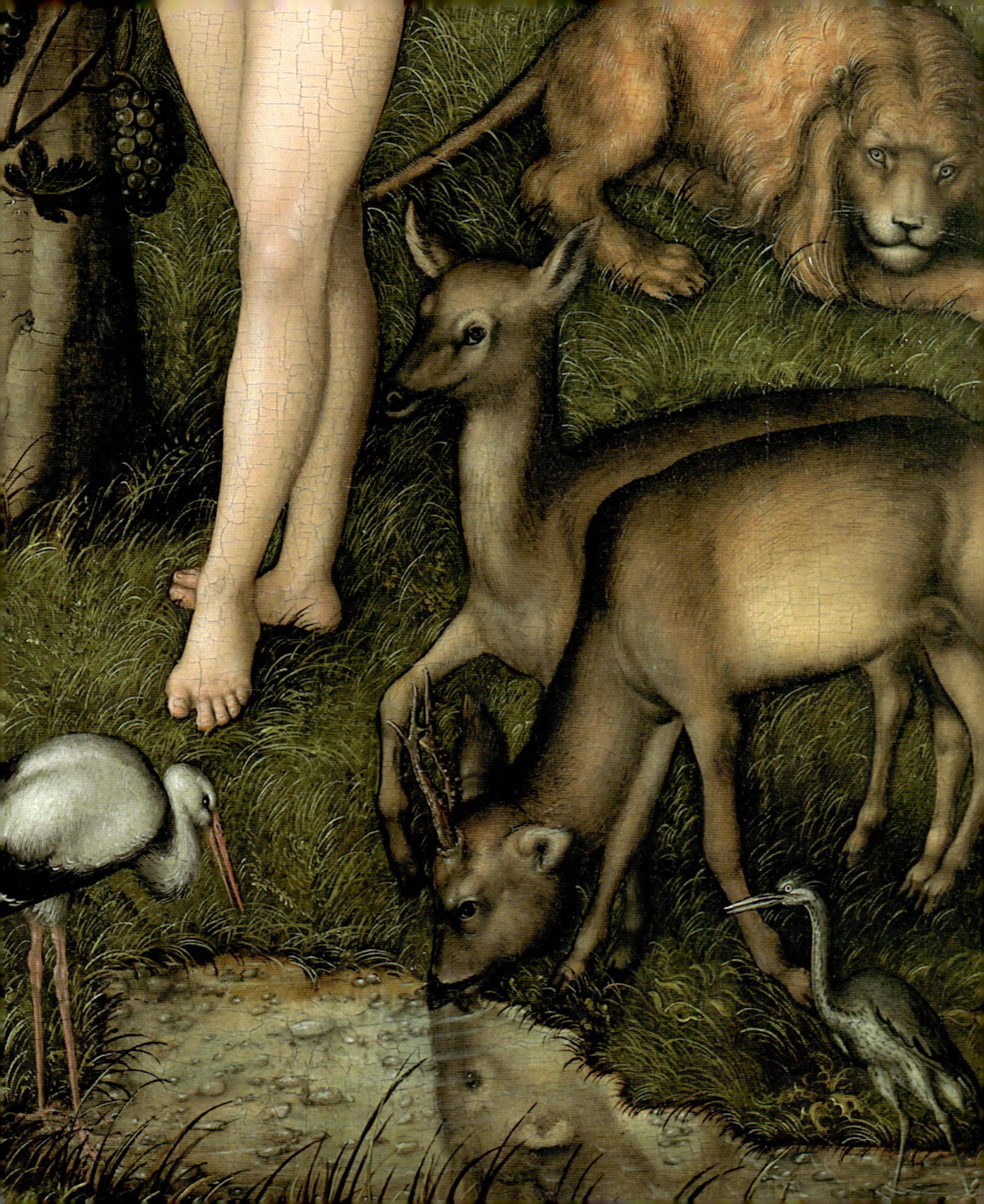

Acknowledgements

This exhibition would not have been possible without the generous loans and support from the following:

The Ashmolean Museum, Oxford
The British Library, London
The British Museum, London
The J. Paul Getty Museum, Los Angeles
Gemäldegalerie Alte Meister, Staatliche Kunstsammlungen Dresden
Kupferstichkabinett, Staatliche Museen zu Berlin
Kupferstichkabinett, Staatliche Kunstsammlungen Dresden
Musée du Louvre, Paris
The National Gallery, London
The Royal Collection, Her Majesty the Queen Elizabeth II

These important paintings, drawings and prints could not have been exhibited in London without the Government Indemnity Scheme and we extend our thanks to Gregory Eades and his colleagues.

The curators also wish to thank especially the external contributors to the catalogue, Susan Foister, Gunnar Heydenreich and Anne Woollett, as well as Yvonne Szafran, Uschi Payne, Paul Holberton and Philip Lewis, and members of the Courtauld Institute of Art Gallery staff, past and present. Research institutions and museums have been unfailingly supportive of our work, and we recognise the help of the Witt and Book Libraries at the Courtauld Institute, as well as the National Gallery, Warburg Institute and British Libraries.

We would also like to acknowledge the help of our supportive friends and colleagues:

Hazel Aitken, Scott Allan, Hein-Th. Schulze Altcappenberg, Karen Ashworth, Pamela Barr, Graeme Barraclough, Giulia Bartrum, Holm Bevers, Rachel Billinge, Julia Blanks, Sue Bond, Iris Brahms, Michael Brand, Lynne Brindley, Xanthe Brooke, Julian Brooks, Christopher Brown, Robert Bruce-Gardner, Aviva Burnstock, Peter Carey, Mary Ellen Cetra, Emma Chambers, Hugo Chapman, William Clarke, Ron Cobb, Patricia Collins, Paul Crossley, Louisa Dare, Emma Davidson, Kathleen Doyle, Albert Elen, Mark Evans, Chris Fischer, Andrea Fredericksen, Alexandra Gerstein, Geraldine Glynn, John Goldfinch, John Goodall, Antony Griffiths, Katy Hadwick, Colin Harrison, Emma Hayes, Kate Heard, Lee Hendrix, Mara Hofmann, Wolfgang Holler, Nicola Kennedy, Thomas Ketelsen, Joseph Koerner, Hanne Kolind Poulsen, Karin Kolb, John Lowden, Henri Loyrette, Neil MacGregor, Harald Marx, Mark McDonald, Susie Nash, Scott Nethersole, Barbara O'Connor, Natalia Owdziej, Simona Pizzi, Erwin Pokorny, Sue Pratt, Janice Reading, Achim Riether, Michael Roth, Clare Richardson, Andrew Robison, Angela Roche, Christian Rümelin, Amanda Sarroff, Charles Saumarez Smith, Karine Sauvignon, Peter Schade, Scott Schaefer, Claudia Schnitzer, Stephanie Schrader, Jennifer Scott, Joanna Selborne, Desmond Shawe-Taylor, Olaf Simon, Marika Spring, Kate Stonor, Margret Stuffmann, Cecilia Treves, Carel van Tuyll Van Serooskerken, Ernst Vegelin van Claerbergen, Lucy Whitaker, Jon Whiteley, Timothy Wilson, Barnaby Wright, Martin Wyld.

Lucas Cranach the Elder
(Kronach, around 1472–1553 Weimar)
Chronology of Life and Work

1472 4 October: Traditional date of the birth of Lucas Maler in Kronach, son of Hans Maler (Hans the painter). Cranach's surname comes from the town of his birth. His first paintings were probably made under the influence of his father.

Around 1502 Cranach lives and works in Vienna, where his circle includes the humanists Conrad Celtis and Johannes Cuspinian.

1504 Cranach begins to sign his works with the initials *LC*.

1505 14 April: Date of Cranach's first surviving payment as court painter to the Elector of Saxony, Frederick the Wise.

1508 6 January, Nuremberg: Elector Frederick of Saxony grants Cranach the Heraldic Letter, permitting him to bear a coat of arms (the winged serpent).

July–November: Cranach travels to the Netherlands. He visits the court of Margaret of Austria, Governor General of the Low Countries, and meets the Holy Roman Emperor Maximilian, as well as the future Emperor Charles V. He is back working in Wittenberg in May 1509.

16 December: Christian Scheurl delivers an address on the superiority of the sciences. This is published in October 1509 with a dedication to Cranach.

1509 Cranach's illustrated catalogue of the Elector's reliquary collection in the Schloss and Universitäts Kirche, Wittenberg, is published.

1512/13 Cranach marries Barbara Brengbier, daughter of a Gotha town councillor.

1513 Birth of his son Hans Cranach.

1513–15 Cranach and ten assistants work on the decoration of Hartenfels Castle, Torgau.

1515 Birth of Lucas Cranach the Younger.

Together with Dürer, Baldung, Burgkmair and others Cranach contributes drawings to the Emperor Maximilian's *Prayerbook*.

1518 Cranach purchases the 'Cranach-hof', no. 1 Schlossstrasse, Wittenberg.

1519 Cranach appointed town councillor of Wittenberg, a post he holds intermittently until 1544/45.

1520 December: Cranach granted the Electoral Apothecary Privilege.

1521 28 April: Luther writes to Cranach from Frankfurt, indicating that he will go into hiding. Appearance of the *Passional Christi und AntiChristi*, which Cranach illustrates for Luther.

1522 September: Appearance of the September Testament, Luther's earliest translation of the New Testament. It is illustrated with woodcuts by Cranach (see fig. 14).

1523 The deposed King Christian II of Denmark stays as a guest in one of Cranach's houses. Cranach operates a book-printing workshop with Christian Döring in Wittenberg (until 1525/26).

1524 Cranach accompanies the Elector Frederick to the Reichstag at Nuremberg. He is portrayed by Albrecht Dürer (fig. 1).

He works for the Cardinal (and Grand Master) Albrecht of Brandenberg, Archbishop of Mainz and Magdeburg (figs. 15 and 16), an opponent of Luther's.

1525 5 May: Death of the Elector Frederick. Cranach commences work for the new Elector, Johann the Steadfast.

13 June: Cranach is a witness at the marriage ceremony of Martin Luther and Katharina von Bora in Wittenberg. Cranach's wife was also present at the ceremony.

3 August: Cranach sends Elector Johann scale drawings for the tomb of Frederick the Wise.

1526 7 June: Cranach stands as godfather to Martin Luther's first son, Johannes.

Date of the Courtauld *Adam and Eve*.

1532 Death of Johann the Steadfast. Cranach is employed by his successor, Elector Johann Frederick the Magnanimous.

1537 9 October: Death of Cranach's elder son, Hans, in Bologna.

1537/38–1543/44 On several occasions, Cranach holds the office of Mayor of Wittenberg.

1540 Death of Cranach's wife, Barbara.

1547–50 Following Johann Frederick's defeat by the Holy Roman Emperor Charles V at the Battle of Mühlberg, Cranach loses temporarily the title of court painter and his annual salary.

1550 23 July: Cranach joins Johann Frederick in Augsburg. He remains in exile with the imprisoned Elector. He meets Titian, Charles V's painter of choice, and apparently produces a portrait of him.

1552 Cranach moves with Johann Frederick to Weimar. In November, he is once again appointed court painter, on condition that he will only serve Johann Frederick and his sons.

1553 16 October: Death of Lucas Cranach the Elder in Weimar, aged eighty-one. He is buried in St Jacob's Cemetery.

1586 27 January: Lucas Cranach the Younger is buried in Wittenberg city church.

The Artist known as Lucas Cranach

CAROLINE CAMPBELL

The artist whom we know as Lucas Cranach the Elder (fig. 1) was born in the small town of Kronach in Northern Franconia, from which he took his name. Very little is known for certain about Cranach's life until his early thirties – even what he was called. He may simply have been known as Lucas son of Hans the painter. He is said to have been born on 4 October 1472, yet his actual date of birth may have been as late as 1475. Cranach's early artistic training remains as elusive as the true date of his birth, although it is highly likely that he was apprenticed to his father Hans, and worked for some time in Kronach. Because of the lack of documentation, Cranach's *Wanderjahre* have been the subject of intense speculation, and a persistent tradition states that he visited Albrecht Dürer (1471–1528) in Nuremberg (see essay by Gunnar Heydenreich). His own work demonstrates clearly that he was familiar with Dürer's graphic work from an early date,[1] but the first firm proof of his existence can be found in Vienna in 1502.

Cranach probably spent less than two years in Vienna, but this period is of great significance for his career and development. His new confidence in his artistic identity can be seen in the fact that in Vienna Cranach first assumed the name by which he has been known ever since, and used these initials (LC) to sign his work. He was closely associated with a circle of humanist writers, notably Johannes Cuspinian, whom he painted with his wife in 1503 (Winterthur, Oskar Reinhart Collection; FR 6 and 7*), and designed woodcuts for the printer Winterburger. Cranach's painted work in Vienna is notable for the importance he placed on strong forms and outlines (seen, for example, in *The Stigmatisation of Saint Francis*, Vienna, Akademie der Bildenden Kunst; FR 3), and the dominant role of landscape in his compositions, including *The Crucifixion* (Munich, Alte Pinakothek; FR 5). Although his style would change radically, these qualities remained crucial to his work to the end of his artistic career.

The year 1505 witnessed the most significant event in Cranach's career. He was appointed court painter to Frederick the Wise, Elector of Saxony (1463–1525; see fig. 2). Unlike his immediate predecessor, the Italian painter and printmaker Jacopo de' Barbari (see cat. 22), Cranach remained almost without interruption in this position until he died. He moved to Wittenberg,

Fig. 1 Albrecht Dürer, *Portrait of Lucas Cranach the Elder*, 1524
Silverpoint on paper, 16.2 × 11 cm
Bayonne, Musée Bonnat

* FR + no. refers to the catalogue raisonné of Cranach's work by Friedländer and Rosenberg (see bibliography).

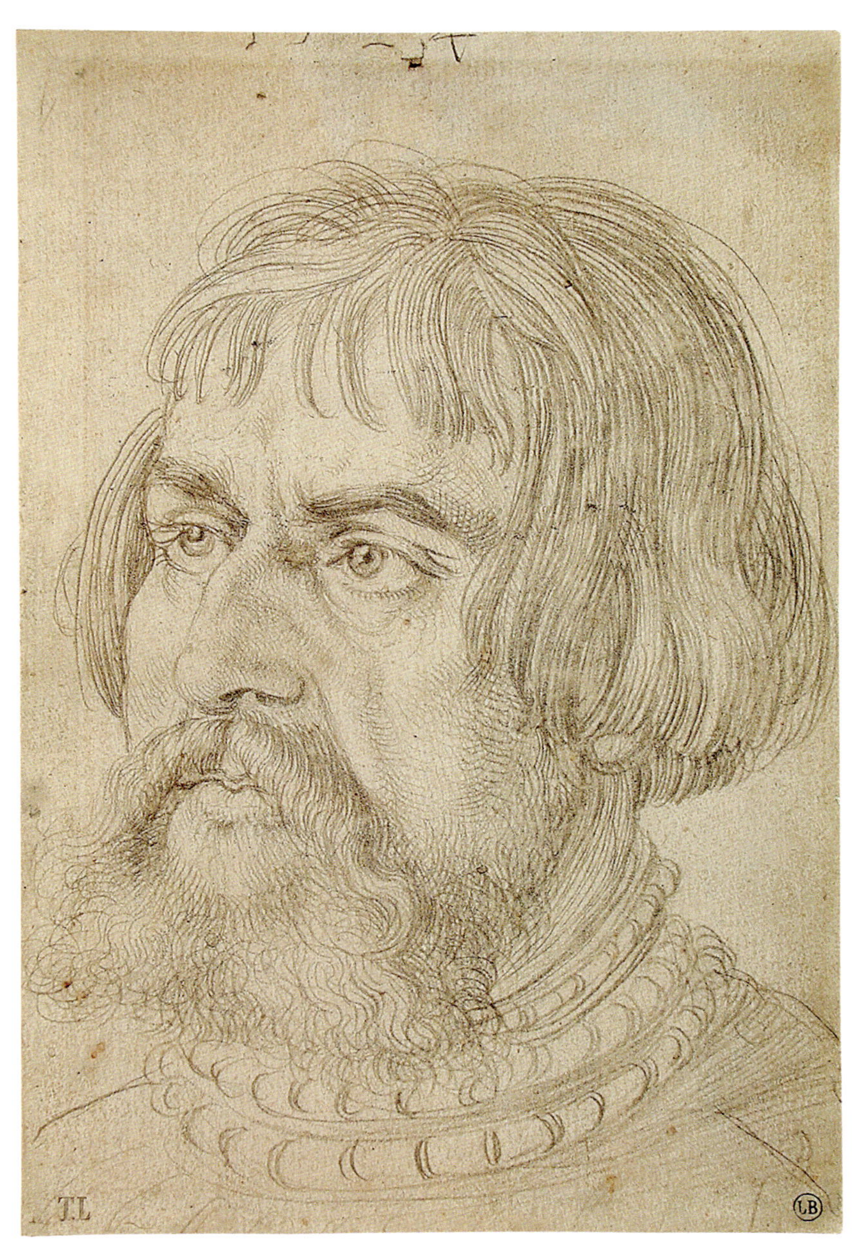

the Saxon city which was Frederick's principal seat, and began to make himself indispensable to his princely patron. Although the Elector and his successors always claimed a large portion of his time and production, Cranach seems at this point in his court service to have identified his artistic production (and his artistic self) almost exclusively with the Elector. The arms of Saxony and the Elector appear on practically all his production as a printmaker at this date, including the unusually large two-block woodcut *The Stag Hunt* (cat. 18); *Saint John Chrysostom* (cat. 16), Cranach's only non-portrait engraving; and the two-tone or chiaroscuro woodcut *Venus and Cupid* (cat. 15), on which Cranach seems to have deliberately falsified the date so that he could claim the invention of this novel printing technique. Such technical variety and innovation suggests that, even if these prints were not made directly for the Elector, Frederick was eager that the fact that Cranach was in his service and worked under his protection should be more widely known. Cranach's long employment at court accounts for his special interest and ability in depicting the hunt and its associated activities. Sadly much of this work, including wall paintings of hunting scenes made for the Elector and other members of the court, has not survived. However, some idea of its probable appearance is given by several extant panel paintings of hunting at the Saxon court, including one in Vienna (fig. 3), which represents Elector Frederick the Wise and Emperor Maximilian participating in a stag hunt, and the present cat. 17 and 18.

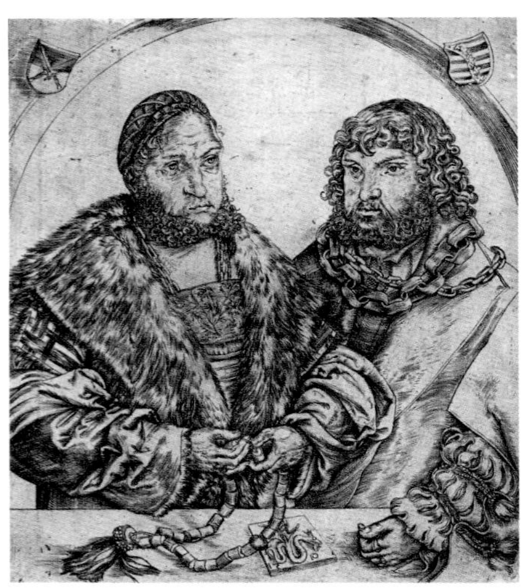

Fig. 2 Lucas Cranach the Elder,
Frederick the Wise and Johann the Steadfast, Dukes of Saxony, 1510
Engraving, 13 × 11.7 cm
London, The British Museum

Acting on the instruction of his master, Cranach travelled from July to November 1508 in the Netherlands, where he met the Holy Roman Emperor Maximilian and the future Emperor Charles V, and visited the court of Margaret of Austria at Mechelen. Shortly before, he had received from the Elector the privilege to bear a coat of arms, which carried the symbol of a winged serpent. This appears on the vast majority of paintings produced by Cranach and his expanding workshop (see fig. 11, p. 31), and it became the symbol of his artistic identity. On his return to Wittenberg at the end of 1509 Cranach made several of his most important paintings, including a life-size *Venus and Cupid* (St Petersburg, State Hermitage Museum; FR 22). This and the related print of the same subject, which probably dates from the same year (cat. 14, 15), set the template for Cranach's depiction of the beautiful female body – somewhat influenced by the recent discoveries of ancient sculpture, but very streamlined, stylised and inoffensive. This type is so constant in Cranach's art that little separates his depiction of one female or goddess from another – whether the subject represents an exemplary or a disreputable woman. Depictions of Eve, Venus, Diana and unspecified nymphs blend seamlessly into each other. This typology also influenced his female portraiture. It is hard to find a Cranach woman who is at all individualised: whether the wife of the Saxon Elector, or an anonymous court lady, they all share the same essential features.

Cranach enjoyed high social standing in the city of Wittenberg as well as at court, and he became increasingly prosperous. A tax return of 1528 states that he was one of the two richest men in the city. This wealth was not generated simply by his work as a painter but also by other business interests. These included his control of the Electoral apothecaries privilege from 1520, and the ownership of a printing press with the goldsmith Christian Döring in the mid 1520s. He purchased a very substantial house in the town centre (the 'Cranach-hof'), and in 1519 was elected for the first time to the town council, on which he sat intermittently until 1544–45. Wealth and status enabled him to make a good marriage, to Barbara Brengbier, the daughter of a Gotha town councillor, and subsequently to arrange prestigious matches for his children. By 1513 his talented first son, Hans, named after his paternal grandfather, was born (sadly to die young in Bologna in 1537). Lucas the Younger was born two years after Hans. He was to continue the painting workshop until his death. In 1520 Cranach's daughter Anna was born. Her godfather was the Wittenberg University theologian Martin Luther (1483–1546), perhaps the single most influential individual of sixteenth-century Europe.

The two men were close friends, and Cranach's personal Lutheran sympathies cannot be doubted. Cranach produced the most numerous and important images of the former Augustinian, in the form of paintings,

Fig. 3 Lucas Cranach the Elder, *The Stag Hunt of the Elector Frederick the Wise*, 1529
Oil on poplar, 80 × 114 cm
Vienna, Kunsthistorisches Museum

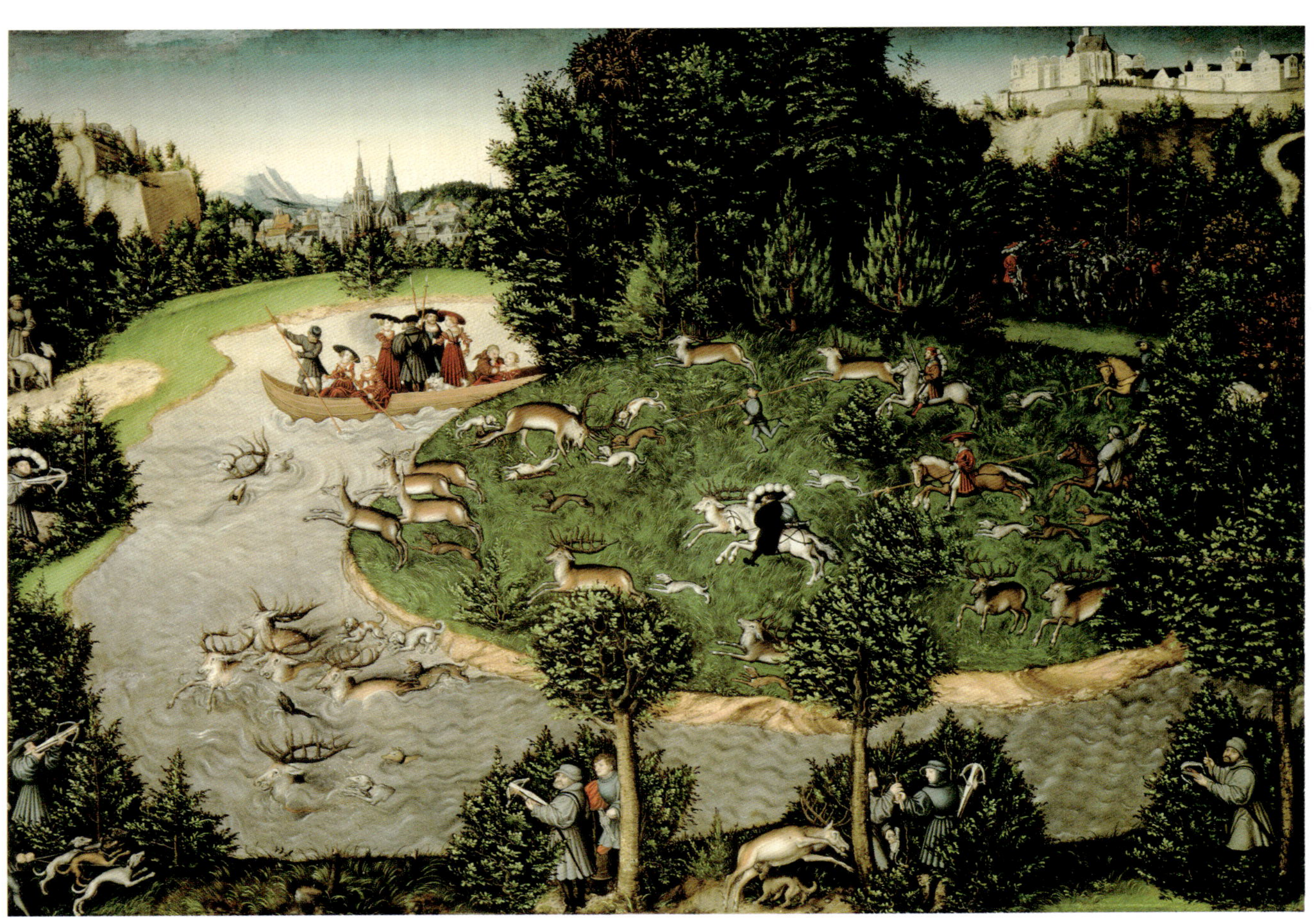

engravings and woodcuts (including fig. 4) – as a monk, in hiding as Junker Jorg at the Wartburg Fortress in 1522, as a learned cleric or as the husband of the erstwhile nun Katherina von Bora. For the first edition of Luther's translation of the New Testament in 1522 (called the September Testament after the month of its publication) Cranach designed woodcut illustrations to accompany the Book of Revelations (see fig. 14, p. 39). He also supported the publication financially. From the 1520s onwards Cranach and his shop produced paintings and book illustrations which were specifically Lutheran in iconography, such as *The Fall and Salvation of Man* (fig. 36, p. 93), or that were intended solely for Lutheran publications (cat. 20). However, Cranach did not work simply for Luther and other Protestant reformers. Many of his works (such as cat. 1) were deliberately designed so that they could be used by all Christians. His most significant patrons included the Catholic Albertine branch of Saxon princes and Cardinal Albrecht of Brandenburg, a notorious enemy of Luther. Cranach made a considerable number of portraits of Cardinal Albrecht (including figs. 15 and 16, pp. 40, 41) as Saint Jerome, depicting him as pious, learned and devout. The cardinal's church in Halle was dedicated in 1523, and in the following years Cranach designed a large number of altarpieces for this new foundation, most of which were executed by members of his workshop.[2]

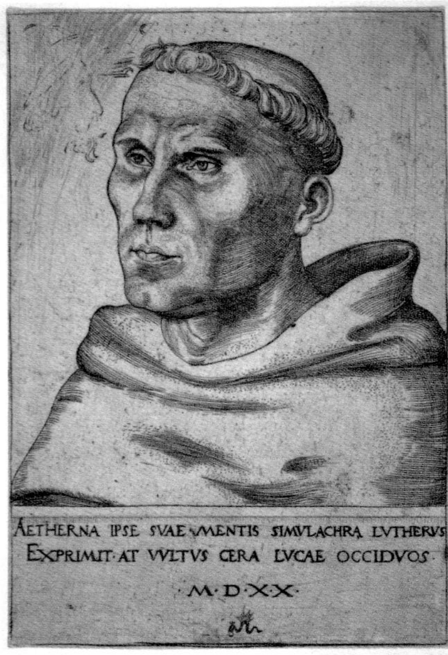

Fig. 4 Lucas Cranach the Elder, *Bust portrait of Martin Luther in 3/4 profile*, 1520
Engraving, 11 × 9.7 cm
London, The British Museum

Another of Cranach's most significant connections was his association with many members of the faculty at Wittenberg University, which had been founded by the Elector Frederick in 1502. A few years after the artist's arrival in Wittenberg the Nuremburg lawyer and Wittenberg professor Christian Schuerl delivered a panegyric of Cranach (published the following year, in 1509), in which he compared the artist in conventional humanist terms to the ancient Greek painters Apelles and Zeuxis.[3] Philip Melanchthon (1497–1560), Professor of Greek at the University, was another close associate. In 1521 Melanchthon and Cranach worked together on the *Passional Christi and Antichristi*, conceived by Luther and developed using Melanchthon's texts and Cranach's illustrations. Several years later Melanchthon wrote to his fellow Wittenberg humanist, Stigel: "I enjoyed your poem, it is as if you had illuminated with bright colours the sentence which I had only outlined. This makes me think of Lucas the painter, to whom I sometimes used to give sketches of scenes from the Bible."[4] From the mid 1520s Cranach specialised in devising paintings of certain mythological themes, including *Cupid complaining to Venus* (cat. 2), *The Nymph of the Spring* (for example, FR 259), *The Judgement of Paris* (for example, FR 41), *The Close of the Silver Age* (fig. 20, p. 46) and *The Golden Age* (such as fig. 21, p. 50). These cannot be understood in ignorance of the intellectual circle in which Cranach moved in Wittenberg. For example, the genesis of *Cupid complaining to Venus*, with its moralising inscription loosely based on the supposed nineteenth *Idyll* of Theocritus (a Greek verse of the third century BC), is closely connected to the activities of Melanchthon and his associates, who at the same time were writing moralised versions of this poem in Latin.[5]

Over twenty-seven depictions by Cranach and his workshop of his *Cupid complaining to Venus* survive. This is not unusual: in fact, most of Cranach's more popular subjects survive in several versions. There are over fifty paintings of *Adam and Eve* by the Cranach shop, and in 1532 alone the master received an order from the new Elector Johann Frederick (1504–1554) for sixty pairs of portraits of the Elector's deceased father and uncle. Scheurl praised Cranach's ability to paint speedily, which placed him ahead of his contemporaries, and also the scale of his workshop: "Wherever one turns, in every nook and cranny there is a picture".[6] Awareness of the size and productivity of Cranach's Wittenberg workshop has prejudiced scholars since the end of the nineteenth century, for they have equated the existence of this large enterprise with a worrying standardisation, and even a decline of artistic quality. Flechsig refused to recognise a single 'Cranach' as being by Lucas the Elder after 1520.[7] Even those like Friedländer and Rosenberg, who were eager to emphasise the quality of much of Cranach's production, looked upon his life in Wittenberg as a great falling-off from the potential suggested by Cranach's Vienna years.[8] Art historians have aspired primarily to discern the hand of Lucas the Elder in paintings bearing the Cranach insignia. Although a very understandable concern, it betrays an imperfect recognition of the way a painter's workshop functioned in sixteenth-century Europe. Like that of his Italian contemporary Pietro Perugino (*c.* 1452–1523), who operated several *botteghe* in different cities, the success of the Cranach enterprise can be seen in our near inability to make secure judgements about the authorship of the best-quality products of the shop. It is not surprising that scholars have wished to identify these with the hand of the master, but neither technical nor connoisseurial studies have yet provided indisputable means of confirming this supposition. Thus Cranach's signature or mark must not be interpreted as a symbol of individual artistic expression but as the 'gold standard' guarantee of the reliable products of a productive workshop.

In 1547 the Elector Johann Frederick of Saxony was defeated by the Holy Roman Emperor Charles V at the Battle of Mühlberg. Johann Frederick lost not just the battle, but many of his territorial possessions and his personal liberty. He was imprisoned by the Emperor at Augsburg and Innsbruck. Cranach lost his position as court painter – since no proper court existed – and took the decision to follow his erstwhile master into captivity. At Augsburg he met Charles V's favourite painter, the Venetian Titian (*c.* 1490–1576), who was engaged in portraying the Emperor's son and heir, Philip of Spain. Cranach is said to have made a portrait of Titian, but it does not survive.[9] In 1552 Johann Frederick was freed, and settled in Weimar with his newly reappointed court artist. Within a year Cranach was dead. His legacy lived on in the Wittenberg workshop, which flourished for over thirty years after its founder's death, and continued to produce pictures in his manner until the demise of Lucas the Younger in 1586.

NOTES

This account of Cranach's life and oeuvre is heavily indebted to Koepplin and Falk 1974, Friedländer and Rosenberg 1978, Schade 1980 and Heydenreich 2002.

1 Heiser 2002, p. 65.
2 See Schauerte 2006.
3 Schuchardt 1851–71, I, p. 29.
4 *Ibid.*, p. 81.
5 Pérez D'Ors 2007, p. 89.
6 Schuchardt 1851–71, I, p. 34 (translation by Gunnar Heydenreich). Cranach was paid for the sixty portrait pairs in May 1533 (see Schade 1980, p. 435).
7 Flechsig 1900a, p. 7.
8 Friedländer and Rosenberg 1978, p. 16 (see essay by Stephanie Buck).
9 Schuchardt 1851–71, I, pp. 206–08; Crowe and Calvacaselle 1877, II, pp. 203–04.

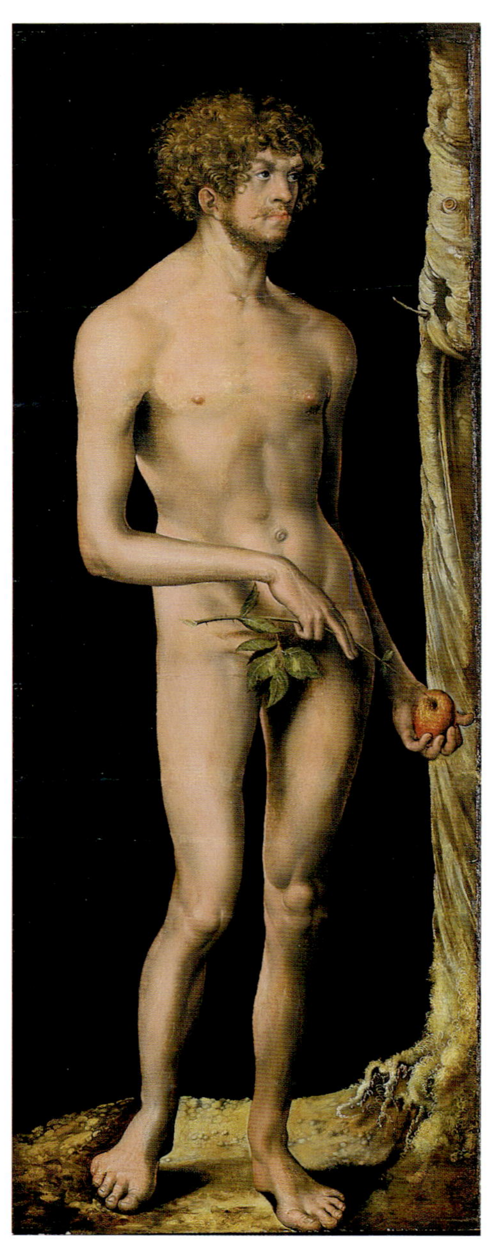

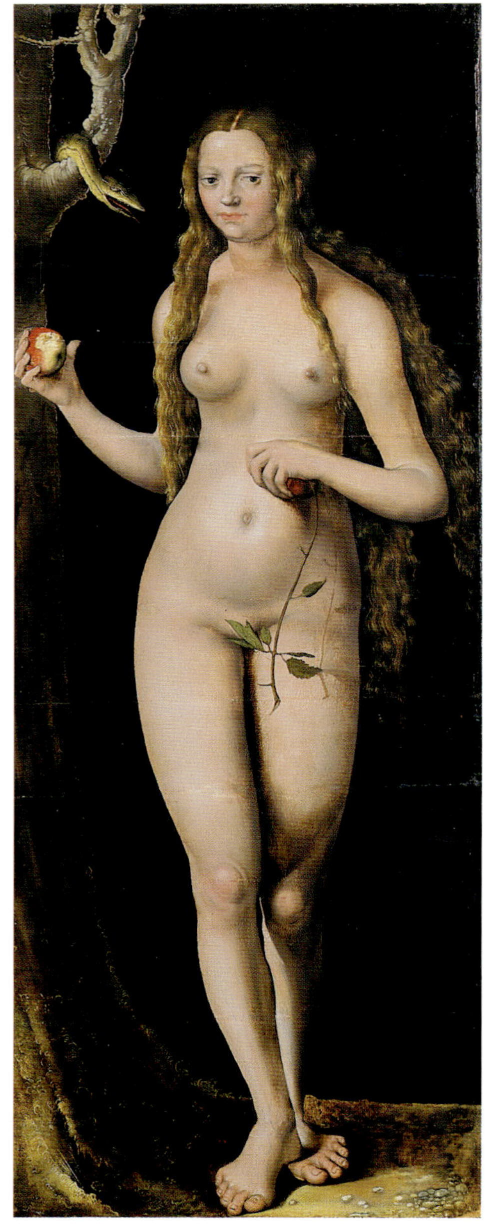

Adam and Eve in the Making

GUNNAR HEYDENREICH

Lucas Cranach the Elder painted the Fall of Man in numerous versions during his career as a court painter in the service of the Saxon Electors between 1505 and 1553. Today more than fifty paintings are known, and they represent only a small fraction of the works originally produced.[1] It was a subject that remained popular for more than four decades, despite the development of new religious thinking during the Reformation. Little is known about the conditions of their commission, but some paintings' provenances suggest that representations of Adam and Eve were painted for a broad class of clients in both religious and secular contexts. Cranach's artistic and aesthetic approach was influenced by a wide spectrum of sources. His earliest pictorial solutions reflect new Renaissance ideals as well as rivalry with his contemporaries. Subsequently the necessity to fulfil the Electors' intentions of decoration and representation encouraged Cranach to adopt new approaches. He was only able to realise the large number of paintings required, for instance, by developing an efficient system of delegation, standardisation and variation. Within these constraints he created his own style and maintained remarkable quality, for which his paintings continue to receive recognition today.

ADAM AND EVE BY CRANACH AND DÜRER

In 1509 the Wittenberg University professor Christoph Scheurl made reference to the artistic competition between Cranach and Albrecht Dürer.[2] The Saxon Elector Frederick III the Wise commissioned works from both artists, and there were several paintings by each in the Wittenberg Castle church. The nature and the degree of association between Cranach and Dürer, however, remain controversial. Both artists were about the same age and Cranach's early works reflect a close scrutiny of Dürer: drawing inspiration from his woodcuts as much as his paintings, Cranach reworked numerous motifs in new contexts (see, for example, cat. 1).[3] While some scholars reject the suggestion that Cranach worked in Dürer's workshop,[4] others have argued that Cranach's evident degree of access to Dürer's paintings implies that Cranach could well have been present in his studio.[5] It is also possible that Cranach, like Dürer, spent a period in Michael Wolgemut's workshop,[6] and conceivably he spent time in Nuremberg both before and after his stay in Vienna.[7]

Technical evidence gained in recent years from the examination of numerous paintings by Cranach and Dürer lends support to the idea of a connection between the painters at the workshop level.[8] A striking example is the use of

Fig. 5 Lucas Cranach the Elder, *Adam* and *Eve*, around 1508–10
Two panels, each 139 × 53.9 cm
Besançon, Musée des Beaux-Arts et d'Archéologie

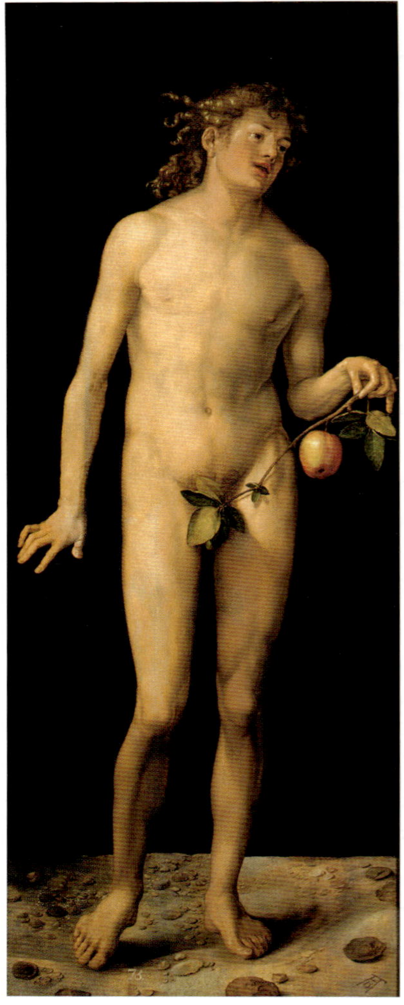

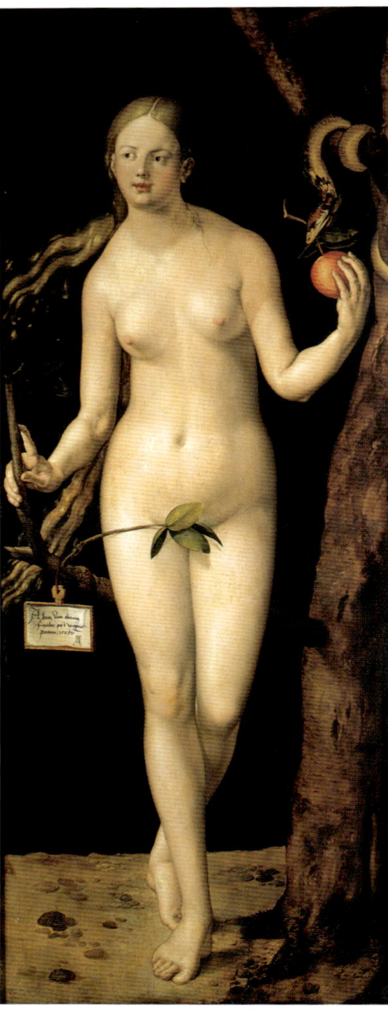

Fig. 6 Albrecht Dürer, *Adam* and *Eve*, 1507
Two panels, 209 × 81 cm and 209 × 80 cm
Madrid, Museo del Prado

unusual reddish preparatory layers by both. For his portrait of Oswolt Krel of 1499 (Munich, Alte Pinakothek) Dürer chose a reddish ground layer made of red lead and lead white. Cranach used the same preparation for his *Saint Jerome*, dated 1502 (Vienna, Kunsthistorisches Museum; FR 4); this type of preparatory layer appears to be exceptional within the oeuvre of both artists. Typically, each preferred a white ground bound with animal glue and with calcium carbonate as a filler, which was widely used by painters north of the Alps. The surface quality of the smoothed ground was then modified with intermediate layers thin in pigment. The use of a white *imprimatura* was widespread in medieval panel painting and integral to the practice of Cranach's contemporaries – including Dürer,[9] Memling,[10] Michelangelo[11] and Titian[12] – at the beginning of the sixteenth century. Judging from extant works, Cranach applied a reddish *imprimatura* on a white chalk-glue ground for the first time on his *Crucifixion* of 1503 (Munich, Alte Pinakothek; FR 5). Wolgemut and Dürer had used this technique only a few years earlier. Dürer chose this particularly efficient painting technique again for his *Christ among the Doctors* of 1506 (Madrid, Museo Thyssen-Bornemisza), inscribed as having been completed in five days. Thus he modelled volume by applying highlights and shadows over a medium flesh tone rather than a white ground. This technique was also preferred by Cranach, whom Scheurl praised for his extraordinary speed in completing paintings. Since the use of a red ground or *imprimatura* could not have beeen deduced by examination of finished paintings, this indicates Cranach's familiarity with this practice, which was routine in contemporary Nuremberg workshops.[13]

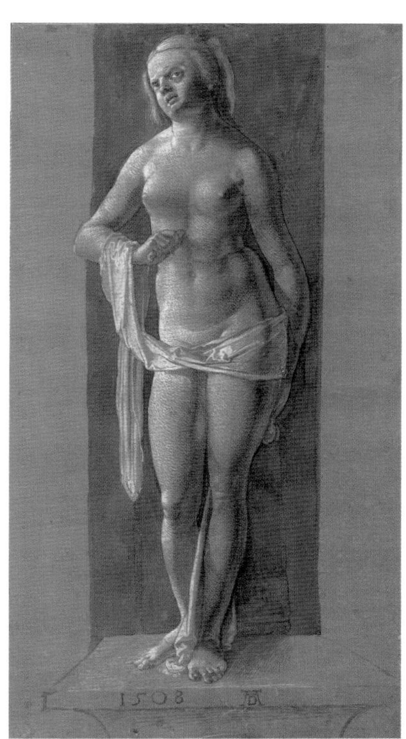

Fig. 7 Albrecht Dürer, *Lucretia*, 1508
Brush and ink with white highlights on green prepared paper, 42.2 × 22.6 cm
Vienna, Albertina

The hypothesis that Cranach studied Dürer's paintings in detail and was familiar with his techniques is further substantiated by a comparison between Dürer's depiction of *Adam and Eve* of 1507 (fig. 6)[14] and Cranach's earliest version of the same subject in the Musée des Beaux-Arts et d'Archéologie in Besançon (fig. 5), which until very recently was dismissed by scholars.[15] Cranach relies on design elements similar to those of Dürer: Adam and Eve, for example, are each painted on a separate panel and stand on stony earth in front of a black background. Both pairs rely on the same perspective, which represents the feet from above and the faces from slightly below.[16] Some details, such as Adam's legs and feet – as well as their illumination – appear almost identical in the two paintings. Dürer's painted version follows his engraving of 1504 (cat. 23), from which Cranach may have also taken inspiration. However, the obvious points in common between Cranach's and Dürer's paintings prove that the engraving cannot have been the sole source. Cranach possibly also knew Dürer's drawing of *Lucretia* of 1508 (fig. 7).[17] The motif of her right hand plunging the dagger into her chest appears to be re-used in Cranach's *Eve*: Eve holds an apple in her left hand in almost the same pose. In contrast to Dürer's *Adam and Eve*, however, Cranach chose to depict a different narrative moment: Dürer represents Eve taking the apple from the snake, while in Cranach's conception Eve has already eaten from the fruit she intends to pass on to Adam.

WORK IN PROGRESS

Cranach's *Adam and Eve* in Besançon (fig. 5) is on two panels, each measuring 139 × 53.9 cm; they are significantly smaller than those used by Dürer (209 × 80 and 209 × 81 cm). The technical characteristics of Cranach's panels are comparable to his early Wittenberg works: the planks are joined in contrary direction to the largest dimension of the panel, as was characteristic for most works he completed between 1505 and 1510–12.[18] Rather unusually for the period, however, some joins were partly covered with fibres before the ground was applied. This practice is found in panels Cranach painted before he was employed in Wittenberg, and again after 1515.[19] However, from then until about 1520, fibres were applied in a direction contrary to that of the boards, and only subsequently do we find the application of tow, either on the joins or irregularly. Tow was frequently applied to panels from the workshop of

Michael Wolgemut. Dürer's *Eve* was also prepared in a similar way, though it remains unclear whether this reflects exchange between the painters, as this stage of work was usually completed by carpenters.

Neither of the original frames for these pairs of panels (figs. 5 and 6) has survived. Thus the material evidence of their original setting, including information about the intended distance between panels, has been lost. The distance between Dürer's *Adam* and *Eve* panels is indeterminable from the image, although recently Christian Schoen has suggested that the ideal distance between them would be at least 2.5 metres.[20] In Cranach's version the stem of the tree reaches across both panels, suggesting that they formed a unified space divided only by the width of the two adjoining frames or by an architectural decoration which covered the area in between. Cranach continued this practice, for instance, in his Neustadt Altarpiece (1511–13; Neustadt on Orla, Johanneskirche; FR 47A), in which the composition of Christ taking leave of his mother is continued from one panel to the next, and in the life-sized marriage portraits of Duke Heinrich the Devout of Saxony and the Duchess Katharina of Mecklenburg (1514; Dresden, Gemäldegalerie; FR 60, 61), where the sheath of the Duke's sword reaches from one picture into the next.[21]

In accordance with his usual practice, the underdrawing of Cranach's Besançon *Adam and Eve* (fig. 5) was made with a pointed brush and a black pigment in a liquid medium.[22] Cranach drew outlines and volumes with a series of curved strokes, following an initial sketch. Although this is no longer detectible with the naked eye, it is evident in the infra-red reflectogram (IRR). Precision of detail and anatomical accuracy are subordinated to expressiveness, elegance of contour and harmony of composition.[23] The underdrawing delineates individual forms without conclusively determining the borders for the application of the paint. In this approach Cranach differs from Dürer, who designed his *Adam and Eve* with a meticulous underdrawing, in which volumes and lighting were carefully fixed with layers of parallel hatching.

Whereas Dürer appears to have progressed undeviatingly from the first to the last brushstroke, Cranach repeatedly corrected forms and colours in his early works. For instance, he painted Eve's right foot, positioned in the underdrawing adjacent to the left (fig. 8), so that the heel rested on her left foot, but he failed to reflect the shift in the right leg from supporting to free in the movement of the hip. The resulting ambiguity contravenes the classical *contrapposto* employed by Dürer, but also accentuates the precariousness of Eve's position.

In line with typical practice of the day, the underdrawing was followed by a lead white based *imprimatura*, which was applied with a wide brush. Cranach began his pictures with a light-coloured flesh paint. This was applied freely, beyond the contours fixed by the underdrawing: the brushstrokes are clearly visible. Cranach continued by modelling greyish and brownish shadows into this layer. Highlights containing high proportions of lead white were used to clarify the form and illumination. Modulation was completed with final glazes

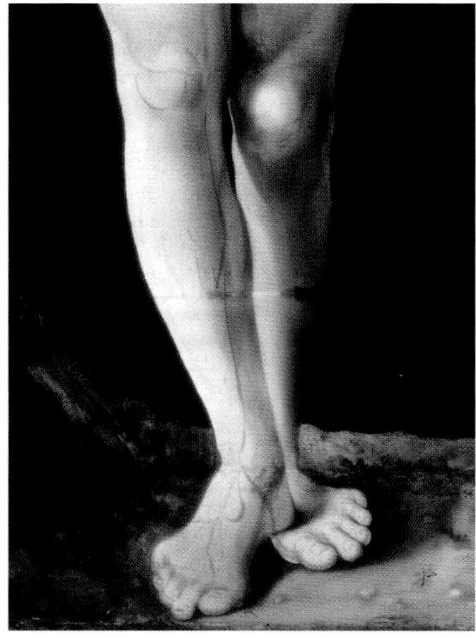

Fig. 8 Infra-red reflectogram, detail of fig. 5

and highlights. X-radiographs confirm Cranach's rapid and remarkably free technique. He can certainly be characterized as a 'fast' painter in comparison with Dürer, who often applied paint with a pointed brush in a hatching fashion.

In the Besançon paintings Cranach's representation of light and shadow is dramatic, relative both to Dürer's and to the fall of light in nature. He accentuates contours with light-coloured lines; shadows are deeply darkened. The bodies therefore not only form silhouettes against the background but also resonate with the indefinite black space behind them. Both Cranach and Dürer added fine graphic details with small pointed brushes, though much of this has been lost owing to later abrasion. Cranach additionally used his fingers to manipulate the wet paint, for example to model the bark of the tree trunk. This imprint of his skin created a fine surface texture, as also in his portrait of Johannes Cuspinian (1502–03; Winterthur, Oskar Reinhart Collection; FR 6). This technique is barely discernible in later works by Cranach, but interestingly has a parallel in Dürer's *Lamentation over Christ* (*c.* 1500; Munich, Alte Pinakothek).[24]

COMMISSION AND PROVENANCE

Dürer dated his panels of *Adam and Eve* to 1507 and Cranach may well have studied them in his workshop, perhaps between 21 October 1507 and 27 January 1508, when there is no evidence of Cranach working for the electorate court in Wittenberg.[25] There is evidence that he was in Nuremberg on 6 January 1508, for the bestowal of his personal coat of arms by Elector Frederick III.[26] He had not yet arrived back in Nuremberg, on his return from the Netherlands, by 7 October 1508. By 23 November 1508, he was working in Wittenberg again.[27] If Dürer's paintings had left the workshop before November 1507, Cranach may have seen copies in the studio.[28] The patron and intended location for Dürer's *Adam and Eve* are not known, although it has been suggested, on little evidence, that they were commissioned by the town council of Nuremberg for the town hall.[29] A text of 1516 written by Johannes Dubravius mentions a panel of Adam and Eve painted by a German artist, Albert (Albrecht Dürer), belonging to Bishop Johann Thurzo in Breslau (now Wrocław).[30] According to Dubravius, the owner had acquired the painting directly from the artist for 120 *Gulden*. Debate continues whether or not Dubravius was referring to Dürer's panels of 1507. He writes of a single panel on which Adam and Eve were painted with the tree between them, while the paintings now in Madrid show them on separate panels with the tree on the outer right edge, next to Eve.[31] Perhaps Dubravius merged Dürer's 1504 engraving (cat. 23) and the 1507 paintings in his description. However, it is equally possible that the painting in Wrocław was another work, whether painted by Dürer or indeed by another artist – such as Cranach. Dürer's *Adam and Eve* cannot be identified with certainty until it appears in 1604 in Prague.[32]

Cranach's *Adam and Eve* (fig. 5) was first noted in a 1607 inventory of the gallery of the Granvelle palace in Besançon.[33] Given their measurements ("seven and half feet high, three feet ten thumbs wide"), the two panels can clearly be identified as the paintings today in the Besançon museum.[34] The inventory was conducted in 1607, soon after the death of François Perrenot de Granvelle, comte de Cantecroix, and recorded all the furniture, books and works of art in the Granvelles' possession at the time. The Granvelle palace housed large portions of the famous collections of Cardinal Antoine Perrenot de Granvelle (1517–1586) and his father Nicolas Perrenot de Granvelle (1484–1550). Nicolas, a chancellor of the Holy Roman Empire under Charles V, was one of the Emperor's most trusted advisers in Germany.[35] Antoine was involved in the settlement of the terms of peace after the defeat of the Schmalkaldic League at the Battle of Mühlberg in 1547. In 1550 he succeeded his father as Imperial Secretary of State; in this capacity he accompanied Charles V in the war with Maurice of Saxony and in the flight from Innsbruck.[36] Both father and son, then, may have been familiar with Cranach's work; Antoine may even have met him in person when both were in Innsbruck in 1551, if not earlier.

It is even possible that the Granvelles commissioned Cranach to paint *Adam and Eve*. However, the panels are neither dated or signed – common practice for many works Cranach created for the Wittenberg court at this time – and they may have entered the Granvelle collection years after their completion. There is indeed documentary evidence that in 1549 Cranach's imprisoned patron Johann Frederick I of Saxony presented *The Martyrdom of the Ten Thousand*, which was painted in 1508 by Albrecht Dürer for the Wittenberg Castle church, to Nicolas Perrenot. According to letters between Johann Frederick and his sons of 25 June and 26 December 1548,[37] Dürer's painting was stored in Cranach's house, and the artist was asked to pack it securely to send it via Antwerp to Johann Frederick in Brussels; thence it entered the Granvelle collection.[38]

PARALLELS AND DIVERGENCES

The close relationship between Dürer's and Cranach's earliest paintings of the Fall supports the thesis that Cranach developed his version as a synthesis of Dürer's inventions[39] and his own between 1508 and 1510. However, it is overly simplistic to explain Cranach's entire artistic development in terms of Dürer's influence. His compositions and techniques reflected numerous other influences, and were also in large part original.[40] His work clearly refers to Netherlandish panel painting, for example, particularly after his journey to Mechelen of 1508.[41] However, I wish to argue that the exchange between Cranach and Dürer was much more intense than has previously been assumed. It went beyond the stylistic appropriation of motifs and elements and included the use of materials and techniques. This level of exchange suggests that there was interaction between the painters' workshops. The two artists probably met, Cranach visiting Dürer's studio. It seems possible that Cranach even worked there for some time.

Of course, despite numerous parallels in motifs and techniques between Dürer's and Cranach's versions of Adam and Eve, these paintings also illustrate divergent artistic objectives and working methods. Dürer painted his panels directly after his return from his second trip to Italy. He composed the human body with anatomical correctness and ideal proportions, following classical standards. Cranach instead sought beauty and harmony in the outline. While Dürer's pair stand in a classical *contrapposto* pose, Cranach's are slightly twisted, giving a sense of movement and ambiguity. Dürer's beautiful, smooth-skinned Adam is lost in thought, while Cranach's, with thick curly hair and a beard, glances unequivocally at Eve. Cranach contrasts the form and colour of the bodies of Adam and Eve and of them both with the gnarled and scarred bark of the tree.

The different temperament of the two artists is also apparent in their working practice. Whereas Dürer prepared his paintings with detailed studies[42] and elaborate underdrawings, which already indicate light and shade, Cranach instead sketched his figures with few outlines and made changes during the painting process, as in the case of Eve's pose. It seems that Cranach was indeed the "fast" painter of Scheurl's eulogy.

ADAM AND EVE IN WITTENBERG

Around 1510–12 Cranach moved his workshop from the castle into the city of Wittenberg.[43] Presumably, this new location offered greater entrepreneurial freedom. The court painter increased his pictorial production in the next decade for a larger group of clients. The subject of Adam and Eve was especially popular, on both panel and canvas.[44] Sizes ranged from very small to nearly life-size depictions. Usually Adam and Eve were painted on two separate panels forming diptychs, which in some cases could be closed like a book, as in the version in Leipzig.[45] This particular work is preserved with its original, deeply hollowed frame. Its vertical and top scotia mouldings contrast with a flat rainsill base, reinforcing its resemblance to a window. Larger diptychs were probably intended to be displayed permanently within a frame or architectural setting. This idea is supported by their weight as well as by the rough finish on their reverse, which was to be hidden against the wall.

However, several of Cranach's earliest versions of this subject were painted on a single panel.[46] The chronology of these paintings has been disputed. While Friedländer and Rosenberg describe the Munich version (fig. 27, p. 66) as the earliest (about 1510–12),[47] Werner Schade places the Warsaw painting (FR 44) a little earlier, at around 1510.[48] The technical details of the latter panel help to establish a more secure chronology. The Warsaw panel consists of four boards joined crosswise to the larger dimension, whereas the Munich panel is joined in a vertical direction, as was Cranach's practice after he had moved his workshop to the city and employed a new carpenter, who used different techniques. The Warsaw *Adam and Eve*, therefore, is probably the earlier version.

Cranach seems to have encouraged minor variations – for example in the poses of the figures or in the background, painted black or with landscape and animals – in each version. While some elements were repeated very frequently, it seems as if there was a workshop principle to avoid direct copies of complete paintings. It is assumed that Cranach's Würzburg *Adam and Eve* (FR 113) adopts motifs from Dürer's 1504 engraving (cat. 23) that were transmitted via the painting of *Adam and Eve* of about 1507–08 by Jan Gossaert (Madrid, Museo Thyssen-Bornemisza). However, a precise determination of the chronology and the relationship between such panels is to some extent hypothetical, as relatively few paintings have survived and new discoveries continually readjust assumptions about the transmission of painted motifs.

COMMISSION AND DELEGATION

The Saxon Electors probably commissioned the majority of Cranach's paintings of this period, though the artist undoubtedly benefited from a growing number of commissions from the merchant class and bourgeoisie, in addition to those from the aristocracy and secular and religious authorities.[49] During the disturbances in Leipzig in 1593, in which Lutherans attacked the house of the Calvinist trader Adolph Weinhausen, it is documented that several works of art were destroyed, including "a most valuable painting of Adam and Eve by Dürer, which was chopped with an axe".[50] Although it is questionable that the painting was really by Dürer rather than by Cranach or another painter, the report provides evidence that bourgeois clients acquired such subject-matter.

Cranach delivered numerous altarpieces to town and village churches in Saxony, some of which probably included panels of *Adam and Eve*. There are such panels also painted on the reverse, which suggests that they originally formed the folding wings of triptychs. Surviving examples include the panels of *Adam and Eve* with *Christ as the Man of Sorrows and the Virgin* on the reverse of about 1518–20 in Vienna (FR 112A). While these were probably made as the wings of a central painted panel, it is also conceivable that the central part of the altarpiece was carved. Again, the tree, stretching across from one to the other panel, suggests that *Adam* and *Eve* occupied the outside of the wings and would have been adjacent when the retable was closed.[51] The panels are joined from several boards of lower-quality limewood. Some irregularities, probably knots or resinous deposits, remained present while others were replaced with another piece of wood. On both sides there are strips of fibrous material applied crosswise to the joins. The subsequent application of the ground layer was so thin that after smoothing these fibres became partly exposed and can today be discerned in the paint surface. It appears that Cranach's standards of technical care were sometimes lowered for commissions from outside the court.

Cranach was able to fulfil multiple tasks at the court only through an efficient system of delegation. Close examination of his surviving panels suggests that there were various divisions of labour in his workshop. These would have reflected the competence of particular assistants, time constraints, the nature of the commission, the format, the need for preliminary studies and models, the significance of individual passages within a painting and, last but not least, the status of the patron. There was a clear hierarchy among the assistants, as is reflected in documentation which distinguishes apprentices (*Lehrjungen*) from hirelings (*Lohnknaben*), helpers (*Knechte*) and journeymen (*Gesellen*).[52] These collaborators, possessing a range of qualifications and often hired on a temporary basis, were paid differently. It is clear that Cranach realised large-scale projects with the help of numerous assistants, as in the case of his commission to decorate the Schloss Hartenfels at Torgau. Within his Wittenberg workshop Cranach employed journeymen with higher qualifications who produced panel and canvas paintings both for commissions and for the open market. Typically there were also two or three boys serving apprenticeships in the Wittenberg workshop; these, after a short trial period, would normally last three years. Apprentices were quickly involved in painting. In a letter dated 4 April 1521 Duke Johann Frederick requested that he be sent a panel by "his

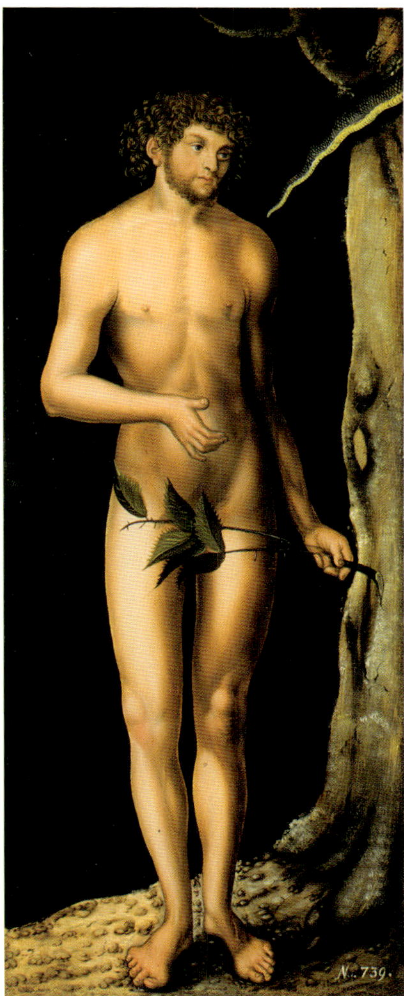

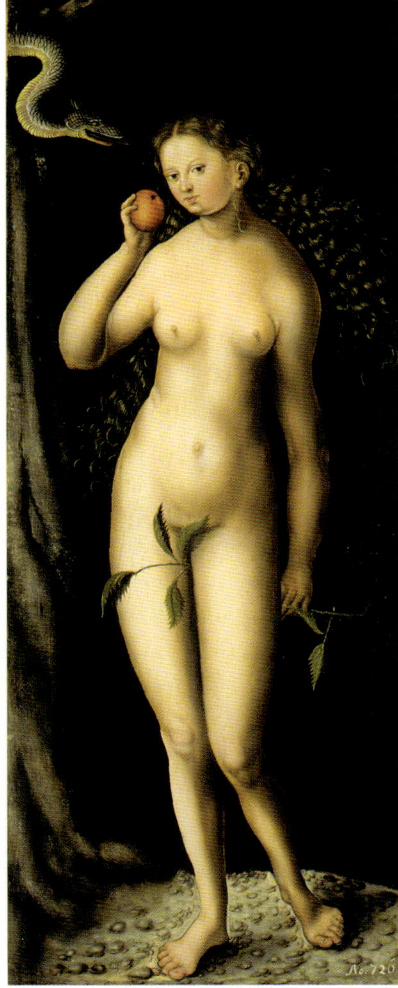

Fig. 9 Workshop of Lucas Cranach the Elder, *Adam* and *Eve*, around 1512
Two panels, 72.8 × 29.3 and 72.6 × 29 cm.
Vienna, Kunsthistorisches Museum

painter" so that he could see "all the good things he has been learning".[53] On 24 April 1545 Cranach sent a painting of the Virgin to the court chamberlain Hans von Ponickau with the comment "made by your painter".[54] Cranach must have been satisfied with the progress the boy had made, because he remarks in the letter that he "had not helped in any way. The boy did it on his own so you can see how much progress he has made." Two panels of *Adam* and *Eve* of about 1512 today in Vienna (fig. 9) might, in fact, be in part the work of an advanced apprentice.[55] There are signs of some division of labour between the underdrawing and the actual painting: the painting itself follows outlines that appear to have been drawn confidently in great flourishes, yet does so rather clumsily and with less understanding of form. Like many other works of the day, these paintings were not signed. Thus it remains open whether this work was considered a product of Cranach's workshop or of a specific apprentice.

In order to maintain consistent pictorial quality within the workshop, Cranach seems to have refined some of his techniques. For example, female faces were often created with light flesh paint that was stippled with a short, blunt bristle brush. This allowed the artist to create a smooth, continuous surface with gradual, imperceptible shifts from highlight to shadow. Flesh tones modelled in this way appear in the x-radiograph as smooth, but with pronounced virtual relief. On higher magnification the relief dissolves into very small islets of paint. It was, no doubt, difficult for Cranach to convey his rather impulsive style of painting to other workshop members. The stippling technique, by contrast, would have been relatively easy to copy, and therefore became the predominant method for modelling flesh tones in the second decade of the sixteenth century. It seems that this technique with which Cranach trained his workshop members was rather time-consuming, but guaranteed a homogenous workshop production. The highest-quality works from later decades suggest that Cranach himself used this technique less schematically.[56]

THE *ADAM AND EVE* OF 1526

The *Adam and Eve* in the Courtauld Institute of Art Gallery (cat. 1) was painted on a panel measuring 117.1 × 80.8 cm.[57] This size is the second largest of the six standard panel formats that were preferred in Cranach's workshop between 1520 and 1535.[58] The introduction of standard-sized panels had the advantage that the carpenter could produce them independently of individual commissions, and therefore more economically. The system seems to have been instituted as a consequence of increased demand in the workshop in the 1520s. Standardised panels also had implications for painting methods. For example, they forced painters to harmonise the design within the predetermined vertical and horizontal limits of the panel. Their use confirms once again Cranach's choice of self-imposed restriction for the sake of workshop efficiency. The fact that different subjects were painted in standard formats and, conversely, the same subjects were painted in various formats further suggests that he regularly produced works without specific commissions.

The panel for *Adam and Eve* was made up of six planks laid vertically. It has a rebate along the edges, which traditionally served to insert the panel in an engaged frame. The original frame, which has not survived, probably had grooved mouldings into which the tapered edges of the panel were inserted. According to traditional medieval practice, such frames were applied before the panel received its ground and the frame was gilded. For example, in 1507, Dürer passed the wooden panels for the Heller Altarpiece to a *Zubereiter*, who applied the ground and carried out the gilding of the frames before Dürer started to paint.[59] Cranach altered this practice. Many of his panels were framed during or after the painting process. In cases where the panel was inserted into its frame before the ground was applied, the priming barb appears close to the edges of the panel. In the Courtauld *Adam and Eve* panel, as in many others, we find several traces of paint on the bare wood outside the barb. This suggests that the panel and the frame were separated again after priming. The presence and appearance of the paint suggest in fact the use of a temporary frame,[60] and this hypothesis is further supported by incisions in the ground along the barb[61] and by black painted borders.[62] The incised lines may have indicated areas yet to be painted[63] or may have been intended to prevent damage to the ground when the frame or interim frame was removed.[64] The black edges may have provided a visual border to direct the painting process. In the case of *Adam and Eve*, the presence of paint on the left and right edges, but not on the top and bottom, may suggest that two grooved wooden battens, rather than a complete frame, held the panel during the painting process. The practice of adding frames after paintings were completed relates to Cranach's use of standard-sized formats, which might be employed for a variety of subject-matter and for different frame designs.

STANDARDISATION AND VARIATION

In line with traditional medieval workshop practice, Cranach possessed an extensive store of patterns and models, some his own, some created by others. Individual motifs and compositions might be used for decades. He and his assistants drew on the wealth of patterns in a collage-like montage and variation of motifs. Patterns were reliable guides and a guarantee of quality. Some of them can readily be recognised within paintings, whether to the same scale, reduced or enlarged, reversed or not, or slightly altered.[65] For example, the lying red deer and lion in the Courtauld *Adam and Eve* reflect a woodcut of 1509 (cat. 12).[66] Both of these animals were depicted many times in various other paintings as well. In addition, the stork, grey heron and horse appear in quite similar fashion in the Vienna *Garden of Eden* (fig. 37, p. 94).

Drawing with a pointed brush and black pigment in a liquid medium on the ground, Cranach fixed the outlines of figures and animals of the Courtauld painting with only a few strokes.[67] For example, Eve's head was initially positioned slightly further to the right. Occasionally it seems that shadows were indicated with washes of diluted ink or paint. The infra-red reflectogram (fig. 33, p. 74) reveals that the back of the sheep was modelled with shades of grey before being covered with the flesh paint of Adam's right leg.

The essential pigments in the flesh paints are lead white, vermilion, vegetable-derived carbon black, iron oxide and a brown organic colorant. Cool lights or half shadows occasionally contain azurite (significant amounts of calcium salts have been found in almost all flesh paints examined to date).[68] Cranach differentiated the bodies and faces within his paintings by varying pigment combinations, layer sequences and brushwork. Each form was built individually in several layers, evident in alternating and overlapping layers of paint. In some sections the background covers flesh tints, while in others the flesh paint encroaches on the background.[69] This confirms Cranach's tendency to develop each painting as a whole, often switching from one detail to another, but not completing individual parts one after another. For example, in leaving reserves for the foliage of a tree (verdigris, carbon black) when applying paint for the sky (lead white, azurite, lead-tin yellow), he calculated not only the final visual result but also the potential savings of time and pigment. Early works commonly left eyes omitted until after the flesh was modelled, at which point eyeballs were added in stereotypical fashion with lead white and blue pigment.[70] When creating reflected light in the pupils, Cranach relied not only on observations from nature, but also on common formulae. There is no other explanation for the light in Eve's eyes in the Courtauld painting,[71] which is divided into four and thus reflects the mullion and transom of a window, although the figures are depicted in a landscape. A similar formula was used in several earlier and later works.[72]

The borderline between Cranach's creative painting process and spontaneous changes in plan is not obvious. The term pentiment (subsequent amendment) can be variously defined,[73] and the 1526 *Adam and Eve* (cat. 1) shows how difficult its application can become. The correction of Adam's left hand, which was initially touching his forehead, can be characterized as a change of plan (fig. 10). By contrast, most of the animals were painted on a white ground before the green meadow was finished; only the stork, horse and grey heron have been painted upon the green ground.[74] Does this reflect the typical working process, a subsequent amendment, or even perhaps a correction by a different hand? The foreground elements are pressed against the picture plane. The red deer, lion and boar are of comparable size and appear to be placed on top of, rather than behind, each other. Perhaps Cranach added the smaller animals not only to fill remaining empty space, but also to create a more realistic perspective and tonal balance (see also p. 38, essay by Stephanie Buck). Without the horse, which is painted on a much smaller scale, there would be little sense of spatial recession in the background. The stork's thin legs and grey heron's beak enrich the spectrum of forms, just as their colours create a tonal balance with other animals, like the white sheep. In short, Cranach worked and reworked his compositions, including the Courtauld *Adam and Eve*, during the painting process to achieve a final sense of harmony and beauty.

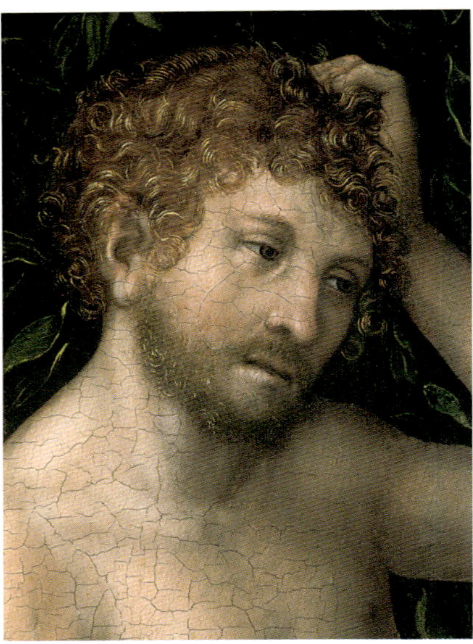

Detail of cat. 1

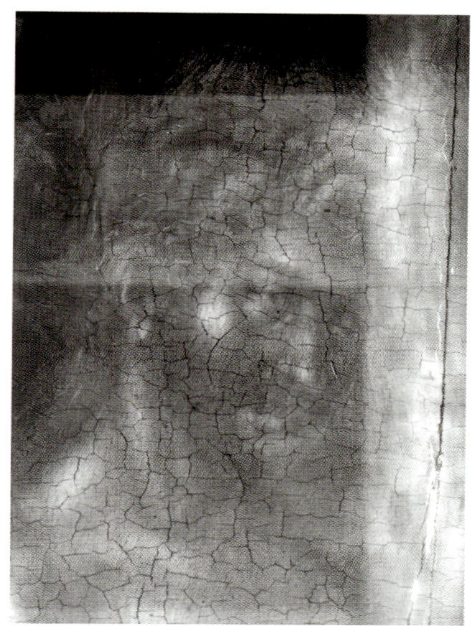

Fig. 10 Detail of x-radiograph of cat. 1.

Given the working process of Cranach's shop, it is certainly possible that multiple hands contributed to the creation of this painting. Uneven quality in the rendering of some animals and vegetation could suggest, in fact, the participation of several painters. Assistants often took part in works by Cranach, and in turn, Cranach contributed to works by his assistants.[75] However, a clear delineation between the work from Cranach's own hand and that of his collaborators is difficult to establish, as a primary aim of workshop practice was to eliminate the possibility of separating hands on the basis of differences in quality.

At its completion, the Courtauld *Adam and Eve* was signed with a winged serpent – the trademark and 'stamp of quality' for paintings produced by Cranach and his workshop – and dated 1526. The division of labour in his workshop allowed for collaborators to sign and date paintings. A comparison of contemporaneous serpent signatures (fig. 11a–f) leaves no room for doubt that different hands were entitled to apply this trademark. There are differences not only in the shape of the serpents but also in the styles of writing the numbers.[76] The *2* formed in the shape of a z, as in the *1526* in the Courtauld painting, is often associated with paintings of higher quality and may have been executed by Cranach himself.

There are numerous extant versions of *Adam and Eve*, and modern technical analysis can provide new insights into the way they were made. Research into the *Adam and Eve* panels at Besançon has changed our understanding of Cranach's earliest approach to this subject-matter and has shed light on the artistic exchange between Cranach and Dürer. Both painters sought the title

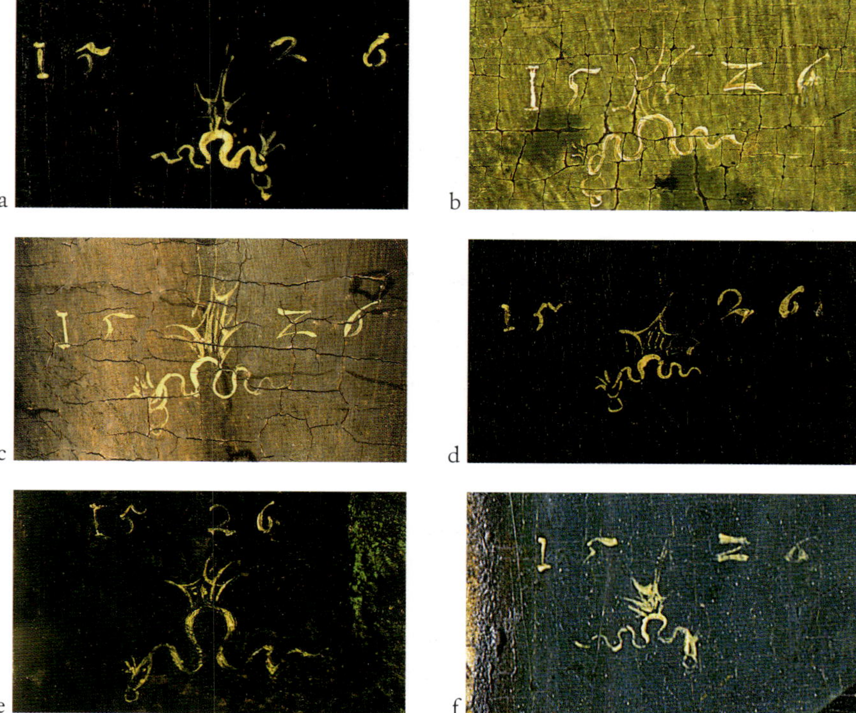

Fig. 11 Six different signatures from 1526:

a) Detail from *Portrait of a Man (von Schleinitz?)*, 1526. Weimar, Kunstsammlungen
b) Detail from *Elector Johann the Steadfast*, 1526. Otterlo, Stichting Kröller-Müller Museum
c) Detail from *Adam and Eve*, 1526. London, Courtauld Institute of Art Gallery
d) Detail from *Princess Sibylle of Cleves*, 1526. Weimar, Kunstsammlungen
e) Detail from *Picture of a Nude Boy*, 1526. Dresden, Staatliche Kunstsammlungen, Gemäldegalerie Alte Meister
f) Detail from *Martin Luther*, 1526. Eisenach, Wartburg-Stiftung

'the Apelles of Germany', though Dürer was ultimately the one to achieve it. Cranach, who probably never visited Italy, devised new approaches. In accordance with his temperament he pursued the idea of speed as an indication of artistic skill, a topos of praise in antiquity.[77] In collaboration with Melanchthon and Luther Cranach developed numerous new subjects for painting in Renaissance Germany. By producing large numbers of paintings in a standardised manner it seems that Cranach transposed into painting the idea of the woodcut as a medium for spreading pictorial information. Cranach thus not only fulfilled the expectations of his patrons but also supported a wide distribution of the new currents of thought that acompanied the Reformation in Germany. However, unlike woodcuts, Cranach's painted repetitions of popular subjects such as Adam and Eve were not viewed as copies, but as variations. They enabled him to maintain high quality, winning him the praise of the Saxon Electors and others. It would seem that Cranach neglected interest in antique ideals such as anatomy and human proportions – some of the main achievements of the Renaissance – in favour of visual sophistication in his paintings, which today makes him appear rather modern, and ensures his continued popularity.

NOTES

My thanks to Emily Scott and the Department of Paintings Conservation at the J. Paul Getty Museum.

1 Cf. Friedländer and Rosenberg 1978; Witt Library, London, and Getty Research Library, Photo Study Collection, Los Angeles.
2 Scheurl 1509.
3 Bonnet 1992, p. 260; Erichsen 1994; Marx 1997; Marx 2005–06.
4 Koepplin and Falk 1974, I, p. 118.
5 Grimm, Erichsen and Brockhoff 1994, p. 293; cf. also Marx 1997. The close relationship between Dürer and Cranach is also apparent in the fact that for stylistic reasons Anzelewsky attributed to Cranach the *Portrait of a Young Man* (Anton Neubaurer?) which previously had been ascribed to Dürer (Anzelewsky 1999). However, technical examination has provided no evidence that Cranach painted the portrait.
6 Grimm, Erichsen and Brockhoff 1994, p. 293.
7 The payment of 50 *Gulden* to Lucas Cranach in Nuremberg in 1505, mentioned by Koepplin and Falk (1974, I, p. 112) referring to Gurlitt (1895, p. 113) cannot be confirmed despite further study of the account books of the Wittenberg court. See also Heiser 2002, pp. 87, 100–01.
8 See Heydenreich 2007.
9 Goldberg, Heimberg and Schawe 1998, p. 289.
10 Périer-d'Ieteren 1994, p. 74.
11 Dunkerton and Spring 1998, p. 124.
12 *Ibid., p.* 126.
13 It remains to be discovered whether Wolgemut and Dürer also used silk fibres.
14 Madrid, Museo del Prado, P 2177, 2178; cf. Bonnet 2001, pp. 185–96; Schoen 2001.
15 Besançon, Musée des Beaux-Arts et d'Archéologie, inv. 896.1.54.
16 Cf. Schoen 2001, p. 37.
17 Vienna, Albertina, inv. 17533, 42.2 × 22.6 cm; cf. Bonnet 2001, pp. 201–04; Schröder and Sternath 2003, pp. 373–76.
18 One defect in the wood is replaced with a rectangular insert.
19 Heydenreich 1998, pp. 181–200; Heydenreich 2007, pp. 67–71.
20 Cf. Schoen 2001, p. 37.
21 Cf. Heydenreich 2007, pp. 81–82.
22 Cf. *ibid*, pp. 104–13.
23 Cf. Bonnet 1992, p. 263.
24 Goldberg, Heimberg and Schawe 1998, p. 44, fig. III.20. Dürer used fingerprints to create structures, for example, in the rock formations.
25 Schade 1974, pp. 403–04.
26 Schuchardt 1851, I, pp. 51–54.
27 Schade 1974, pp. 403–04.
28 Several scholars have speculated that the copies which are today in the Landesmuseum Mainz might have been produced in the Dürer workshop. Cf. Schoen 2001, pp. 144, 150–55.
29 Cf. Hampe 1928, p. 42; Anzelewsky 1971, p. 209; Schoen 2001, pp. 117–21.
30 Schoen 2001, pp. 120, 292–93.
31 While for example in 1971 Anzelewsky related this source to Dürer's *Adam and Eve* (1971, p. 209), in a later edition of 1991 he rejected this hypothesis and considered that this description might even refer to a panel by Cranach (Anzelewsky 1991, p. 214). More recently Schoen again assumes that the document refers to Dürer's panels in Madrid (Schoen 2001, p. 121).

32 To date the earliest source which is not disputed is Carel van Mander (*Het Schilder-Boeck*, Haarlem 1604). He mentions the panels in the ownership of the Emperor Rudolf II in Prague; Schoen 2001, p. 145.
33 "*Un Adam, de Lucas Cranac, d'haulteur de sept piedz et demy, large de trois piedz dix polces, molure de chasne, nº 159*" and "*Une Eve, de Lucas Cranac, d'haulteur de sept piedz et demy, large de trois piedz dix polces, molure de chasne, nº 160*": Castan 1866, p. 126. See also Gauthier 1901, p. 339: "*LV SUNDER (Lucas), dit Cranach, de Cranach. 1472–15…, 164. Adam; 7 pieds ½ sur 3 pieds 10 pouces (nº 159). 165. Eve; memes dimensions (nº 160)*".'
34 Chudant 1929, p. 24.
35 *Encyclopaedia Britannica*, 1977, IV, p. 50.
36 *Ibid.*
37 Thüringisches Hauptstaatsarchiv Weimar, Ernestinisches Gesamtarchiv, Reg. L. fol. 191 B. 7. Nr. 5: Johann Frederick I writing to his sons (transcribed by Junius 1926, pp. 233–34); Reg. L. fol. 231–239 C. 1, fol. 9–10, Johann Frederick and Johann William writing to Lucas Cranach (Junius 1926, p. 234; Schade 1974, no. 376, p. 442)
38 Anzelewsky 1971, p. 212.
39 Cf. also Dürer's earlier depictions of the same subject (Bonnet 2001; Schröder and Sternrath 2003).
40 See Bonnet 1992, p. 249; Erichsen 1994, p. 299; Bierende 2002.
41 See Hentschel 1948, pp. 39–40; Degen 1953, pp. 198–99; Koepplin 2003, p. 66 *et alibi*.
42 Including an *Arm of Eve* of about 1507, The Cleveland Museum of Art, 1965.470; see Schoen 2001, pp. 38–45.
43 See Lücke 1998, pp. 11–59.
44 See Friedländer and Rosenberg 1978; "*Die tucher sein noch zu vor rechen … Adam und Efa …*", Thüringisches Hauptstaatsarchiv Weimar, Ernestinisches Gesamtarchiv, Reg. Aa 2975, fol. 19r.
45 Leipzig, Museum der Bildenden Künste, inv. 1269.
46 Friedländer and Rosenberg 1978, nos. 43, 44, 44A, 113, 114 etc.
47 *Ibid.*, no. 43.
48 Schade 1974, p. 459; Friedländer and Rosenberg 1978, no. 44.
49 Amongst others, the merchants Heinrich Ackermann of Frankfurt and Raymund Fugger of Augsburg owned Cranach paintings (Zülch 1935, p. 311; Busch 1973, p. 85).
50 Heller 1827, p. 184; Schoen 2001, p. 173.
51 Schütz 1972; see for example Hans Memling's *Adam and Eve* (about 1485) in the Kunsthistorisches Museum, which is also painted on the reverse of the wings of a small triptych.
52 Heydenreich 2007, pp. 280–87.
53 Letter from Duke Johann to Elector Frederick III the Wise: see Kolde 1881, p. 45.
55 Thüringisches Hauptstaatsarchiv Weimar, Ernestinisches Gesamtarchiv, Reg. Rr. 937. fol 10, Cranach writing to Hans von Ponickau: see Schuchardt 1851, I, pp. 175–76.
55 Vienna, Kunsthistorisches Museum, inv. 929.
56 Friedländer and Rosenberg 1978, nos. 29, 33, 49, 135, 150, 214A, 407.
57 The panel consists of six wooden planks of varying widths, joined vertically.
58 Heydenreich 1998; Heydenreich 2007, pp. 39–47.
59 Dürer writing to Jakob Heller on 28 August 1507 (Rupprich 1956, I, p. 64).
60 Friedländer and Rosenberg 1978, nos. 146, 312B, 313B, 338A, 348 – a portrait of Martin Luther (1534, Swiss private collection) – etc.
61 See also *ibid.*, nos. 9, 10, 16, 18, 30, 48, 58, 92, 132B, 285D, 314D etc.
62 See also *ibid.*, nos. 11, 14, 18, 20, 21, 74A, 86, 122, 168, 191 etc.
63 FR 314D, *Elector Frederick III* and *Elector Johann the Steadfast* (1532), Weimar, Kunstsammlungen.
64 Bartl and Gärtner 1997, pp. 27, 194, 529, 557.
65 See the dog in Friedländer and Rosenberg 1978, nos. 34 and 73; the head of John the Baptist and Holofernes in FR 32, 33, 73, 230, 231, 232 etc, or the *Studies of Wildfowl* in Dresden, Kupferstich-Kabinett, with FR 272–75 and FR 290 (Schade 1961–62; Schade 1974, p. 49).
66 Jahn 1972, p. 292.
67 Presumably because of the high degree of dilution the carbon-based ink or paint is hardly detectable by infra-red reflectography. I am grateful to Caroline Campbell for having provided me with the infra-red reflectogram.
68 Heydenreich 2007, pp. 133, 170.
69 Friedländer and Rosenberg 1978, nos. 17, 20, 68: *Adam and Eve*, *c.* 1512–20, Vienna, Kunsthistorisches Museum.
70 FR 1–16, 19 ; blue pigment not detected in FR 17, 31.
71 The same formula is used for the eye of the red deer.
72 FR 30, 160, 191.
73 Wolters distinguishes between different types of such amendments: "The external ones to improve individual elements ought to be described as 'rectifications', those which intrude on the structure of the picture, recasting it from inside, ought to be called 'alterations'" (Wolters 1938, p. 57). According to Van de Wetering (1997, p. 42), the term *pentimento* should be reserved for changes made to a painting that has already been partly or fully worked up.
74 Similar phenomena are discernible for example on FR 99: cf. Michaelis 1989–90, pp. 123–24.
75 See Heydenreich 2007, pp. 289–98.
76 For example 1525: Friedländer and Rosenberg 1978, nos. 168, 185, 199 and *Lucretia*, Staatsgalerie Aschaffenburg, 13256; or 1526: FR 176, 178, 189D, 191, 210, 294, 296, 304, 305, 306, 311, 311B etc.
77 Pliny the Elder 1978; cf. Bierende 2002, p. 283.

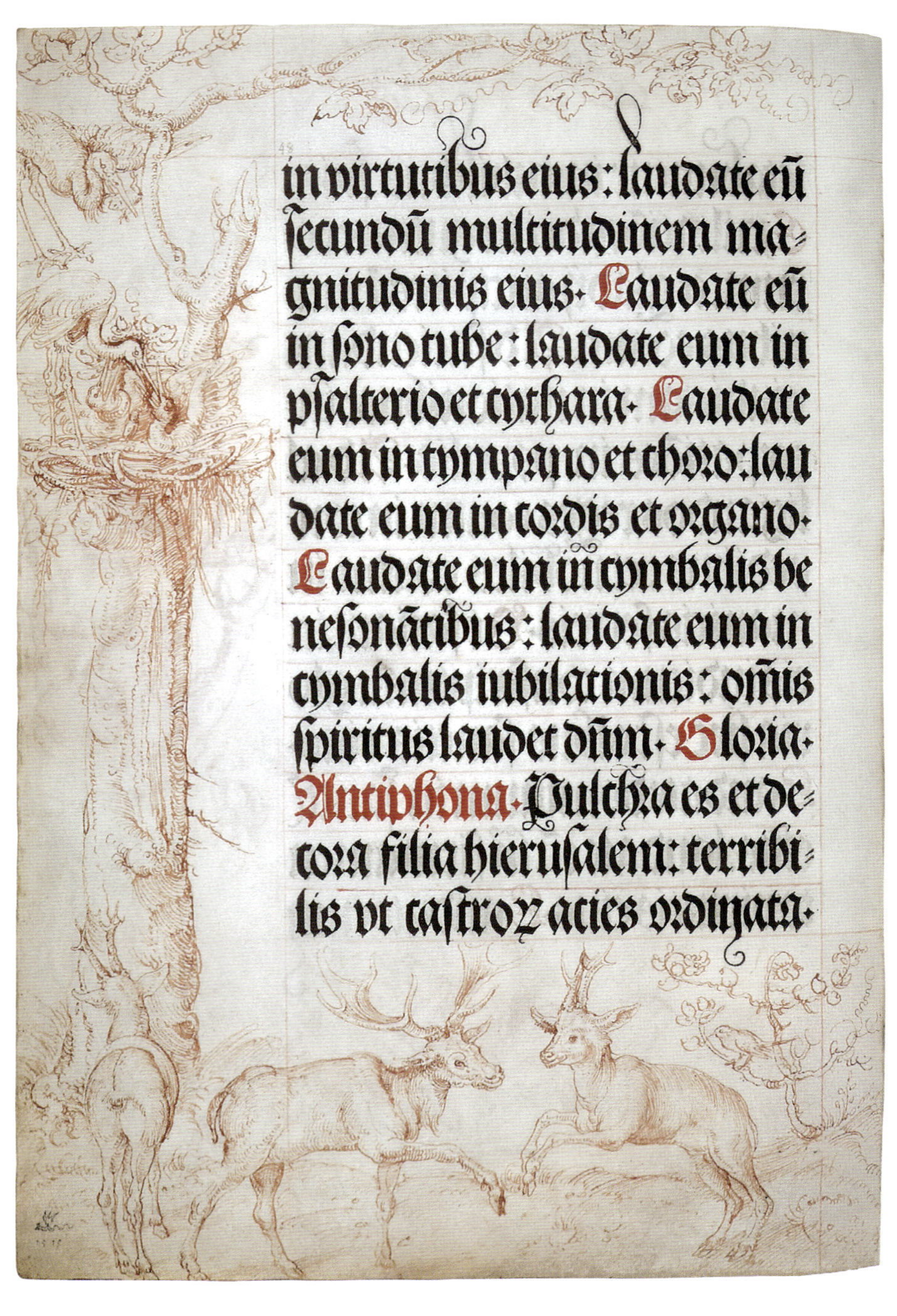
in virtutibus eius: laudate eũ
secundũ multitudinem ma-
gnitudinis eius. Laudate eũ
in sono tube: laudate eum in
psalterio et cythara. Laudate
eum in tympano et choro: lau
date eum in cordis et organo.
Laudate eum in cymbalis be
nesonãtibus: laudate eum in
cymbalis iubilationis: omis
spiritus laudet dñm. Gloria.
Antiphona. Pulchra es et de-
cora filia hierusalem: terribi-
lis vt castroꝝ acies ordinata.

STEPHANIE BUCK

Framing the Image: Lucas Cranach's *Adam and Eve* and Book Illustration

> "Dürer, Holbein and Cranach – the great trinity of German painters, according to the traditional and outdated view. Critics were preparing to oppose this general assessment of Cranach when they suddenly found themselves confronted with works that re-established and revived his reputation. He had taken his place in history as the 'master from Saxony', the friend of Luther, the orthodox Protestant painter in the Protestant north-east of Germany; his well-known paintings, found in galleries all over the world, gave an impression of sound craftsmanship without a trace of the tensions and spiritual struggles of the Reformation period; they were immediately recognizable, and invariably elicited a fleeting, superior smile."[1]

With these words Max J. Friedländer, eminent connoisseur of early German and Netherlandish art, introduced his monograph on Lucas Cranach in 1932. This text has shaped the perception of Cranach's oeuvre in art-historical scholarship, owing not only to Friedländer's authority as the director of one of the leading art museums in the world, the Berlin Gemäldegalerie, but also to the powerful and persuasive language he used to characterise the individual style and expression of a work of art. Friedländer's appraisal begins positively, effusively praising Cranach's (then recently discovered) early oeuvre, from before 1505, when he became court painter to the dukes of Saxony in Wittenberg. In Friedländer's words, compositions from this creative period "disturb us and seem to recall the time when primitive nature and primitive man were one and indivisible".[2] Clearly affected by the appreciation of German Expressionism in his own time, Friedländer continues with an often-cited outburst of disappointment in evaluating Cranach's later work:

> "Had Cranach died in 1505, he would have lived in our memory as an artist charged with dynamite. But he did not die until 1553, and instead of watching his powers explode, we see them fizzle out .... As a dreamer Cranach promised what in cold reality he was unable to fulfil. The works of his Wittenberg period make one think of a smooth, shiny chestnut that has broken out of a prickly green shell. The impassioned symphony of nature gives way before a cool, precise, rational exposition."[3]

Friedländer's assessment of Cranach's stylistic development continues to be important. His critique of Cranach, though widely embraced by art historians,[4] has, however, recently been challenged by scholars willing to adopt an approach that takes into account the documented success of Cranach's Wittenberg workshop, which produced multiple versions of a single subject, all of them of high quality.[5] While this object-based line of research focuses on his workshop practices, another aims to elucidate Cranach's later images in the light of both humanist and classical sources,[6] and by this means to arrive at a more positive evaluation of his mature style.

Fig. 12 Emperor Maximilian I's Prayerbook, 1515, fol. 57v
Pen and red-brown ink on parchment, 27.8 × 19.4. cm
Munich, Bayerische Staatsbibliothek

Among those adopting this latter approach is Hanne Kolind Poulsen, who has suggested interpreting Cranach's late oeuvre against the backdrop of Martin Luther's perception of images as texts with unambiguous meanings that refute any possibility of misunderstanding or personal interpretation.[7] Poulsen's view is based on the crucial observation that Cranach's works from the Wittenberg years largely reject the principles of linear perspective, generally understood to be an essential element of Renaissance imagery. By denying views into the distance, Cranach created flat picture spaces, stressing the two-dimensional plane. The figures are clearly outlined, an appearance Poulsen deems "anti-realistic".

However, Poulsen's one-sided interpretation of this phenomenon in Cranach's later oeuvre is somewhat problematic. As the author herself points out, tendencies toward "simplification" can clearly be seen in Cranach's work prior to 1522, when Luther first defined the role of pictures in the Reformed Church.[8] The style also appears to have been acceptable to Cranach's Catholic patrons, such as Cardinal Albrecht of Brandenburg, who certainly did not subscribe to Luther's views about images.[9] Moreover, in Cranach's diverse compositions, such as his female nudes and his allegories of the Old and the New Testament, the imagery is anything but one-dimensional and clear-cut. On the contrary, it evokes as many different readings today as it presumably did in Cranach's own time. However, Poulsen's comparison of the pictorial structure of Cranach's late works with that of texts has proved useful on another level.

ADAM AND EVE

The Courtauld Institute of Art Gallery's *Adam and Eve* (cat. 1), executed in 1526, is a perfect example of Cranach's mature painting style, practised when he was firmly established as a court painter of the dukes of Saxony at Wittenberg. The distinctive flatness of the picture space recalls medieval tapestries. The figures of Adam and Eve and the animals are clearly outlined and arranged next to one another with little overlapping. Surrounded by the relatively homogeneous green of the foliage, each form is conceived individually. The bushes and the tree are integrated into this pattern, as is evident at the upper left, where the branches and leaves of the trees do not overlap. The stag and the deer to the left of Adam and Eve, and the roebuck, the hind, the lion and the boar to their right are staggered in space. The white horse, though reduced in size to suggest its placement in the distance, adheres to the same formula.

Understood as a two-dimensional image, Cranach's panel refutes Leon Battista Alberti's definition of a picture as an "open window".[10] The metaphor of the "open window", as a means by which to structure the viewer's perception of perspective, was intended to function "in the same way as the surface of a window behind which the representation of a three-dimensional, homogeneous and logical space stretched far into the distance".[11] Cranach clearly understood this principle, as is demonstrated in the reflection of the roebuck's head in the pool. This detail exemplifies the painter's mimetic skill in capturing the three-dimensional natural world on a two-dimensional picture plane. Following contemporary conventions, the humanist Christoph Scheurl, in his panegyric of 1509, compared Cranach with the great ancient painters Apelles and Zeuxis: "In Austria you once painted grapes on a table with such success that a magpie invariably came flying by in your absence and, indignant of the chicanery, angrily hacked the new work with its beak and claws. In Coburg you painted a stag that foreign hounds always barked at."[12] Cranach's highly sophisticated work combines a refined stylisation of forms with a life-like representation of nature that remains convincing, despite its denial of scientific precision.

To this Cranach's depiction of the figures of Adam and Eve serves as an interesting counterpoint. In contrast to the finely rendered animals, the anatomies of Adam and Eve are anything but accurate.[13] The flow of Eve's long curls, which radiate unnaturally behind her, framing her temptingly beautiful body like a halo, is an expression of artful stylisation that prevails over the need for anatomical correctness.

Yet this stylisation should not be interpreted simply as a purely formal characteristic of Cranach's style in general or of the Courtauld painting in particular but also as an artistic strategy to liberate the depiction of the biblical narrative of the Fall of Man from the nature of a scene that is bound by time and space. The isolation of the figures and the resulting stylisation create an emblematic quality and imbue the picture with a sense of eternity. The notion is particularly poignant in the light of this man-made rendering of mankind the moment before it was made fallible. According to Christian belief, Original Sin is inherent in mankind. The concept is outlined in the book of Genesis: Adam and Eve, having eaten from the forbidden Tree of Knowledge, broke the only rule God had given to his creation. By breaking the law, man lost Paradise and gained consciousness of his own being, expressed in the realisation of being naked.

Cranach depicts Adam and Eve at this crucial moment of temptation, about to forfeit Paradise, unaware of their preconditioned nature. The apple unites the figures. With his left arm raised to his head, Adam is shown contemplating whether or not to eat the fruit and thereby trust in the promise of gaining knowledge and become like God. When stripped of the temporal details of the narrative, the image becomes a metaphor for this human condition. Like Adam, the viewer is asked to contemplate his own fallibility. The vines concealing the figures' nakedness – as opposed to the fig leaves that Adam and Eve will use after having eaten the apple – are integrated into the setting as part of the vegetation. By concealing the figures' genitals, Cranach follows contemporary rules of decorum and renders the picture suitable for pious reflection. However, the grapevine simultaneously recalls the New Adam, Christ, who will eventually free man from Original Sin through his Passion.[14]

THE 'FRAME'

In the context of Late Gothic imagery, this multi-layered interpretation extends to the animals as well.[15] On a literal level, they refer to God's creation in the Garden of Eden, while on an allegorical level they symbolise moral values. As Caroline Campbell (see cat. 1) has shown, the reading of these images – for example the lion, the two partridges and the boar – is not always definitive. It is possible that learned contemporary viewers – including, no doubt, the patron – avidly debated their multiple meanings.[16] On a third level, the animals provide points of reference to the world of the artist and his patrons. Except for the lion, the animals depicted in *Adam and Eve* were native to Cranach's Germany; indeed, he studied some of them, like the red deer and the partridges, during hunting trips (see cat. 6). By placing these familiar creatures in the Garden of Eden, Cranach helped to interrelate the image's subject with the world of the patron.

The animals' special role is underscored by the composition, in which the tree trunk, flanked by Adam and Eve – the primary subject – marks the central axis. The animals are arranged around this centre and, together with the apples in the tree, create a frame. This compositional structure is not unique to the Courtauld's *Adam and Eve* but was a strategy Cranach employed in several pictures.

This characteristic Cranach framing device is revealed through comparison with Dürer's compositions, which often served as models for Cranach. In Dürer's engraving of 1504 (cat. 23), for example, Adam and Eve are also surrounded by animals. By showing the figures from different angles, including foreshortening, Dürer opened up the picture space to give the illusion of depth. By vigorously cutting off the crown of the apple tree, the artist placed the human figures in convincing proportion to their surroundings and structured his image as an Albertian 'open window' providing a fragmentary view into nature. Cranach, on the other hand, conceived the elements of his picture individually and distributed them as patterns across a single plane, paying careful attention to their interrelationships. This arrangement might explain the odd placement of the sheep in the early stage of the work, visible in the infra-red reflectogram (see fig. 33, p. 74). The position of the sheep is comparable to that of the elk in Dürer's engraving: it is parallel to the picture plane behind Adam and the central tree, and thus delineates the foreground. Perhaps with this model in mind, Cranach placed the sheep in a similar position, presumably transferring the complete figure of a sheep from a drawing and then superimposing the figure of Adam. As no part of the sheep's body is visible in the zone between Adam's legs, the animal does not appear to stand behind Adam but rather to his left, thereby relegating the sheep to the 'frame'.

Cranach's decision to create a framing device by arranging significant pictorial elements around the central figures becomes evident when comparing Dürer's woodcut of the Apocalypse of around 1496–98, known as *The Vision of the Seven Candlesticks* (fig. 13)[17], to Cranach's variation of 1522 (fig. 14),

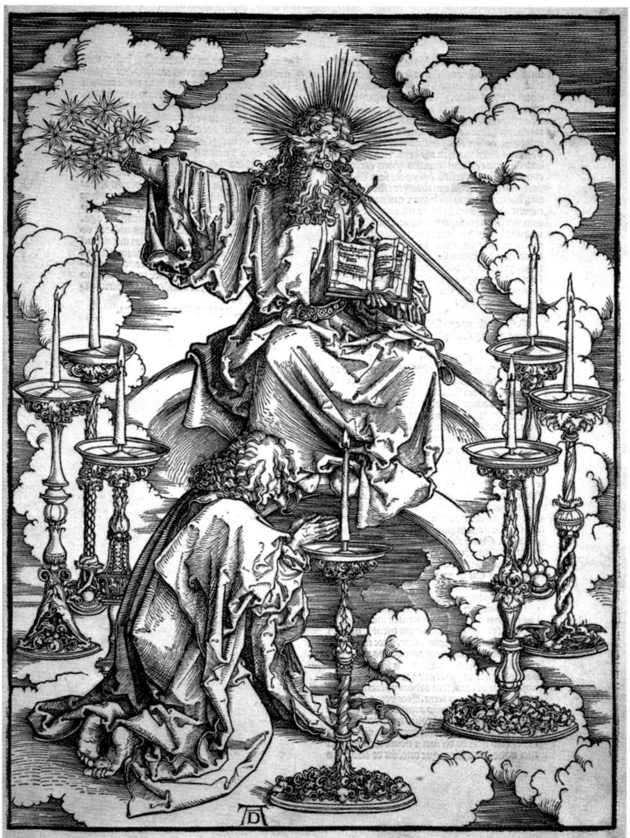

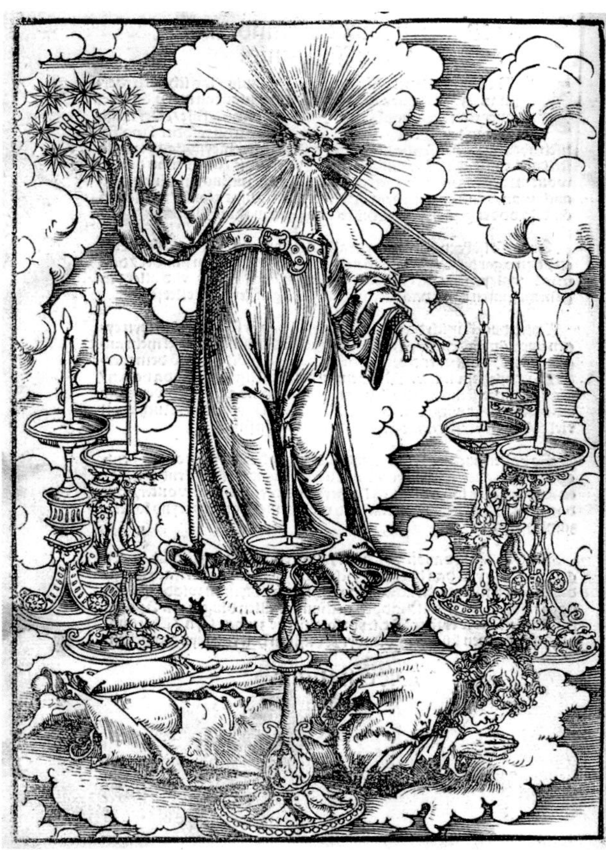

ABOVE LEFT
Fig. 13 Albrecht Dürer, *The Vision of the Seven Candlesticks*, 1496–98
Woodcut, 29.5 × 28.4 cm
London, The British Museum

ABOVE RIGHT
Fig. 14 Lucas Cranach the Elder, *The Vision of the Seven Candlesticks*, 1522
Woodcut, 25 × 17 cm
London, The British Library

published in Luther's September Testament.[18] In Cranach's woodcut, the seated God the Father has been replaced by a standing figure and the kneeling Saint John, seen from behind in Dürer's woodcut, lies across the foreground. These changes not only renounce the foreshortening of the figures, thereby stressing the flatness of the picture plane, but restructure the image entirely. Unlike Dürer, Cranach conceived his depiction around a key figure, placed in the centre, and a frame, to which Saint John is relegated. While Dürer's version explores the relationship between Saint John and his vision of the apocalyptic God as a coherent composition, Cranach's makes Saint John's vision the central motif. Saint John thus becomes an ancillary figure. With respect to the viewer, however, this framing figure has considerable significance and creates new avenues of communicating the meaning of the narrative.

This pictorial structure can be further understood in the context of the religious imagery of the 1520s and in light of Luther's perception of images as visual aids to help the viewer reflect intellectually on biblical stories rather than as objects to facilitate devotion. Such popular 'naïve' devotional objects were criticised not only by Luther but also by Erasmus of Rotterdam in his famous *Praise of Folly*, first published in 1511, as foolish behaviour akin to superstition.[19] Moreover, as Tacke has stressed, Cranach's style also accommodated those who disagreed with Luther's view, as the artist and his

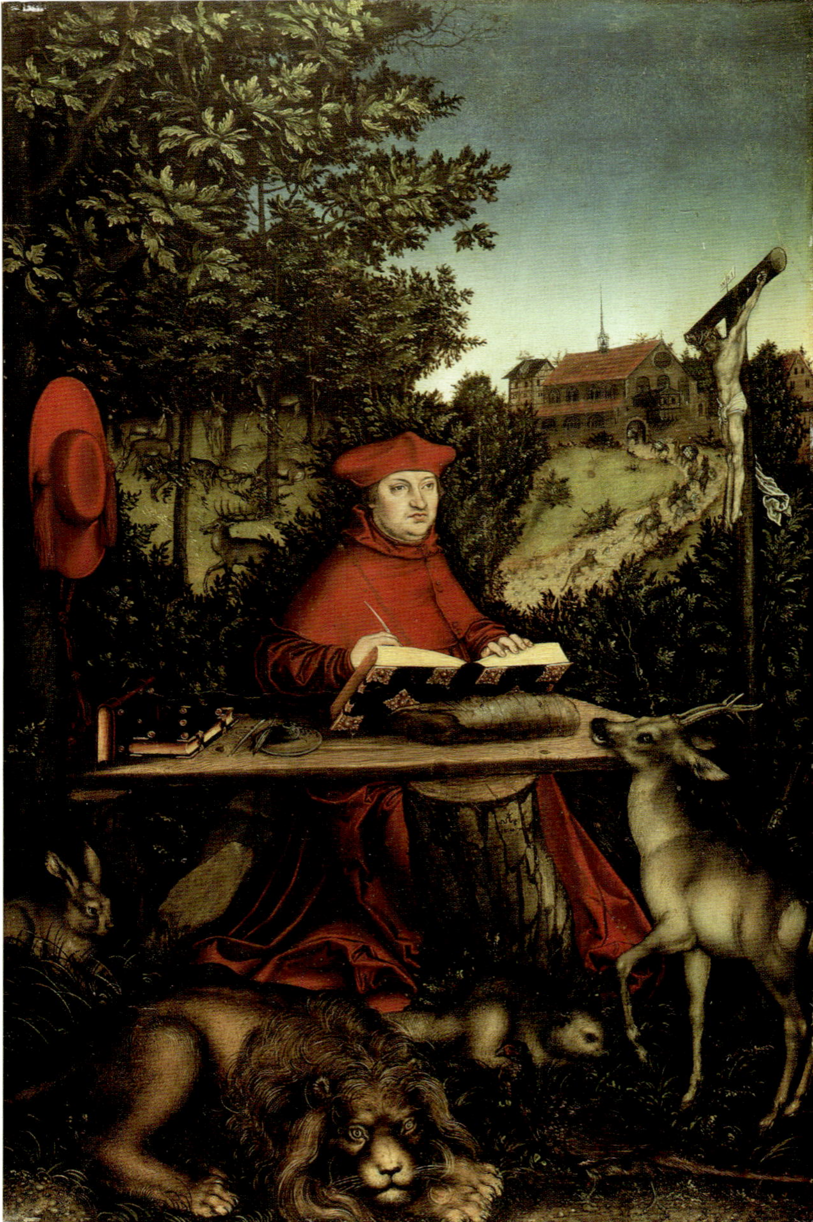

Fig. 15 Lucas Cranach the Elder, *Canon Albrecht of Brandenburg as Saint Jerome, outdoors*, 1527, Oil on limewood, 57 × 37.6 cm Berlin, Gemäldegalerie

workshop executed nearly one hundred and eighty paintings for Cardinal Albrecht of Brandenburg.[20]

Perhaps the most telling examples of Cranach's use of this pictorial structure are two portraits of this mighty Catholic dignitary in the guise of Saint Jerome in the wilderness and Saint Jerome in his study, in Berlin and Darmstadt respectively (figs. 15 and 16),[21] both contemporary with the Courtauld *Adam and Eve*. Regardless of the specific iconography of depictions of the saint's legend, Cardinal Albrecht of Brandenburg is consistently shown as an erudite church father rather than as an ascetic who flagellates himself

Fig. 16 Lucas Cranach the Elder, *Canon Albrecht of Brandenburg as Saint Jerome, indoors*, 1525
Oil on limewood, 116.5 × 77.5 cm
Darmstadt, Hessisches Landesmuseum

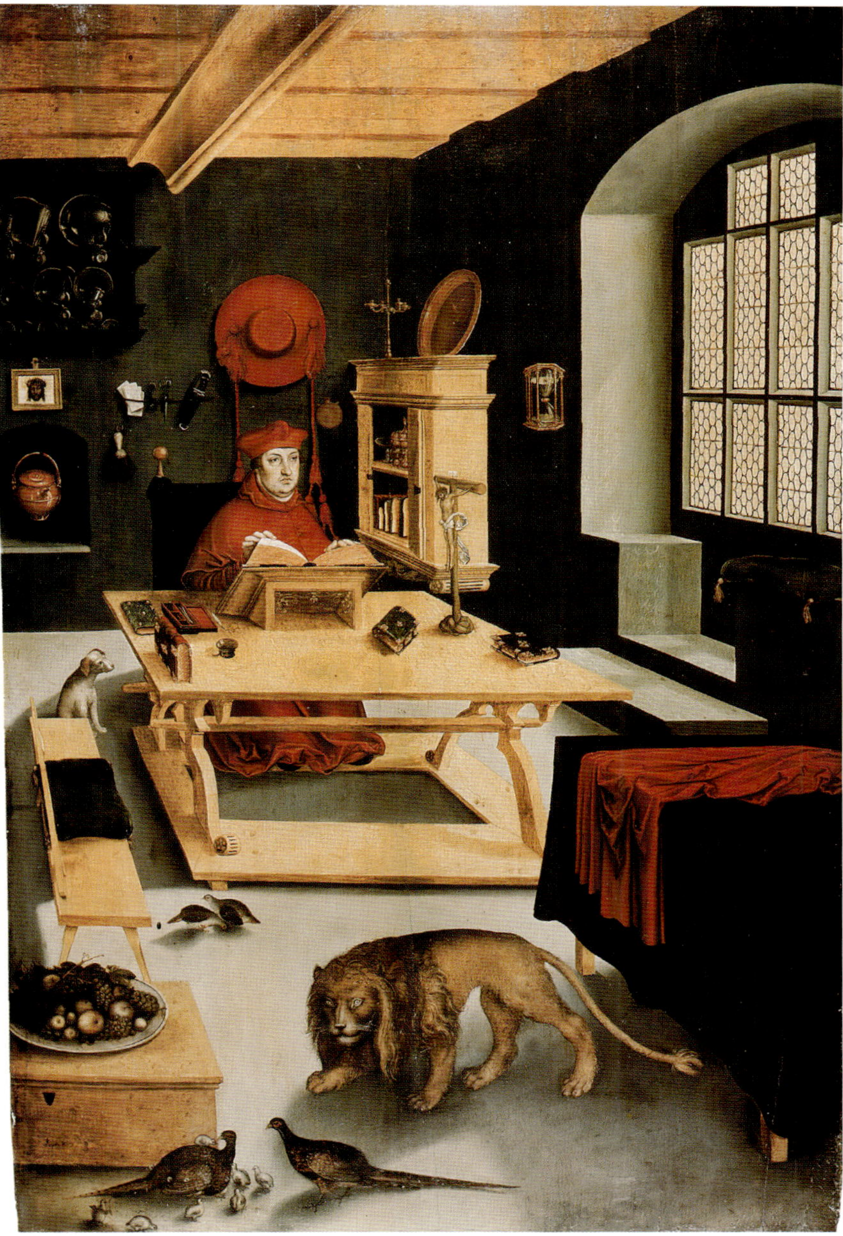

before the crucified Christ. As in *Adam and Eve* and *The Vision of the Candlesticks*, the main figure is placed in the centre, and is framed by elements that celebrate Albrecht of Brandenburg as a humanist scholar and are thus crucial to the narrative and act as pictorial embellishments. In the Berlin panel, animals are placed at the bottom and at the sides, grouped with the cardinal's hat and a sculpture of the crucified Christ. The zone above Saint Jerome is reserved for a clearly divided strip of sky, trees, and buildings.

While the Berlin painting reiterates Cranach's typical flat space – even though a middle ground is included – the Darmstadt panel shows that

Cranach was well aware of the rules of linear perspective, as demonstrated by the use of orthogonal lines that meet at a vanishing point to the left of the picture of a *vera* icon pinned to the back wall. Yet even in a composition that follows the demands of a 'Renaissance' picture in the Albertian mode, Cranach deliberately employs perspective in the service of his framing device by placing most elements – only one book is exempt, which seems to float on the table – either parallel to the picture plane or aligned with the orthogonal lines, avoiding overlapping. A clear pattern emerges in which the cardinal is encircled by a frame of animals, books, cushions, and objects fixed to the wall.

In the Darmstadt painting, the key figure is not placed along a central axis, thereby rendering the sides of the frame unequal in width. This scheme, however, is not arbitrary but follows the well-established layout of a book page, which, in the case of a recto, shifts the central square reserved for the text or the main picture to the left (often, but not always, according to the 'golden section'), framed by borders that were either left blank for annotations and commentaries or were lavishly decorated. The border and the central picture or text co-existed on the page as separate units yet corresponded in a variety of ways. In the early sixteenth century this relationship had been explored in depth in Netherlandish, German, French and Italian book illustration, both in painted manuscript illuminations (fig. 17) and in prints (fig. 18).[22] Cranach was familiar with this form of decoration, as he had operated a printing press with Christian Döring in Wittenberg from 1523 until about 1525–26. More importantly, in 1515 he belonged to a prolific group of artists, headed by Albrecht Dürer, that was asked to decorate the borders of Maximilian I's Prayerbook with pen-and-ink drawings.[23] Without directly referring to the texts he illustrated, Cranach chose instead to depict mostly animals – deer, storks, foxes, elks, and monkeys. On folio 57v (fig. 12) the border can be interpreted as a flat but continuous picture space. On folio 61v (fig. 19) it is subdivided into four segments – top, bottom, and sides – each treated independently. While the lower border depicts a group of herons at a lake, the left is reserved for candelabra and the small zone above the text is decorated with an ornamental cartouche. Unrelated to the other motifs, the pen lines echo the flourishes of the typeface, newly developed for the Prayerbook. In all Cranach's designs in the Prayerbook individual motifs are arranged in an additive manner with little overlapping. This is also the case in Cranach's designs for woodcut title-page illustrations, which place the text block in the very centre of the page, thus creating side borders of equal width. The title page with the Grunenberg monogram of 1520 (cat. 19) depicts multiple superimposed, unrelated images, as does the one designed in 1525 for Luther's *Das diese Wort Christi* (cat. 20), which presents the familiar stags and deer in a meadow at the bottom and grotesque figural ornaments above.

The structure and motif of Cranach's decoration is embedded in the tradition of border illustrations developed in the last quarter of the fifteenth

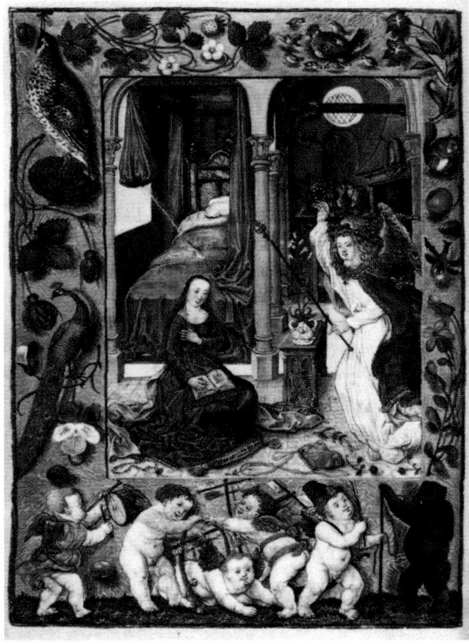

Fig. 17 Augsburg painter, *The Annunciation*, from Narciss Renner's Prayerbook, 1523
Tempera on parchment
Vienna, Österreichische Nationalbibliothek, cod. 4486, fol. 35v

century by the Master of Mary of Burgundy and his followers, known as the Ghent–Bruges school of book illumination.[24] In Germany, the Augsburg Petrarch Master's woodcuts of about 1520, designed as border illustrations (fig. 18), are offshoots of this tradition, as are the miniatures in Narziss Renner's Prayerbook of 1523 (fig. 17),[25] all of which frame a main image with animals and flowers, stylised to various degrees.

In this tradition, the border is conceived as part of the book and the flowers are intended to appear strewn on the page. As *trompe-l'oeil* paintings, they differ from the image in the centre, as it depicts the text or refers to it and as such functions as the text's equivalent. Thus both types of images address different levels of reality and of perception – distinctions which book illuminators frequently played with when employing various strategies to dissolve boundaries between the two zones. The illustration of the Crucifixion in a Book of Hours of about 1480–90 in the Blackburn Museum and Art Gallery (Hart Ms. 20884, fol. 33v) by the Netherlandish Master of Edward VI provides a representative example.[26] The artist used the lower border of the page as a zone to depict the Carrying of the Cross; the figures overlap with the borders of the main miniature, thereby allowing them to move out of the lower border and into the foreground; the side borders are conceived as a flat page strewn with flowers.

Cranach plays with these principles of book illustration on several levels when using the framing structure for compositions like the Courtauld *Adam and Eve*. This structure helped Cranach to stress the primacy of the main figures and their equivalence to the essence of the written text. As they become isolated figures within the setting of the Garden of Eden, they are liberated from the limitations of time and space – an appropriate reflection of the human condition originating in the Fall. The animals add yet another level of meaning to the image by virtue of their traditional iconography. In this respect, it is significant that most of the animals gaze out at the viewer, thus mediating between the main figures – the 'text' – and the world of the viewer. This impact is powerfully underscored by the cropping of the animals' bodies on either side of the picture, as they appear to reach into our space. Here, the animals are conceived as *parerga*, a concept that in ancient rhetoric characterises embellishments and, according to Pliny, ornamentations added to paintings.[27] Without having to give up the Renaissance precept of a panel painting as the depiction of a single scene, Cranach was able to focus on the main subject, Adam and Eve, in a clear, direct manner and still include the embellishments that make the picture enjoyable.

Thus there is yet another level of explanation for this metastructure: the frame – understood as such – provides a space for the painter to illustrate his powers of *trompe l'oeil*. As Victor Stoichita has demonstrated, borders of book illuminations were the origin of still-life painting.[28] Cranach's depiction of animals and of objects shown pinned on the wall in the Darmstadt *Saint Jerome* can be understood within this context. In the Courtauld *Adam and Eve* the reflection of the roebuck in the lower right corner gives us a glimpse of

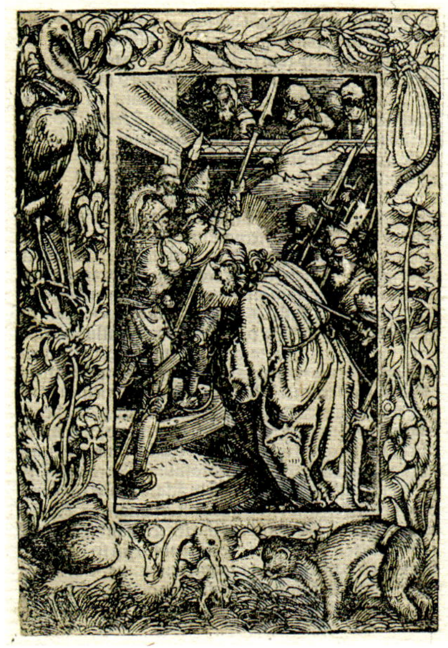

Fig. 18 The Petrarch Master, *Christ carrying the Cross*, around 1520
Woodcut
Oxford, The Ashmolean Museum

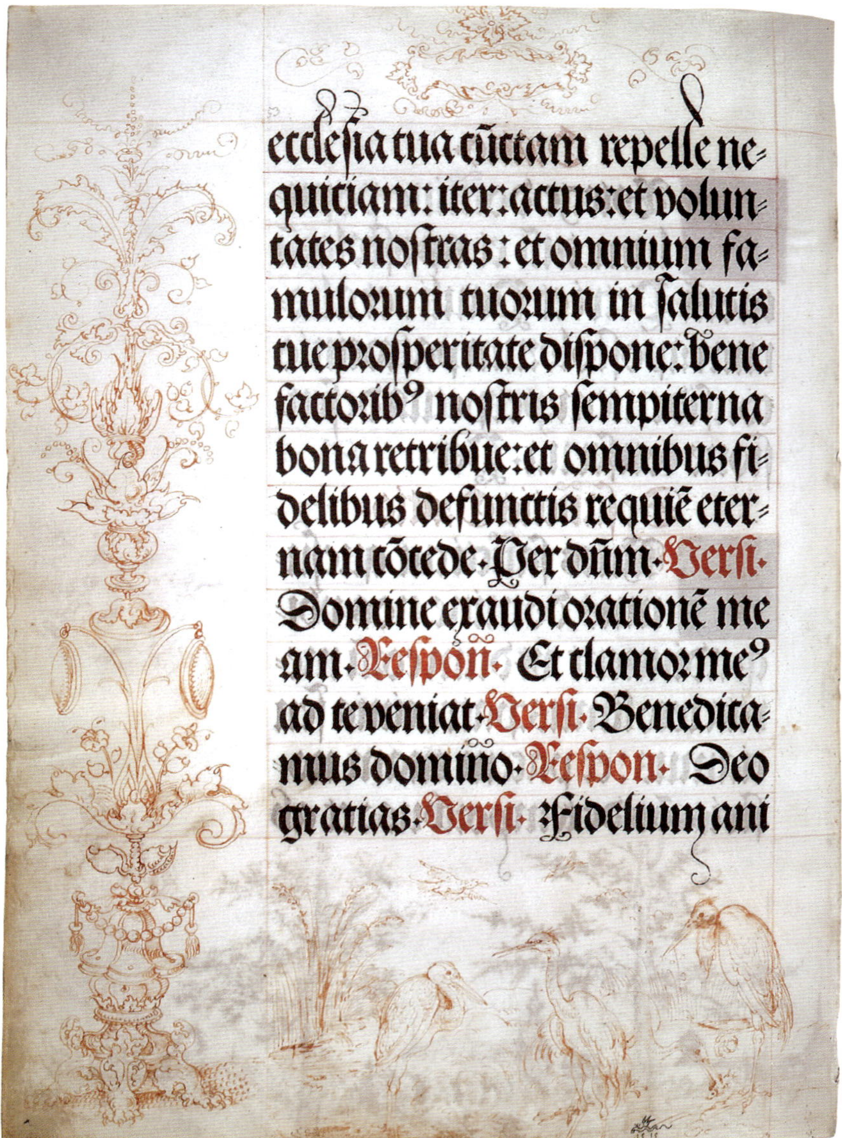

ecclesia tua cūctam repelle ne-
quiciam: iter: actus: et volun-
tates nostras: et omnium fa-
mulorum tuorum in salutis
tue prosperitate dispone: bene
factoribꝰ nostris sempiterna
bona retribue: et omnibus fi-
delibus defunctis requiē eter-
nam cōcede. Per dñm. Versi.
Domine exaudi orationē me
am. Respon. Et clamor meꝰ
ad te veniat. Versi. Benedica-
mus domino. Respon. Deo
gratias. Versi. Fidelium ani

Fig. 19 Lucas Cranach the Elder,
Emperor Maximilian I's Prayerbook, 1515, fol. 61v
Pen and red-brown ink on parchment, 27.8 × 19.4 cm
Munich, Bayerische Staatsbibliothek

Cranach's ability to capture the world in his painting as masterfully as the ancient painters Parrhasius, Zeuxis and Apelles. The fact that it is the painter who challenges the viewer's senses and refers him back to the main subject is made clear when looking at his signature. Cranach's coat of arms, a winged serpent, granted to him by Frederick of Saxony, is placed immediately under the serpent on the forbidden Tree of Knowledge. By self-consciously inscribing his name into the text, Cranach was perhaps challenging the viewer to seek the meaning and wisdom lost during the Fall by contemplating and enjoying his own masterful and tempting creation.

NOTES

My warm and sincere thanks to Pamela Barr and Amanda Sarroff, who helped with the editing of this essay.

1 "*Dürer, Holbein und Cranach: das Dreigestirn der deutschen Maler in der überkommenen und überalterten Vorstellung. Die Kunstkritik machte sich gerade daran, der populären Wertung Cranachs entgegenzutreten, als sie auf Werke stieß, die seinen Ruhm erneuerten und belebten. In die Geschichte war Cranach eingegangen als der sächsische Meister, als der Freund Luthers, der rechtgläubige Maler im protestantischen Nordosten. Die bekannten Bilder von ihm, in allen Galerien der Welt, bieten den Eindruck von einer handwerklich gediegenen Kunstübung, die nichts von der seelischen Spannung des Reformationskampfes verrät. Sie sind leicht kenntlich und werden überall mit gönnerhaft wissendem Lächeln flüchtig begrüßt*": Friedländer and Rosenberg 1932, p. 1; Friedländer and Rosenberg 1978, p. 13.

2 Friedländer and Rosenberg 1978, p. 16.

3 "*Wäre Cranach 1505 gestorben, so würde er im Gedächtnis leben wie geladen mit Explosivstoff. Er ist aber erst 1553 gestorben, und wir beobachten statt der Explosion ein Ausrinnen .... Der wache Cranach hält nicht, was der träumende versprochen hat. Seine Wittenberger Kunst gleicht einer glatten Kastanie, die aus stachlig grüner Schale gesprungen ist. Phlegmatisch verständige und saubere Darlegung tritt an die Stelle leidenschaftlich tönenden Naturlauts*": Friedländer and Rosenberg 1932, pp. 9–10; Friedländer and Rosenberg 1978, p. 16.

4 For a recapitulation see Kolind Poulsen 2003, pp. 130–31.

5 See Campbell in this volume (cat. 1). See also Hinz 1994, Tacke 1994 and especially Kunz 1994, pp. 98–100. The Cranach workshop is not the only example of this type of 'mass production'; the phenomenon can also be traced in other German workshops, for example in Ulm. See Stuttgart 1993.

6 Matsche 1996, Bierende 2002 and Robert 2003. For the humanist background of the young Cranach see Koepplin 1973.

7 See Kolind Poulsen 2002 and 2003.

8 Kolind Poulsen 2003, pp. 134–36; on Luther's texts see Stechow 1966, pp. 129–30.

9 On Cardinal Albrecht of Brandenburg see Schauerte 2006.

10 Alberti 1972, chapter 19, p. 55: "Let me tell you what I do when I am painting. First of all, on the surface on which I am going to paint, I draw a rectangle of whatever size I want, which I regard as an open window through which the subject to be painted is seen; and I decide how large I wish the human figures in the painting to be."

11 Stoichita 1997, p. 12.

12 Schuchardt 1851–71, I, p. 29.

13 For an interpretation of Cranach's stylisation of nude figures, especially Venus, in the light of humanist rhetoric, see Robert 2003, pp. 112–13.

14 See Campbell in this volume (cat. 1).

15 Houwen 1997; Dittrich 2004.

16 See Campbell in this volume (cat. 1).

17 Schoch, Mende and Scherbaum 2001–04, II, no. 113, pp. 72–73.

18 Koepplin and Falk 1974, I, nos. 222 and 223, p. 340; Strehle and Kunz 1998, pp. 186–87.

19 Erasmus 1979, pp. 63–64: "Closely related to such men are those who have adopted the very foolish (but nevertheless quite agreeable) belief that if they look at a painting or statue of that huge Polyphemus Christopher, they will not die on that day; or, if they address a statue of Barbara with the prescribed words, they will return from battle unharmed; or, if they accost Erasmus on certain days, with certain wax tapers, and in certain little formulas of prayer, they will soon become rich. Moreover, in George they have discovered a new Hercules, just as they have found a new Hippolytus. They all but worship George's horse, most religiously decked out in breastplates and bosses, and from time to time oblige him with some little gift. To swear by his bronze helmet is thought to be an oath fit for a king."

20 Tacke 1992, p. 12.

21 See Friedländer and Rosenberg 1978, nos. 184–85, p. 106. A third panel in the John and Mabel Ringling Museum of Art, Sarasota, Florida, dated 1526, is a variant of the Darmstadt composition: see Friedländer and Rosenberg 1978, no. 186, pp. 106–07.

22 See in general Pächt 1986, especially chapter VII ('The Conflict of Surface and Space: an Ongoing Process'), pp. 173–202; De Hamel 1986, especially chapters 6 and 8, pp. 159–85, 215–44.

23 Giehlow 1907; Leidinger 1922; Rosenberg 1960, nos. 21–28, pp. 19–20; Sieveking 1987; Buck 2006.

24 For the Master of Mary of Burgundy and his circle see König *et al.* 1998; Kren and McKendrick 2003, pp. 126–57.

25 See Koreny 1985, pp. 12–13, 42.

26 Kren and McKendrick 2003, no. 98, p. 342.

27 Stoichita 1997, p. 23.

28 *Ibid.*, pp. 17–18.

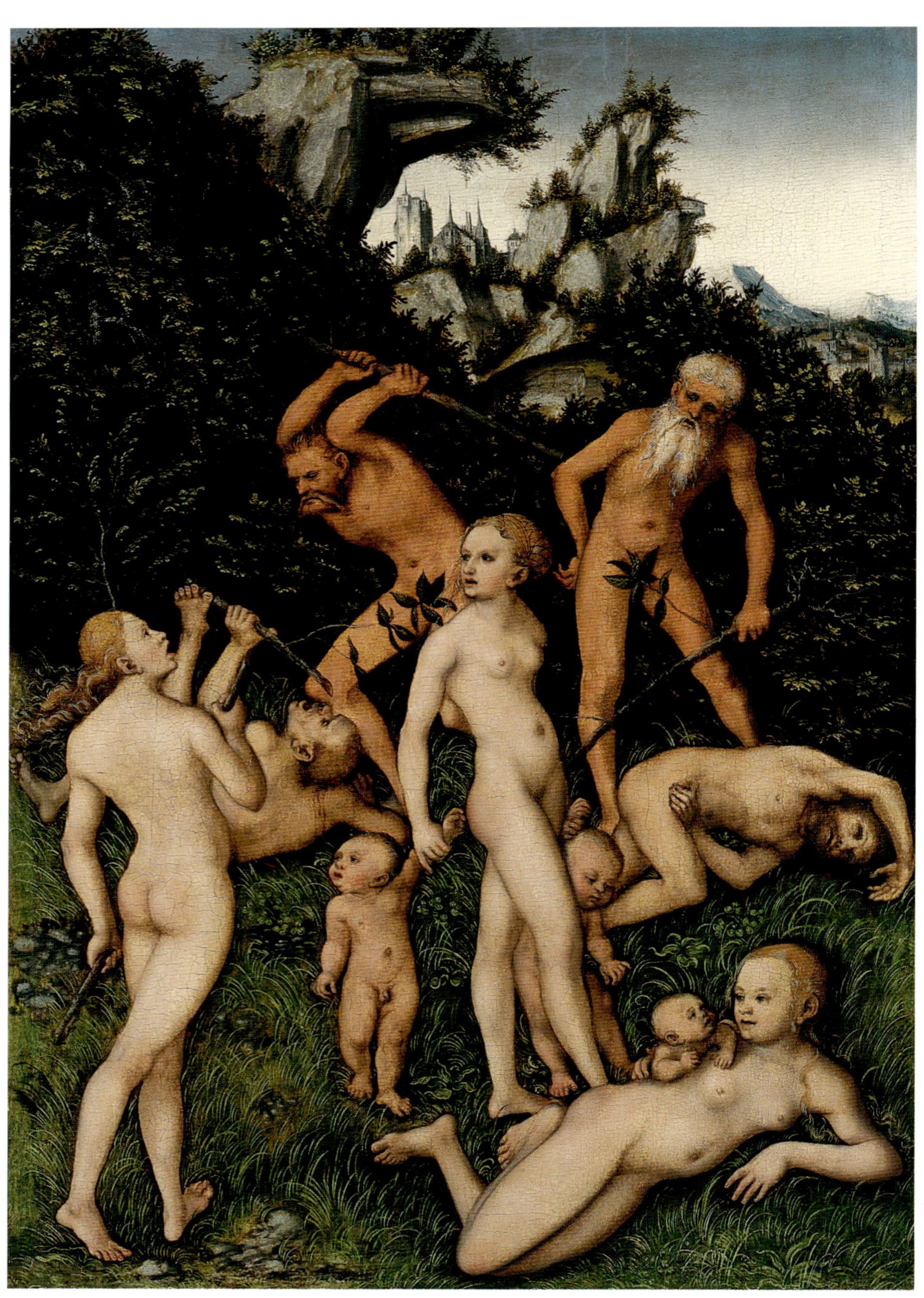

SUSAN FOISTER

Before the Fall: *Adam and Eve* and Some Mythological Paintings by Cranach

Among the most beautiful and widely appreciated of Cranach's paintings today are those which depict nude figures in verdant wooded landscapes, often with distant views of castles perched on elevated crags and reflected in still stretches of water below. The subjects of these paintings are mostly mythological but their treatment of landscape extends to the Courtauld Institute Gallery *Adam and Eve* (cat. 1) in the Garden of Eden, surrounded by animals of all kinds. Highly refined in their painting technique, these pictures are not only superb examples of Cranach's mature painting style, but also show him redefining a traditional biblical subject and inventing new secular representations in a way which involved fruitful exchange between the two, perhaps with the ultimate intention that such paintings, despite their ostensibly diverse subjects, should be displayed and viewed together.

Depictions of Adam and Eve, the first sinners, whose Fall would lead to man's redemption through Christ's death on the Cross, were traditionally included on the shutters of altarpieces telling the story of Christian redemption.[1] Just as Adam's sinfulness was in medieval theology contrasted with Christ's sacrifice, so Eve's responsibility for the Fall of man was set against the Virgin Mary's purity as mother of Christ. Cranach portrayed Adam and Eve on the outsides of panels now in Vienna which depict Christ as the Man of Sorrows and the Virgin on the reverses (see essay by Gunnar Heydenreich); the panels have been dated to about 1518.[2] The earliest versions of Cranach's painted Adam and Eve compositions, however, appear to be those produced as unified compositions on small panels, rather than part of altarpieces. They present the pair on either side of a tree with a serpent, and although they stand on stony ground they are placed against black backgrounds. None is dated firmly, but those in Besançon (fig. 5), Warsaw, Würzburg and Munich (fig. 27, p. 66) have been dated on stylistic grounds from around 1508–9 to 1512.[3] The early history of these panels is unknown, but they appear to have been conceived as independent paintings, and as such can be compared to Dürer's life-size depictions of *Adam* and *Eve* of 1507, now in the Prado (fig. 6), as well as to his famous engraving of the pair dated 1504 (cat. 23).[4]

Cranach's first securely dated representation of Adam and Eve was also a print, the woodcut of 1509 (cat. 12), which differs from these earliest paintings in including a landscape background.[5] Produced at the same time as his woodcuts of secular subjects such as *Venus and Cupid* (cat. 14 and 15) and *The Judgement of Paris*, which feature nude female figures, it suggests an audience for this subject very different from those for altarpieces. Cranach's secularised

Fig. 20 Lucas Cranach the Elder, *The Close of the Silver Age*, around 1530
Oil on panel, 50.2 × 35.7 cm
London, The National Gallery

presentation of Adam and Eve was reflected in, and perhaps stimulated by, images of the nude produced by other artists at the same period in a variety of media, notably sculpture.[6] Adam and Eve became frequent subjects for small sculpted plaquettes in Germany, alongside mythological themes.[7] For Dürer, Adam and Eve provided vehicles for his studies of human ideal proportion. In the case of the Netherlandish artist Gossaert, whose work Cranach must have seen when he visited the Netherlands in 1508, first-hand knowledge of antique sculpture informed the figure style of his highly erotic representations of Adam and Eve.[8] His German contemporary Baldung's representations of Adam and Eve (cat. 24 and 25) and his small paintings of nude women with the figure of death drew less on studies of proportion and the antique and more on a tradition of ostensibly moralising, objectifying presentations of women depicted for male gratification.[9] The portrayal of Eve inevitably offered the opportunity for the male viewer to enjoy the depiction of female nudity while deploring the ability of women to lead men astray from the path of Christian virtue.

If the subject of Adam and Eve provided Cranach with a new opportunity for the pleasurable representation of nude figures in landscapes, the majority of those secular subjects which he produced while working in Wittenberg for the court of the Electors of Saxony from 1506 were far from novel in Northern Europe at this time. Cranach's paintings make visible a category of subject-matter commonly encountered in medieval literature, and which had long been represented in manuscript illumination, tapestries and the decorative arts.[10] For the Judgement of Paris, Cranach, like others, followed a visual model which derived from a medieval text, the *History of the Destruction of Troy* of 1287 by Guido of Colonna, while the nudity of his female goddesses echoes that found in fifteenth-century manuscript illustrations of, for example, subjects from Ovid, popular throughout the Middle Ages. When Cranach first took up the theme of Venus and Cupid in the woodcut of about 1509 (cat. 14 and 15; its date of 1506 is usually argued to have been falsified),[11] the goddess was given her traditional astrological aspect as a planetary deity, with star and scales, mirror and flowers.[12] The composition is reflected in a life-size painting with a dark background, now in the Hermitage (FR 22, dated 1509). Although its production may have been encouraged by humanists wishing Cranach to emulate the feats of Apelles, it bears a moralizing Latin inscription, warning against the dangers of the pleasures of the flesh. Over the ensuing decades, Cranach's presentation of these and other mythological subjects became increasingly reliant on sources which were ultimately inspired by interest in the figure sculpture of classical antiquity. In some cases, therefore (Bacchus or Diana, for instance), his presentation differs from those of earlier times, showing figures nude rather than dressed in the fashions of the period, but the subjects may not have been understood by their courtly audience in any particularly novel manner. For example, in 1517 Albrecht of Prussia ordered a "*Hercules der einen nackenden Kerl zu Tod drückt*", the subject of which clearly parallels a Hercules and Antaeus painted by Cranach ; it may be significant that he describes the subject as an action picture rather than a mythology.[13]

Few payments to Cranach otherwise survive to elucidate the context for his early mythological paintings or for those of Adam and Eve, or to confirm that these subjects were popular with the Saxon and other German courts; nor is there any specific information concerning the market for his prints of these subjects. [14] But a poem of 1508 by the Wittenberg town clerk Andreas Meinhard provides descriptions of the interiors of the castle at Wittenberg, decorated with imagery including the triumphs of Hercules and the stories of Perseus and Andromeda and Jason and the Golden Fleece.[15] A slightly later poem by the Wittenberg poet Philipp Engelbrecht celebrating the marriage of the Elector Johann the Steadfast and Margaret of Anhalt in 1513, for which Cranach and his assistants provided painted decorations, describes their bedchamber decorated with hangings showing subjects including the Judgement of Paris, Apollo and Marsyas, Hercules and Omphale and Lucretia.[16] Even if some of these descriptions might be regarded as idealising rather than literal, they are important in suggesting a courtly context for the production of Cranach's early prints and paintings depicting nudes and secular subjects.

Later documentation of the paintings on canvas which Cranach supplied for the rulers of Saxony and the bills he sent in for paintings on both panel and canvas show that these included the biblical subjects of Adam and Eve and Judith, along with such mythological subjects as Venus, Diana and Actaeon, Lucretia, Hercules and Omphale, the Judgement of Paris and Charity.[17] Although, other than the poems already mentioned, we do not have evidence from Saxony showing how these paintings of nude subjects – mythologies as well as Adam and Eve – were displayed, information concerning other northern European courts is suggestive in this context. For example the inventory taken of Henry VIII's possessions on his death in 1547 records a painting of Adam and Eve immediately following one of Lucretia, suggesting they were shown together; similarly he owned what may have been a single diptych with paintings of Lucretia and Mary Magdalen, both evidently showing beautiful and perhaps scantily clad women.[18] Mythological and nude subjects, similar to those in paintings by Cranach, are listed in other contemporary courtly inventories from northern Europe. For instance, Anthony, Duke of Lorraine had in his palace at Nancy in 1544 paintings of Mary Magdalen, Adam and Eve and Lucretia.[19] For such courtly owners the dramatic action of a Hercules, the seductive charms of a naked Venus, Lucretia or Eve, and the subsidiary motifs of hunting, forests and deer, landscapes and castles, which appear in Cranach's settings of some of these subjects, are likely to have represented their greatest pleasure in owning such pictures.

In the 1520s, however, Cranach developed some subjects directly inspired by the interests of humanists close to the Saxon court, along with a new range of secular subjects including nude figures, all in exquisite landscape settings. In style closely associated with his depiction of the Courtauld *Adam and Eve* of 1526 (cat. 1), the subjects include Cupid complaining to Venus (cat. 2), the

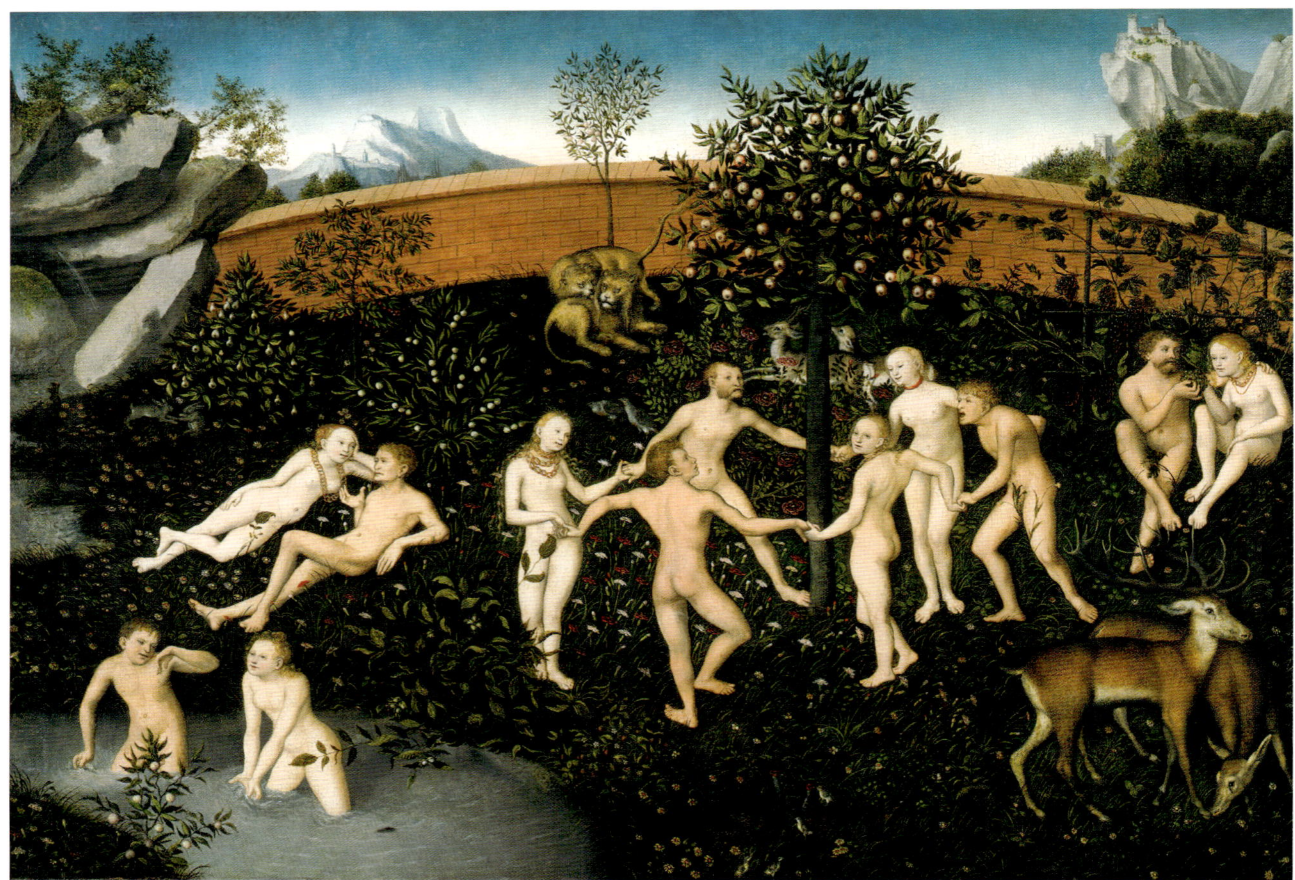

Fig. 21 Lucas Cranach the Elder, *The Golden Age*, around 1530
Oil on panel, 68 × 102 cm
Munich, Alte Pinakothek

'Nymph of the Spring', and Apollo and Diana (cat. 3), as well as representations of primitive people, and related paintings of the Golden Age (such as fig. 21) and the so-called 'Silver Age' (fig. 20). Landscape depiction had always been an important part of Cranach's painterly repertoire, though by the 1520s he had developed an approach to its representation which reflected the methodical nature of his approach to painting in general, differing from the much freer depictions of forests and wilderness in his earliest paintings. The landscapes of the 1520s into which Cranach inserted his Adam and Eve and mythological subjects were largely made up of three principal elements – distant views of castles and lakes, evocative of those owned by his Saxon patrons,[20] cultivated swathes of trees, grass and hedges and, in the middle-ground, forests with deer, evoking the pursuit of hunting. Hunting was certainly of the greatest importance to the courtly owners of paintings by Cranach, and a number of his paintings take it as its principal subject (including fig. 3).[21] While continuing on occasion to place his subjects against a plain background, he now proceeded to insert landscape settings into depictions of subjects previously presented without such adornment, or essayed in this manner only as prints. The Judgement of Paris, first seen as a woodcut, was developed as a painted subject as early as 1512–14,[22] but by the 1520s the subjects presented in landscape settings in a similar manner included both Adam and Eve and Venus and Cupid, as well as many more.

The undated painting of *Cupid complaining to Venus* now in the National Gallery, London (cat. 2), is the most elaborate and elegant of the numerous versions of this subject painted by Cranach and his workshop, and probably the earliest.[23] Venus and Cupid are shown against a lavish and beautiful landscape background. To the left is forest, in which a stag and a hind lurk in semi-darkness. On the right, silhouetted against a brilliant blue sky which shades into the haziness evocative of distance, is a mountainous landscape with a castle perched on a high crag overlooking water, in which a perfect mirror image of the landscape is reflected. Between Venus and Cupid is an economically depicted apple tree burgeoning with fruit,[24] which closely resembles the tree in the Courtauld *Adam and Eve*. Like Eve, Venus holds a branch of the tree with her left hand, while her left foot is supported by a lower branch. To her left is Cupid, clutching a stolen honeycomb and suffering the stings of the bees which have flown out of a large hole in the base of the tree trunk. Whereas the Latin inscription in other versions is presented on a white *cartellino*, making the text easier to read, here, uniquely, it is painted directly against the sky.

As Pablo Pérez d'Ors has recently shown, the Latin text was composed by Georg Sabinus, son-in-law of Philipp Melanchthon, the Lutheran theologian who was Professor of Greek at the University of Wittenberg, and first published in 1536.[25] It is based on lines traditionally attributed to the third-century Greek poet Theocritus, whose supposed *Idyll* XIX, 'The Honeythief', tells how Cupid ran to his mother Venus, complaining of being stung by bees after stealing a honeycomb.[26] When Cupid asked how such a small creature could give him such a large wound, Venus, laughing, told him that the effect was very similar to the wounds that he himself imparted when he shot his darts at humans, and caused them pain. The Latin inscription on the Cranach paintings reads in translation: 'Young Cupid was stealing honey from a hive when a bee stung the thief on the finger. So it is for us: the brief and fleeting pleasure we seek comes mixed with wretched pain to do us harm.'

The Pseudo-Theocritus's text was not unknown in the Middle Ages - an illuminated fourteenth-century copy survives[27] – but it became fashionable among the humanists of Cranach's time, and was easily and amusingly visualised, as well as adapted in their own writing.[28] Dürer's friend Pirkheimer owned a copy of the Greek text (now in a private collection) with an illustrated titlepage usually attributed to Dürer, and dated to about 1504. Dürer illustrated the *Idyll* of the honeythief in 1514 (fig. 22) in the so-called Ambras sketchbook, which included other drawings by Dürer with classical subjects and inscriptions. One of these subjects, also developed by Cranach in a series of paintings, was the Nymph of the Spring: the Latin inscription, which reads in translation: 'I am the nymph of the sacred spring. Do not disturb my sleep, I am resting', though believed to be of classical origin, was a shortened version of an epigram in fact composed in Italy in the late fifteenth century.

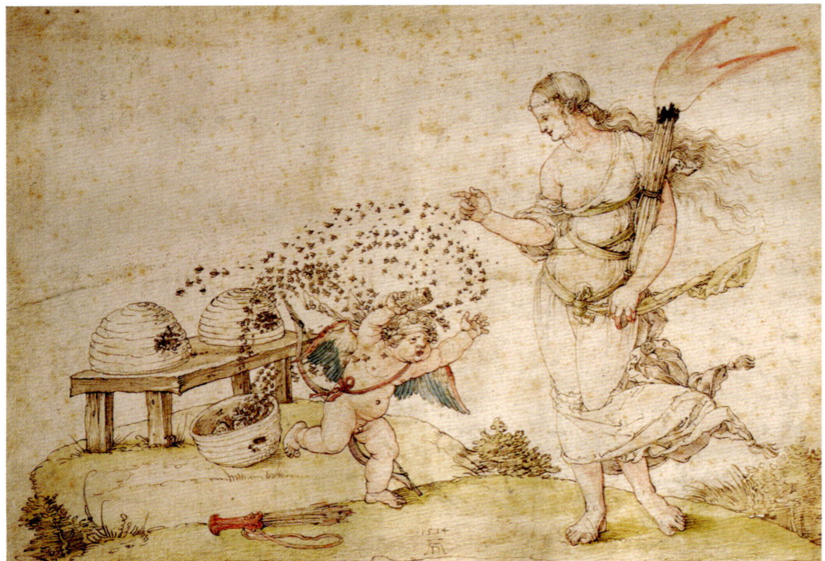

Fig. 22 Albrecht Dürer, *Venus and Cupid the Honeythief*, 1514
Pen and ink, over indications in graphite, with watercolours on paper, 21.6 × 31.3 cm
Vienna, Kunsthistorisches Museum

The 'sleeping nymph' provided another entirely new subject for Cranach, allowing him to present a nude female figure in a landscape in a manner inspired by classical sculpture.[29]

Despite the fact that both Cranach and Dürer took inspiration from the subjects of the Nymph of the Spring and Venus and the Honeythief, the two artists' images of the latter are not at all similar. Dürer presents the subject as a horizontal narrative composition with Cupid running across it towards Venus, an approach that is repeated in his small woodcut of around 1526.[30] In both works by Dürer Venus is clad in a flowing robe, rather than being presented nude, while in neither do his bees reside in a hollow tree: in the 1514 drawing bees pour out of beehives (true to the Greek text), and in the woodcut they emerge from a hole in a post.

While Cranach's version of the subject is strikingly unlike Dürer's, it is very close to some images of his own. Selecting a medium-sized panel to be used in an upright form, Cranach, in keeping with his economical techniques, created a new composition from an older image. The painting's upright format, on Cranach's standard medium-sized panel, allowed him to follow closely on his earlier representation of a nude Venus in the woodcut and painting of 1509.[31] Moreover, as mentioned above, the pose of Venus grasping a branch of the tree mirrors that of Eve, a pose first seen in the woodcut of 1509 (cat. 12). The elegant bend of her left leg was perhaps inspired by the intersection of the bent lower leg of Adam in the woodcut with the upper left thigh of Eve; the boundaries between the two figures being merged in one to form Venus's leg. The National Gallery picture has a red-chalk underdrawing in which Cranach established the outlines of the composition, presumably following a compositional sketch, and perhaps taking account of a template made up from the figures of both Adam and Eve. In the diagram of the underdrawing (fig. 23), recording those lines that are visible (there are no doubt others which have not been revealed), the upper part of Venus's right thigh is outlined. However, we cannot see whether the articulation of the leg underwent any alteration at this stage which might indicate whether Cranach had transferred templates taken from two different figures. The easy manner in which he would switch figures and poses from his Adam and Eve compositions to others requiring nudes is shown in a drawing for the male figure of Hercules, shown from the back rather than the front, but with his arm outstretched in the pose of Eve.[32] Similarly, a drawing for an Adam and Eve composition (fig. 32, p. 71), which shows Eve seated on a stag, echoes the pose of Adam in the 1509 woodcut, but also reflects the pose Cranach conceived for Diana in the painting of *Apollo and Diana* (cat. 3); this appears to be based loosely on the early engraving by Dürer, itself inspired by one by Jacopo de' Barbari (cat. 22), who worked at the Saxon court from 1503 to 1505, immediately prior to Cranach's arrival. The seated pose of Diana in these prints may indeed have first inspired that of Adam in Cranach's woodcut, which was then much later recycled as inspiration for both Eve and Diana.

Cranach's composition *Cupid complaining to Venus* (cat. 2), like its text, seems to wear its learning lightly. The pleasures of the painting are to be found in combined enjoyment of the amusing subject-matter and the moral of the verses, in the elegance of the nude with her sweepingly decorative hat, in the beauty of the beasts lurking in the darkness of the forest and in the contrast of the precisely described distant vistas, themselves reflected in the lake. Although the basis of Cranach's composition was not new, the way in which he adapted it, finally making Venus turn to the viewer, sharing the moral, with her left eye exactly in the centre of the composition, brings text and image together with witty precision. The moralising verse, though more sophisticated in tone, is reminiscent of the warning against the pleasures of the flesh of the 1509 Venus painting: Cupid's pleasure in his stolen sweetness is perhaps to be parallelled by those pleasures enjoyed by the viewer, who should then reflect upon the ensuing pain. As Hanne Kolind Poulsen and Pablo Pérez D'Ors have argued, in Lutheran Wittenberg the suggestion that the viewer could choose between virtue or the pleasure which brings pain may have been brought into particularly sharp focus, and Cranach's visual parallel between Venus and Eve might have been understood explicitly as a means of reflection on Christ's salvation, which freed man from "the seemingly endless spiral of desire and grief".[33]

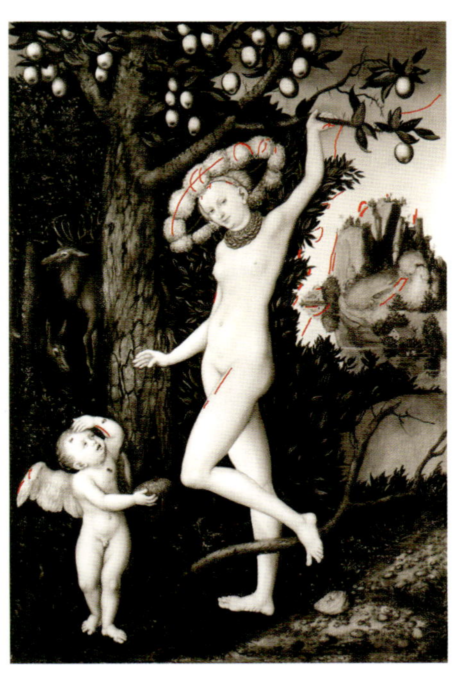

Fig. 23 Diagram, showing areas of red chalk underdrawing on cat.2

By 1526 Saxony was firmly Protestant. Cranach himself, while continuing to produce altarpieces and other works for the Catholic Cardinal Albrecht of Brandenburg, was close to Luther, painting his portrait and that of his wife, the former nun Katharina von Bora. He developed new pictorial subjects that evidently reflect Lutheran ideology, such as the Fall and Salvation of Man, Christ and the Woman of Samaria, Christ among Children, while his interpretation of other subjects might be understood with specifically Lutheran intent.[34] While his depiction of Venus might be understood to make reference to Eve and to the viewer's choice of salvation in Christ, his representation of *Adam and Eve* of 1526 (cat. 1) makes its focus Adam's choice in receiving the apple from Eve. Similarly, in his paintings of the Fall and Salvation of Man, man, the 'miserable sinner' is placed at the centre of the composition, directed to look towards Christ, his salvation.[35] For Luther, Eve was an exemplar of woman's lack of control and her need to be subdued to male authority, as God had prescribed after the Fall.[36] In Cranach's representation of the story of Adam and Eve in Paradise from creation to their expulsion (cat. 5) the Fall itself is depicted in the background of the painting, while the central position is occupied by God's admonishments to Adam and Eve after the Fall, a subject at the heart of Luther's preaching on the theme of God's law and man's sinful nature.[37]

In the late 1520s Cranach developed another series of paintings which also show enticing visions of paradise landscapes, but which depict stories of the origins of humanity evidently based on classical mythology rather than the Bible. Cranach's paintings known under the title of 'The Golden Age' show people bathing and disporting themselves alongside peaceable deer and lions and trees laden with fruit (fig. 21), motifs which have a clear relationship to those representative of Adam and Eve's Garden of Eden. Certainly the descriptions of a sybaritic golden age related by Latin authors such as Virgil and Ovid were well known in the Middle Ages, and it is not necessary to assume that Cranach's paintings were based on the descriptions of the ages of the world in the *Works and Days* of the Greek author Hesiod.[38] The 1598 inventory of the Dukes of Bavaria describes Cranach's subject-matter simply as naked men and women in a garden, dancing and bathing.[39] As well as these images of a 'Golden Age' there are several paintings depicting fauns, satyrs and the life of primitive peoples, including a painting of a faun family with the body of a lion (cat. 4). These compositions include the pictures of fighting people given the title of 'The Silver Age' by Flechsig in 1900, and which again have been assumed to have been inspired by Hesiod.[40] These were puzzling subjects to nineteenth- and early twentieth-century scholars of Cranach. In at least one case it was thought that the subject must be a biblical one related to Adam and Eve: the painting of fighting primitive people at Munster (fig. 24) was assumed to be a pendant to Cranach's Adam and Eve (fig. 29, p. 67) in the same collection, as it was thought to represent Adam and Eve after the fatal quarrel between their sons Cain and Abel.[41]

None of the paintings depicting fauns is dated; the earliest known dated composition of the 'Silver Age' type, at Weimar, is dated 1527, and has been seen as a pendant to one version of Apollo and Diana. Others of this type are one in the Louvre, dated 1535; one formerly in a private collection in Berlin, dated 1529; and those in the Pushkin Museum and in the National Gallery, London, both undated (fig. 20).[42] The last has the fewest figures of these compositions – three naked women with children and four fighting men. The men form two pairs: on the left a man holding a still leafy wooden stake lies on the ground with blood streaming down his back and his mouth open in pain; he is being attacked by a standing bearded man with a long stick. On the right lies a bearded man who has evidently just been beaten to the ground by the white-bearded man standing over him, who also holds a long leafy stick. In the

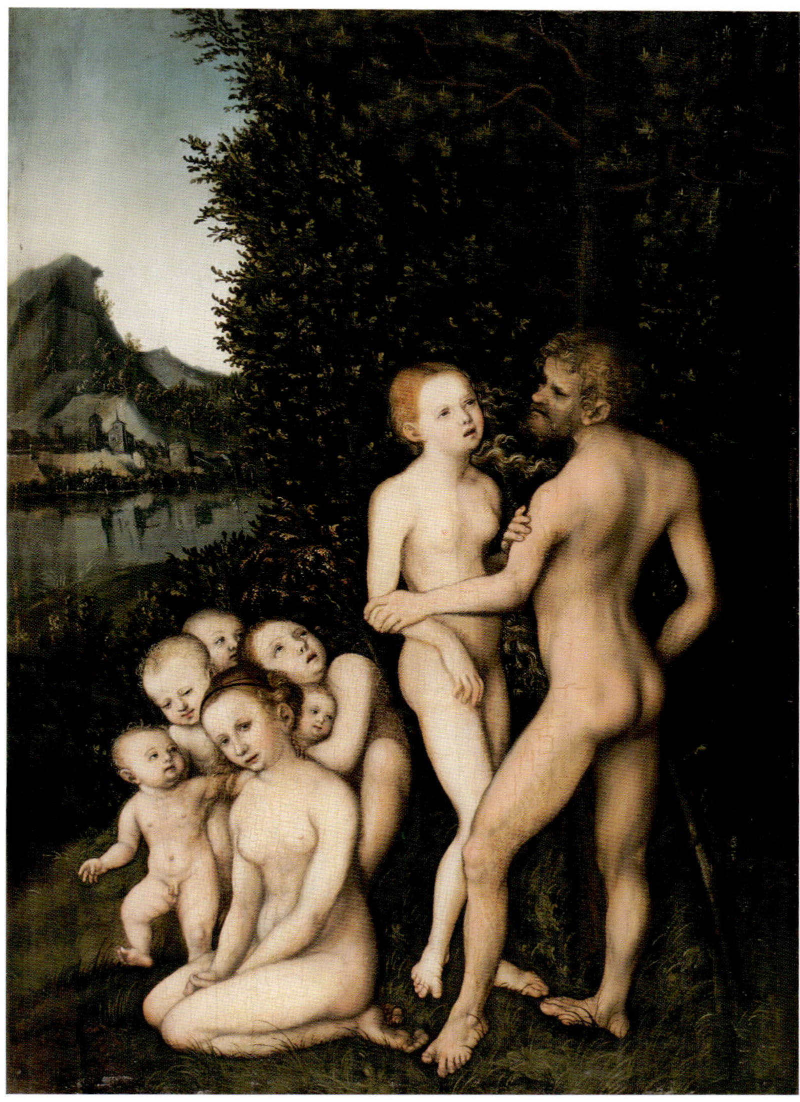

Fig. 24 Lucas Cranach the Elder,
Mythological Scene, around 1530
Oil on panel, 50 × 40 cm
Münster, Westfälisches Landesmuseum

foreground, on the left, a woman turns open-mouthed to look at the scene, and herself holds a stick with the sharper end upwards, as if to defend herself or one of the men. Another woman, standing centrally and grasping the wrists of two babies, appears to be speaking to her. In the right-hand corner of the picture, apparently oblivious to the fighting behind her, a woman reclines in the grass with her baby; it looks up at her over her shoulder, while the baby behind reaches down as if to grab its hair or pluck some grass. There are no fruit trees or animals to be seen, but in the background are the craggy mountains and buildings similar to those of *Cupid complaining to Venus*.

There are several classical authors whose texts have been cited as possible sources of inspiration for Cranach, of whom one is the Greek poet Hesiod. In his *Works and Days* Hesiod gave an account of the Ages of the world, Golden, Silver, Bronze, and Iron, with an age of heroes interpolated between the last two. He described the people of the Silver Age as weak and lacking in consideration for each other and for the gods and creatures such as fauns and satyrs, creatures Cranach portrays in other paintings (see cat. 4).[43] Flechsig first suggested that the subject might have come to Cranach's attention through some version of the text made by a German humanist poet at the Wittenberg court, which would account for the lack of any real relationship between the Greek text and Cranach's pictures. No such text has ever been found, although an edition of Hesiod had first been published in 1493. As Levey pointed out, Hesiod's account of the Silver Age has little to do with the action of the National Gallery picture, and he suggested that the National Gallery picture might in fact derive from another part of Hesiod's text.[44] He thought it might show the coming of the people of the more warlike Bronze Age, as the men carry spears, and the vanquished seem to have a skin lighter in tone than the victors, who would therefore be men of bronze. The skin colour of these warriors may, however, have more to do with creating the effects of distance in the middle ground of the composition. Neither of these suggestions find support in the text concerning the Bronze Age: there is no reference to any fighting with the Silver Age men, and the passage referring to ashen spears has been interpreted differently by most commentators, as describing a race of men born of ashtrees.[45]

Hesiod's account of the early development of the human race was only one among several such accounts given in classical literature, and it is not known to have generated any visual tradition.[46] Cranach is more likely to have drawn inspiration from other, more commonly available accounts of primitive man. In early sixteenth-century Germany the best known was that given in Ovid's *Metamorphoses*, a popular text in its moralised form in the Middle Ages.[47] Ovid's description of the Ages of the world, like those of other classical authors, showed a progressive deterioration from a Golden Age in which the uncultivated earth freely provided produce to sustain the human race. The Silver Age brought the seasons and agricultural cultivation, while the Bronze Age people were fiercer. The Iron Age saw the introduction of trade, mining, warfare and domestic strife. A number of sixteenth-century illustrations to Ovid depict the Silver Age, but they have little in common with Cranach's paintings: in these illustrations, by artists such as the German Virgil Solis (fig. 25) and the Netherlander Marten de Vos, the figures are clothed, have shelters, and are engaged in agricultural activities. Depictions of the Bronze Age show men fighting wearing armour.[48]

In the National Gallery picture the people are naked, and have only tree branches with which to fight. In the distant background are castles and other dwellings of some grandeur which cannot be those of the quarrelling protagonists. If this detail is not merely to be taken as a characteristic element of Cranach's landscape backgrounds it might add some weight to the argument that the subject derives from Ovid: it would then show forest dwellers living in the Bronze or Iron Ages, when building techniques had been mastered, but living a life apart, as they are not themselves using metal weapons.[49]

However, Ovid says nothing to suggest that the forest dwellers fought among themselves.

The *De rerum natura* (Of the nature of things) of the Roman author Lucretius has also been suggested as a possible source for Cranach's depictions of forest dwellers who are in some works clearly fauns with pointed ears (see cat. 4) or satyrs with cloven feet (fig. 26), but in others indistinguishable from the unclothed people in the 'Silver Age' compositions.[50] According to Lucretius the life of early man was distinguished by discomfort, rather than the bounty available to Golden Age inhabitants in the writings of other classical authors, and was gradually improved. In one passage he describes how men's fierce behaviour mellowed after they took women as their mates and produced children.[51] However, knowledge of Lucretius was not widespread in the early sixteenth century, and there appears to have been no visual tradition associated with his text, which was regarded as dangerously anti-religious.[52] Knowledge of Lucretius appears rather to have been mediated through Vitruvius, whose work on building became known in Germany in the later 1520s. German woodcut illustrations to Vitruvius show groups of naked people in families similar to Cranach's. However, like the paintings by Piero di Cosimo, which according to Vasari were made for the house of Francesco del Pugliese in Florence, they tend to focus on the discovery of fire, which is not the subject of any of Cranach's paintings.[53]

Recent discussions of Cranach's groups of fighting men have stressed the importance of considering these pictures in the context of all Cranach's works showing primitive people, including those depicting fauns and satyrs.[54] Nor did Cranach separate them, as is shown by the drawing in Berlin (fig. 26) in which a satyr embraces a woman from a group of primitive people, some fighting,

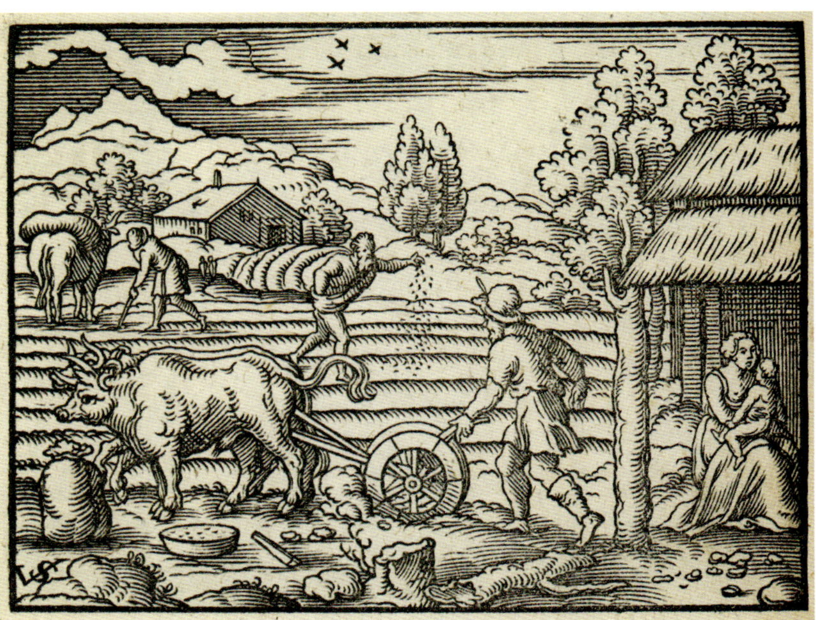

Fig. 25 Virgil Solis, *The Silver Age, from Ovid's 'Metamorphoses'*, 1563
Woodcut, 62 × 81 mm
London, The British Museum

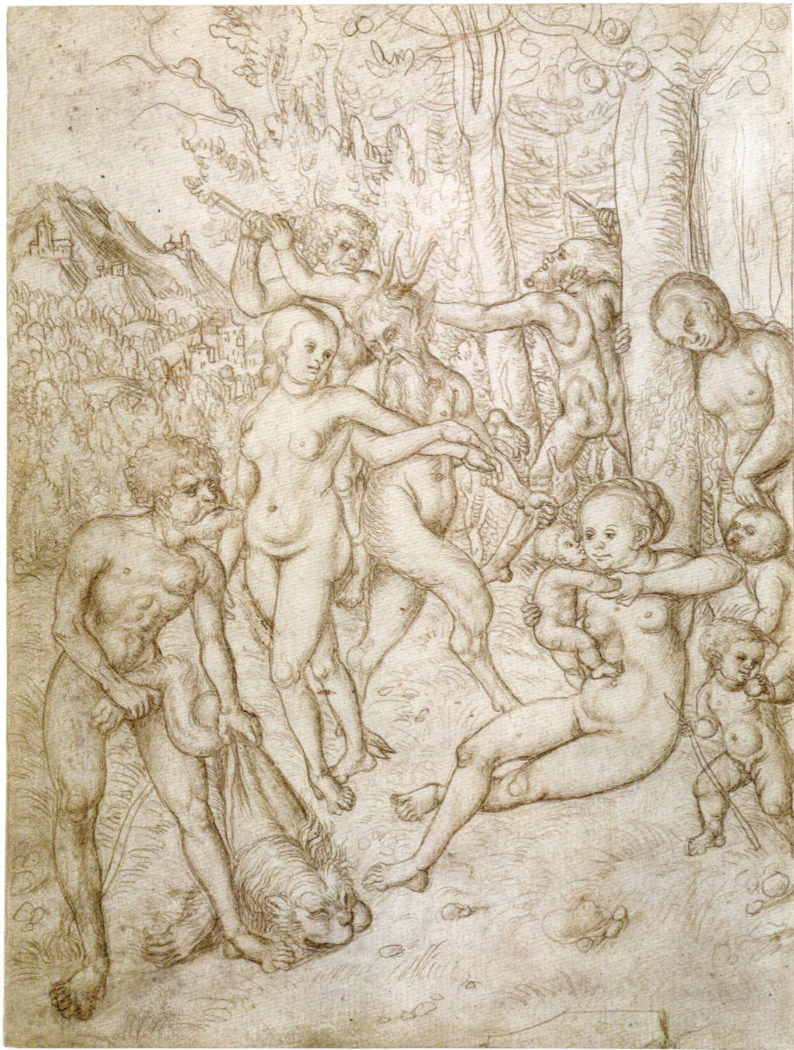

Fig. 26 Lucas Cranach the Elder,
A Satyr with Wild People, around 1527–30
Metalpoint on paper, 19.4 × 14.4 cm
Berlin, Kupferstichkabinett

and a naked man presents a lionskin, echoing the motif seen in the faun family compositions.[55] Early sixteenth-century visualisations of a primitive world included fauns and satyrs and primitive forest dwellers, whose origins can be traced to knowledge of classical texts known in medieval times, such as Virgil and Ovid, as well as the semi-bestial 'wild men', well known in the Middle Ages, with their origins in pagan beliefs and ceremonies. A passage in Ovid, following Hesiod's account of the four Ages, includes a speech in which Jupiter favours destroying the Iron Age people in order to protect the fauns, satyrs and other forest dwellers, the latter perhaps identified in Cranach's time with the 'wild people' often depicted in the late Middle Ages, and apparently still of great interest to Cranach's contemporaries.[56] In Virgil's *Aeneid* there is a short passage in which the Golden Age is described as populating a woodland area in which fauns, nymphs and men sprung from the trunks of trees already flourished.[57] Recent discussions of the German context for the understanding of the depiction of forest dwellers by Altdorfer, Dürer and other artists have suggested that interest in primitive people in Germany in the early sixteenth century might have been stimulated by the accounts of newly discovered lands beyond Europe.[58]

Contemporary visual parallels for Cranach's themes are found in Dürer's engraving of a satyr family or Altdorfer's wild people, and even in earlier prints.[59] The theme of 'wild men' was one which had been used in decoration of many types by German artists and also by Cranach himself (in an early tournament woodcut).[60] Cranach's figures look less wild than Dürer's in his engraving, or Altdorfer's in his painting, perhaps because of the more open setting and because the figures themselves are carefully arranged, in pairs.[61] Yet the figures in the National Gallery picture (fig. 20) especially, with their flowing beards and the carefully decorative arrangement of their leafy branches, resemble the wild men motifs used by Cranach and earlier decorative artists, 'freed' into paintings.[62] Although Cranach's compositions depicting primitive people were not much repeated, in contrast to other subjects, such as Venus and Cupid, they must have been intended to appeal to the same market for which Dürer, Altdorfer and other German artists such as Burgkmair produced images of primitive people. Such paintings might have had resonance both for the hunting-obsessed Saxon courtiers as well as for those sharing the interests of German humanists such as Conrad Celtis in the German forest and in the origins of the primitive German people, mediated through texts such as Tacitus's *Germania*. It has been suggested that, when one or more of Cranach's pictures were hung in the domestic settings for which they must have been intended, their meaning would have been reinforced by their surroundings, by the contrast or tension between the representation of uncivilised life within the picture and civilised life around it.[63] The contrast between the peaceable life of the semi-bestial fauns and the discord created by modern Christians might also have been seen as instructive. Conceivably parallels were also drawn between images of the faun family and the family of Adam and Eve expelled from Paradise.[64]

It is harder to come to any absolute conclusion as to whether the *Faun and his Family with a Slain Lion* (cat. 4), *Adam and Eve* (cat. 1), *Cupid complaining to Venus* (cat. 2) and *Apollo and Diana* (cat. 2), a group of exceptionally beautiful paintings, probably of about the same date, 1526 – and reunited in this exhibition for the first time – were intended as a suite of paintings, to be hung together as a series or as pendants, possibly as part of a room decoration of the kinds suggested in the descriptions of the interiors and furnishings of the castle of the Saxon electors nearly two decades earlier. The Courtauld *Adam and Eve* (cat. 1) is larger than the others, but if the paintings were part of a decorative scheme they might have been designed for different positions, necessitating differing sizes; conversely, Cranach's habit of using standard panel sizes might wrongly suggest the grouping of unrelated pictures made for separate patrons. Yet it is very tempting to suggest that these paintings might have been produced for a particular occasion, and even a particular location. A suitable courtly patron, enjoying themes of landscape, hunting and secular pleasures, with an interest in humanism and certainly supportive of Luther, might have been the young future Elector Johann Frederick the Magnanimous, who married Sibylla of Cleves in 1527, an occasion on which Cranach supplied canvas paintings for the celebrations, subject unknown; there are no records concerning panel paintings.[65]

However, despite close technical similarities and iconographic connections (see also entry for cat. 1), this can remain no more than speculation. What is clear is that after the death of the Elector Frederick the Wise in 1525, with the Reformation well established in Wittenberg, Cranach swiftly created a new repertoire of secular subject-matter for his paintings, at least in part drawing on motifs which had only earlier appeared in his decorative work.[66] Cranach's creative exploration of the subjects of Venus, Adam and Eve and Apollo and Diana at this time is vividly shown by the intermingling of motifs described above, whether or not he intended the products to be viewed together. While still broadly appealing to a courtly audience, like the narrower range of mythological subjects from the early part of his career, at least some of these subjects may well have been intended to have been understood in relation to Lutheran commentary on Christian subject-matter and in the context of debates expressing concern about both secular and religious imagery. The ambivalence which surrounded Cranach's imagery at this period is suggested by the words that Georg Sabinus, the author of the poem Cranach had included in his *Cupid complaining to Venus* (cat. 2), wrote in 1535 in his description of the paintings provided by Cranach and his assistants for the collegiate church in Halle and commissioned by the Catholic Cardinal Albrecht of Brandenburg: the altarpieces included pious images rather than those of Venus, the "impure mother of impure earthly love".[67]

NOTES

I am most grateful to Rachel Billinge and my colleagues at the National Gallery for their collaboration and observations during the examination of paintings by Cranach.

1 For example, see the Liesborn altarpiece, which evidently included such a shutter: Brandl 1993, p. 89.
2 FR 112A; there appears to be no record of the centre panel of the altarpiece.
3 See Gunnar Heydenreich's essay in this volume. Grimm, Erichsen and Brockhoff (1994, p. 345) place Warsaw (FR 44) the earliest (around 1509–10), followed by Würzburg (FR 166), while Friedlander and Rosenberg 1978 argue that Munich (FR 44) is Cranach's first *Adam and Eve*, around 1510–12, followed by Warsaw, of a date around 1512. All these are on a black background, even if – following Dürer – they include the tree.
4 Adam's feet in Cranach's painting in Munich (FR 44) resemble those of Dürer's engraving (cat. 23). For the artistic interchange between Dürer and Cranach see Gunnar Heydenreich's essay in this volume.
5 Bonnet 1994, p. 143.
6 Koepplin 2003, p. 158; see also Koepplin 2003a. For the sculptor Konrad Meit's *Venus and Cupid* see Koepplin and Falk 1974, II, no. 564, pp. 653–54: Meit worked in Cranach's workshop at the Saxon court in the years around 1506–10.
7 Baxandall 1980, pp. 75–78.
8 Pauwels *et al.* 1965, no. 23, pp. 155–56; nos. 60, 61, 62, pp. 303–12.
9 See Koerner 1993, pp. 292–306, 412–14.
10 See Koepplin 2003. It is arguable to what extent this relationship with other arts was unique to Cranach.
11 See Koepplin and Falk 1974, II, pp. 644–50; Landau and Parshall 1994, pp. 191–92.
12 See Koepplin and Falk 1974, II, pp. 641–55; Hinz 2000.
13 Friedländer and Rosenberg 1978, FR 269; see Koepplin and Falk 1974, II, p. 611, where this point is made.

14 On the markets for German prints in the sixteenth century see Landau and Parshall 1994, pp. 347–58.
15 Matsche 1994, pp. 81–82.
16 *Ibid.*, p. 83.
17 See Heydenreich 2002, I, pp. 193–200.
18 Starkey 1998, p. 239, no. 10692, "Item a Table with the picture of Lucretia Romana with thistorye of the same" and 10693, "Item a Table with the pictures of Adame and Eve"; no. 10686: "Item twooe Tables with the pictures of Lucretia Romana in redde robes and lawne sleeves" and no. 10687: "Item twooe Tables with the pictures of Marye Magdaleine in redde roobes like Damaske and a boxe in their handes". Some paintings by Cranach himself may have reached England: for example, among other pictures listed in King Henry VIII of England's collection were not only a portrait of Duke Johann Frederick of Saxony on cloth but also a painting of a man and women with partridges, similar to a type of composition painted by Cranach: see *ibid.* nos. 10715 and 10591, p. 240.
19 Paris, Bibliothèque nationale, MS Collections de Lorraine, no. 462, ff. 104ff.
20 Marx and Mossinger 2005–06, pp. 382–83.
21 See Pérez d'Ors 2005.
22 Fort Worth, Kimbell Museum, acquired in 2004.
23 See Koepplin and Falk 1974, II, p. 600. The earliest dated versions are those at Schwerin (1527) and Copenhagen (1529).
24 Cross-sections show that some of the leaves were first painted with a green paint consisting of lead-white mixed with verdigris under a glaze of copper resinate, and then half of the leaf was painted black.
25 Pérez D'Ors 2007.
26 Bauch 1894 was the first scholar to recognise this.
27 Seznec 1953, p. 163.
28 Koepplin and Falk 1974, II, p.656.
29 Hand and Mansfield 1993, pp. 34–40; Koepplin and Falk 1974, II, pp. 631ff. Cranach's first surviving painted depiction of this type, at Berlin, probably dates from 1515–16.
30 Dodgson 1933.
31 Size D, identified in Heydenreich 1998.
32 Berlin, Kupferstichkabinett, reproduced in Bonnet 1994, p. 147, fig. A93.
33 Kolind Poulsen 2003; Pérez D'Ors 2007; Kolind Poulsen 2000, especially pp. 57–59.
34 Koepplin and Falk 1974, II, pp. 498–522; Kolind Poulsen 2000.
35 Koepplin and Falk 1974, II, pp. 505–10; see also Müller and Kemperdick 2006, pp. 424–27.
36 Genesis 3: 18. For Luther and women see Roper 1989.
37 Marx and Mössinger 2005–06, pp. 200–07.
38 Virgil, *Eclogues*, IV; 110–39 (Virgil 1935, pp. 29–35); Ovid, *Metamorphoses*, I, 89–144 (Ovid 1921, pp. 9–11).
39 Friedlaender and Rosenberg 1978, FR 261, 262; Matsche 1994, p. 85.
40 Flechsig 1900, pp. 268–69.
41 Koch 1913, p. 62, no. 114.
42 Friedländer and Rosenberg 1978, FR264, 265B, 265, 265A and 263.
43 Hesiod, *Works and Days*, 110–40 (Hesiod 1954, p. 13).
44 Levey 1959, pp. 21–22.
45 See Lovejoy and Boas 1935, p. 29.
46 For a comprehensive account of this subject see *ibid.*
47 Ovid, *Metamorphoses*, I, 100–50.
48 Examples includes a series of prints by Virgil Solis, published in 1557 as illustrations to Ovid, and the 1582 Leipzig edition of the *Metamorphoses* illustrated by Johann Steinnar. A series of drawings in Antwerp, Koninklijk Museum voor Schone Kunsten, by Marten de Vos depict the Silver Age as a young woman with agricultural implements and the Bronze Age as a figure in armour.
49 Koepplin and Falk 1974, II, p. 598 make a similar point. For Cranach's contemporary Altdorfer, see Wood 1993, pp. 152–57 and Gaus 1971 pp. 7–15.
50 Koepplin and Falk 1974, II, p. 599.
51 Lucretius, V, 1013 ff. I am grateful to Erika Langmuir for drawing my attention to this passage; see also Koepplin and Falk 1974, II, p. 599; Simon 1965, pp. 52–60.
52 See Reynolds 1983, pp. 218–22.
53 Panofsky 1972; Simon 1965, pp. 52–60.
54 Koepplin and Falk 1974, II, pp. 585–604, especially pp. 599–600.
55 The drawing has sometimes been attributed to Hans Cranach: see Koepplin and Falk 1974, II, no. 497, pp. 598–99.
56 *Ibid.*; see also Bonnet 1994, p.144. For wild people see Bernheimer 1953, Silver 1983 and Wood 1993.
57 Virgil, *Aeneid*, VIII, 314–25.
58 Silver 1983, pp. 5–8.
59 Koepplin 2003 p. 159, fig. 87 (engraving of 1480–90 by the Monogrammist BG).
60 Koepplin and Falk 1974 II, p. 592.
61 See Koepplin and Falk 1974, II, p. 600. In the Weimar picture, dated 1527, the figures are arranged in the most ambitious manner, deliberately showing backs contrasted with fronts and foreshortened figures lying on the ground with heads lying in contrasting directions. These figures are highly reminiscent of the famous engraving of fighting men by Pollaiuolo and are surely adapted from this source (see Foister 2003, pp. 126–27).
62 *Ibid.*, II, pp. 585–93, esp. figs. 302, 303. See also Koepplin 2003.
63 *Ibid.*, II, pp. 600; reiterated by Koepplin in Koepplin 2003.
64 *Ibid.*, II, p. 601, comparing the painting by Fra Bartolommeo today in the Philadelphia Museum of Art.
65 Heydenreich 2002, II, p. 451.
66 Koepplin and Falk 1974, II, p. 593.

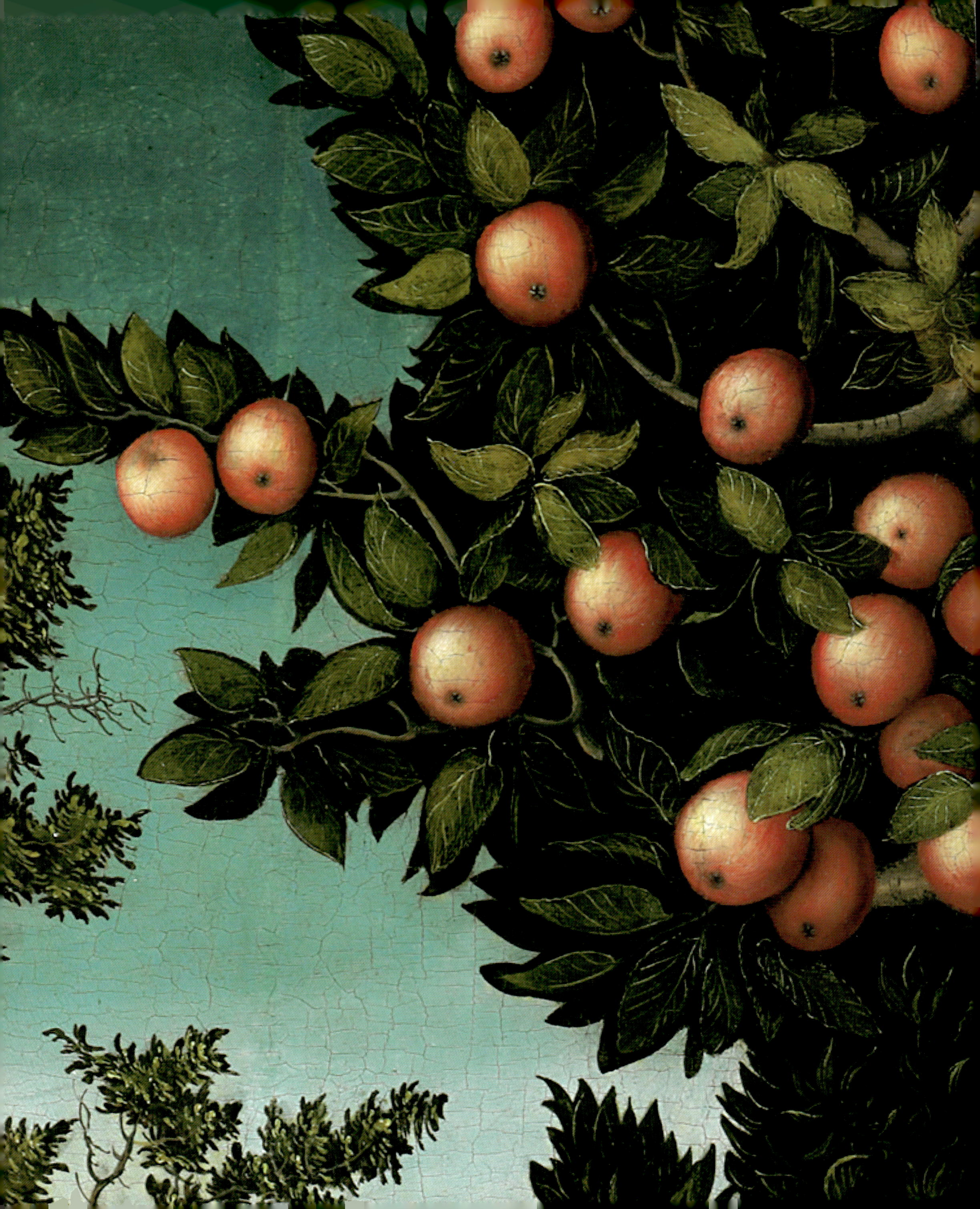

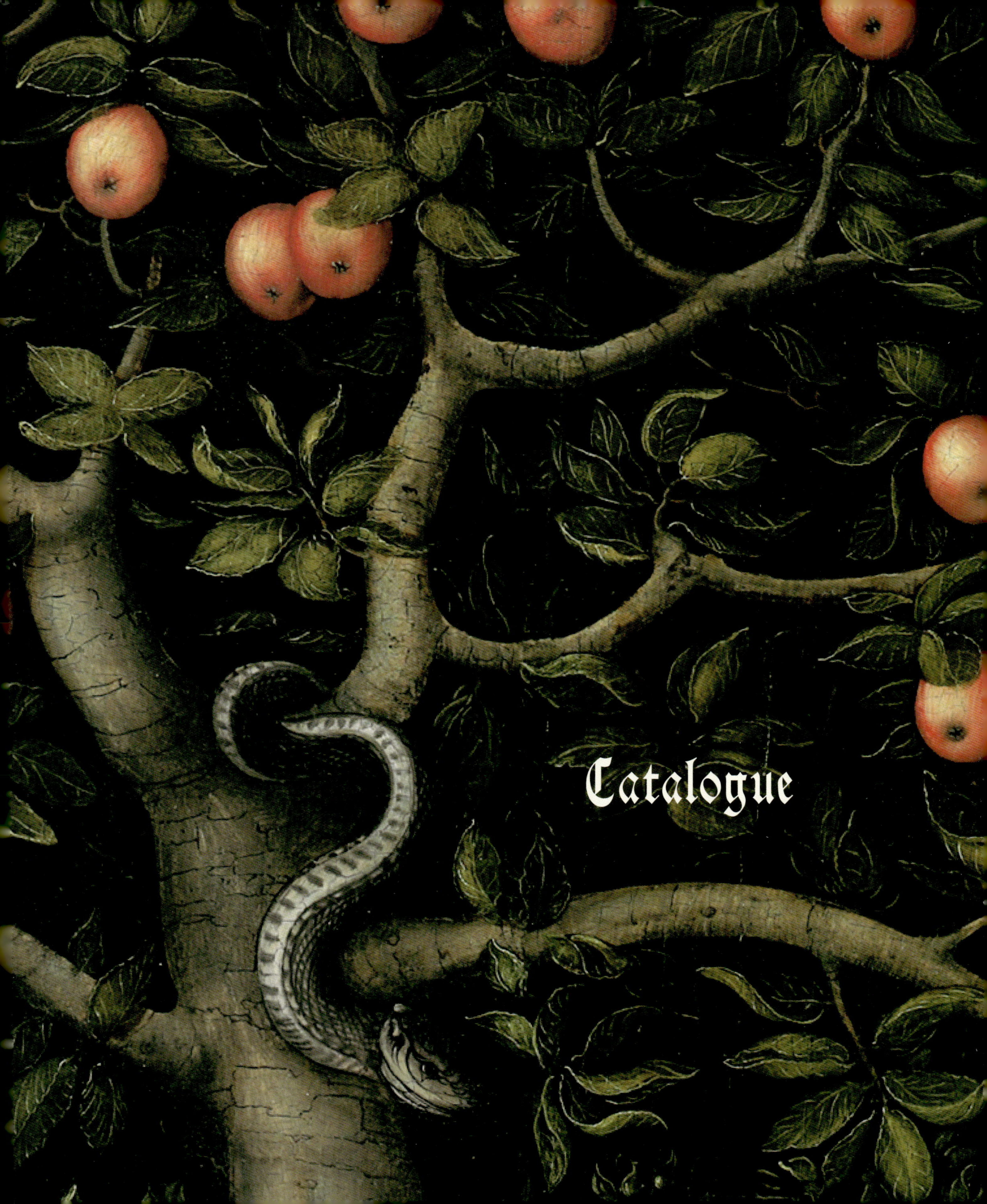

Catalogue

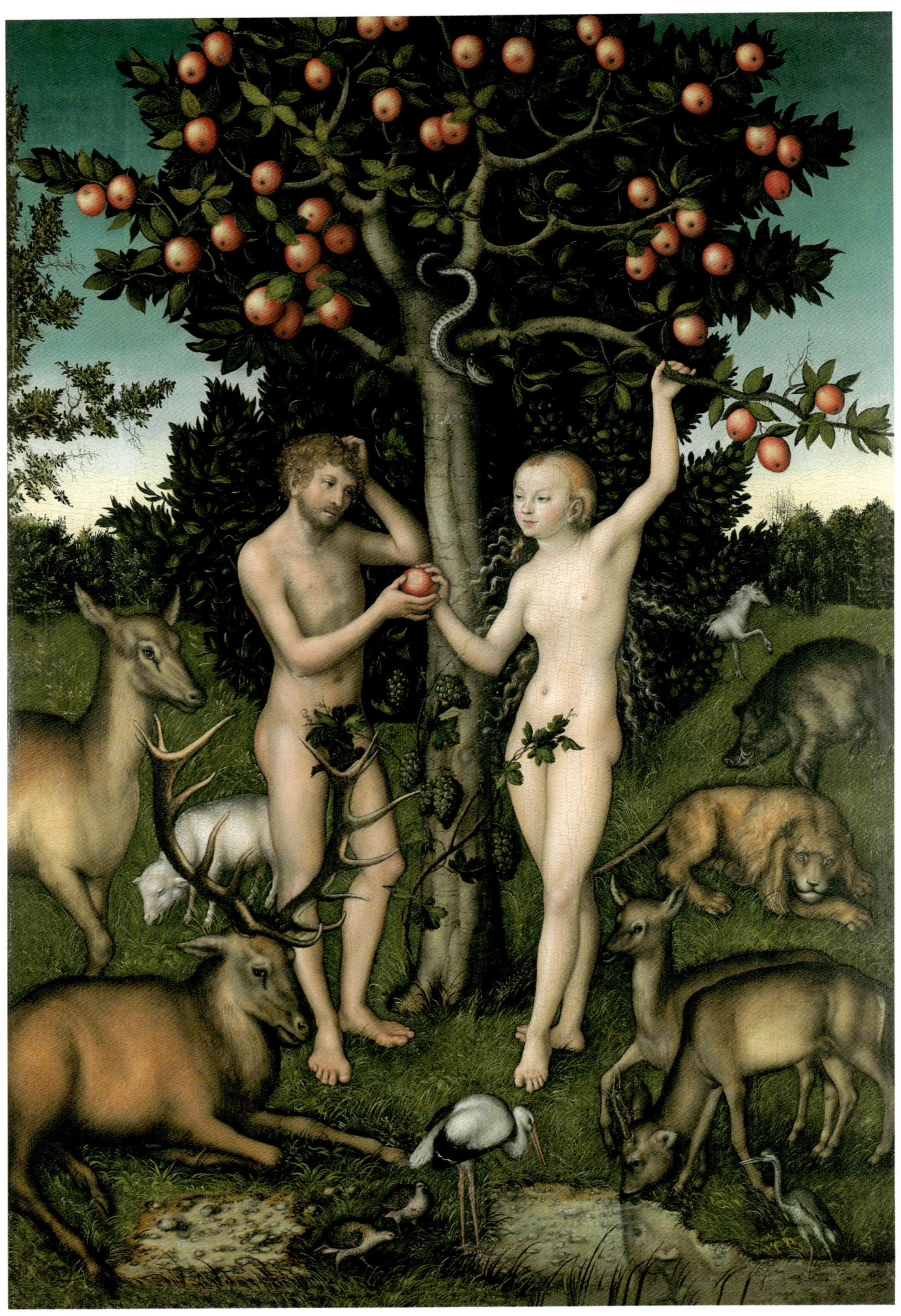

1 Lucas Cranach the Elder (around 1472–1553)

Adam and Eve, 1526

Oil on maple
117.1 × 80.8 cm
Signed with the winged serpent, and dated *1526* on the central tree trunk
London, Courtauld Institute of Art Gallery, P.1947.LF.77

THE OLD TESTAMENT history of Adam and Eve (Genesis 2: 21–25; 3: 1–24) has played a central role in every Christian theology and has always been one of the key narratives of Christian art. Adam's decision to disregard God the Father's commandment and follow his wife's lead in eating the fruit of the Tree of Knowledge had fatal consequences. Rather than being as gods, as the serpent had promised Eve, Adam and Eve's consumption of the forbidden fruit meant that they were expelled from Paradise. Through their foolish disobedience Adam and Eve had destroyed mankind's expectation of salvation, which was to be restored by the 'new' Adam and the 'new' Eve – Christ and Mary his mother, who alone of all women gave birth while still an intact virgin. Only Christ's subsequent sacrifice on the cross could redeem mankind from the slavery of sin and the yoke of mortality to which Adam and Eve had condemned them. This introduced a new covenant between God and Man, which was the basis of Christianity.

The Cranach workshop produced over fifty depictions of Adam and Eve in the Garden of Eden.[1] The painting now in the Courtauld Institute is the only one not to follow either of the two models of representation Cranach had otherwise developed for the subject. His paintings of the 1510s and the large-scale paintings of the 1520s, such as figs. 5 and 27, are heavily indebted to Dürer's painting of 1507 (fig. 6), and depict Adam and Eve in isolation next to the Tree of Knowledge, either against a monochrome background or in a very limited landscape setting. Sometimes Adam and Eve are depicted on separate panels, on other occasions a single support is preferred.[2] In the mid 1520s Cranach began to make numerous small-scale panel paintings of the first couple, set in the depths of the primeval forest which was the German interpretation of the Garden of Eden, and accompanied by one or two animals, normally including a stag.[3] Examples of this type include figs. 28 and 29, where the usual apple tree has been replaced with a precarious pine. The Courtauld painting stands apart from these pictorial formulae. It takes elements from them, but combines them to produce a unique composition which is replicated directly nowhere else in Cranach's work.

Cranach made considerable use of various types of drawings when devising and executing the Courtauld *Adam and Eve*. Many of the animals are based on studies – from life, death and imagination – which were kept in the Cranach workshop. For example, Cranach never saw a real lion and, like all his other depictions of this animal, the lion in this painting is based on a typology he derived from model-books, first found in his 1509 prints of *Saint Jerome*

PROVENANCE
Possibly Habich collection, Kassel; purchased in Kassel by Harold Woodbury Parsons for Edward Perry Warren, Lewes House, East Sussex, 1906; Warren sale, Lewes House (Gorringe of Lewes), 22–24 October 1929, lot 546; bought by J.R. Thomas (Georgian Galleries, London); sold to Lord Lee of Fareham, Richmond; by whom bequeathed to the Courtauld Institute of Art, 1947

SELECTED LITERATURE
Clark and Murray 1962, no. 22; Ruhmer 1963, p. 84, pl. 22; Koepplin and Falk 1974, II, p. 500; Clark 1977, p. 71, fig. 7; Friedländer and Rosenberg 1978, no. 19, p. 108; Campbell 1985, p. 365; Campbell in Farr 1987, pp. 38–39; London 1987; Sox 1995, pp. 20–21, fig. 12; Bradford in Murdoch 1998; Schoen 2001, p. 196 note 76; Heydenreich 2002, I, pp. 80, 173, 177

BRIEF TECHNICAL NOTES
The panel is composed of six vertical members. These were thinned when the panel was cradled, probably in the early twentieth century. Conservation treatment at the Courtauld Institute in the 1980s removed the cradle, which was forcing the panel to warp and crack. It was placed in a panel tray which would allow the wood to move if necessary. Apart from paint losses along the cracks and panel joins, the paint surface is in good condition. The panel has been examined with infra-red reflectography and X-radiography (for an analysis see main text, and essay by Gunnar Heydenreich). The panel's dimensions mean that it belongs to Heydenreich's 'standard format E' (see Heydenreich 2002, I, Table 1, p. 32).

Fig. 27 Lucas Cranach the Elder,
Adam and Eve, 1510–12
Oil on limewood, 59 × 44 cm
Munich, Alte Pinakothek

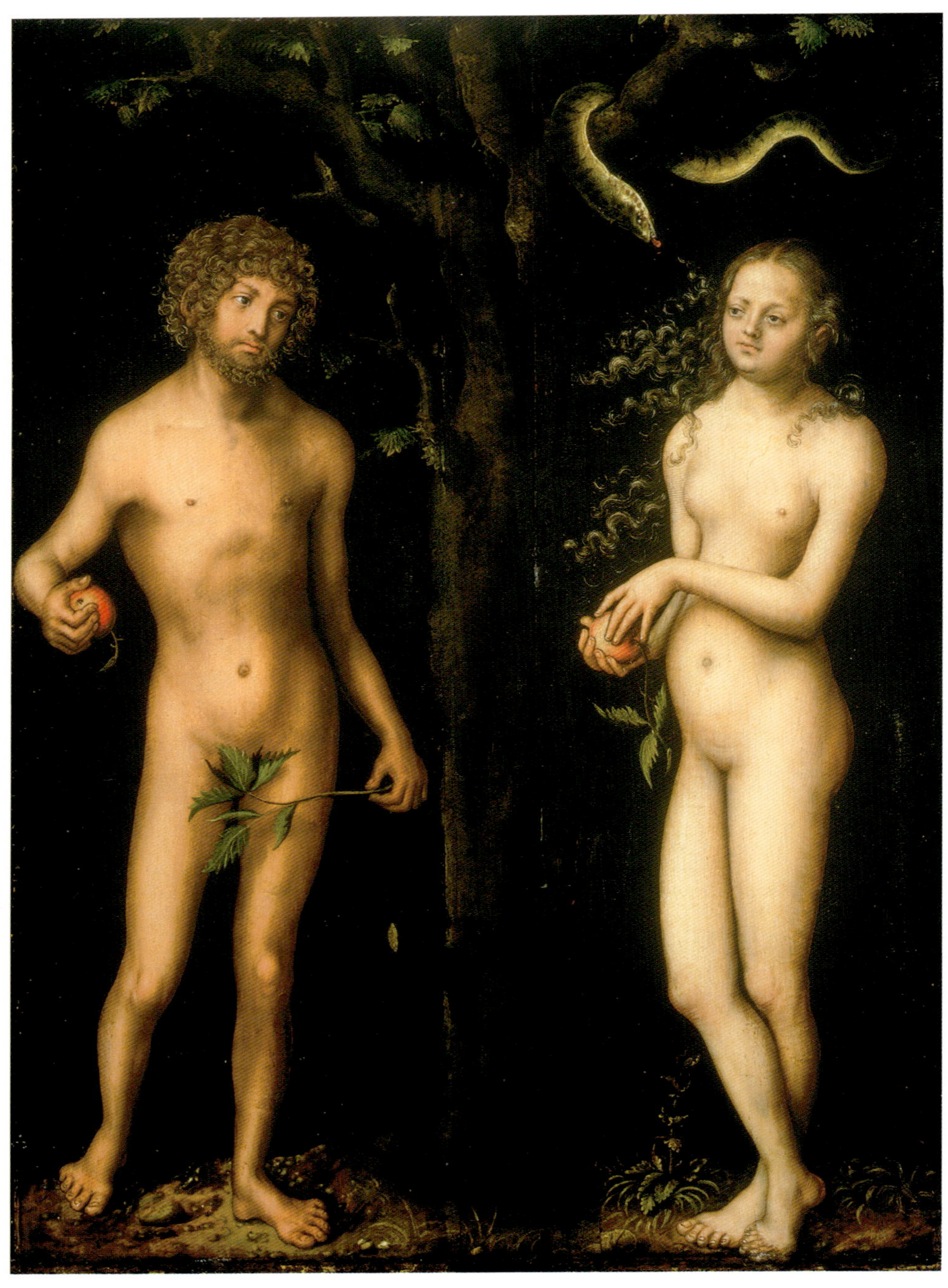

Fig. 28 Lucas Cranach the Elder,
Adam and Eve, 1533
Oil on beechwood, 50.4 × 35.5 cm
Berlin, Gëmaldegalerie

Fig. 29 Lucas Cranach the Elder,
Adam and Eve, 1525
Oil on panel, 50 × 40 cm
Münster, Westfälisches Landesmuseum

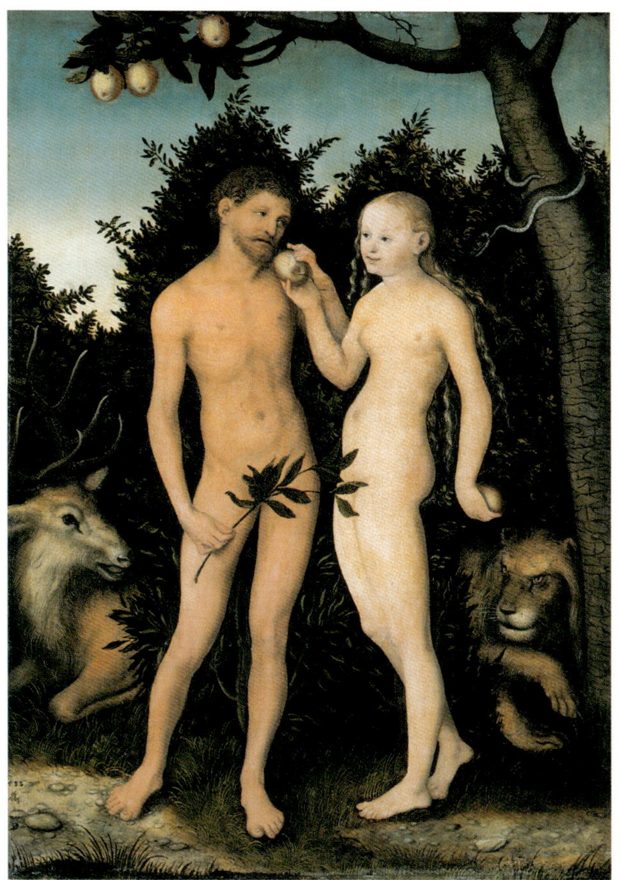

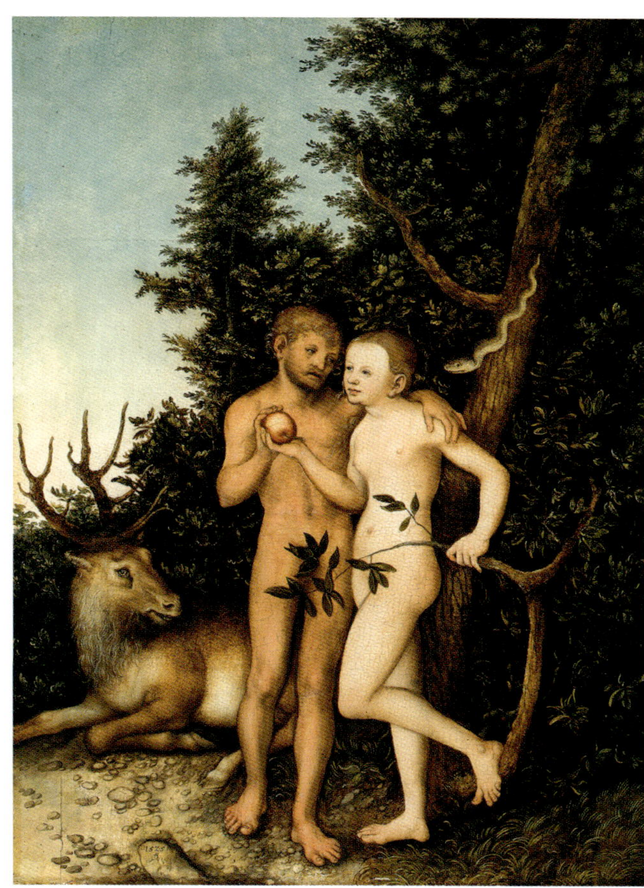

Fig. 30 Lucas Cranach the Elder,
The Penitence of Saint Jerome, 1509
Engraving, 32.1 × 23.5 cm
London, The British Museum

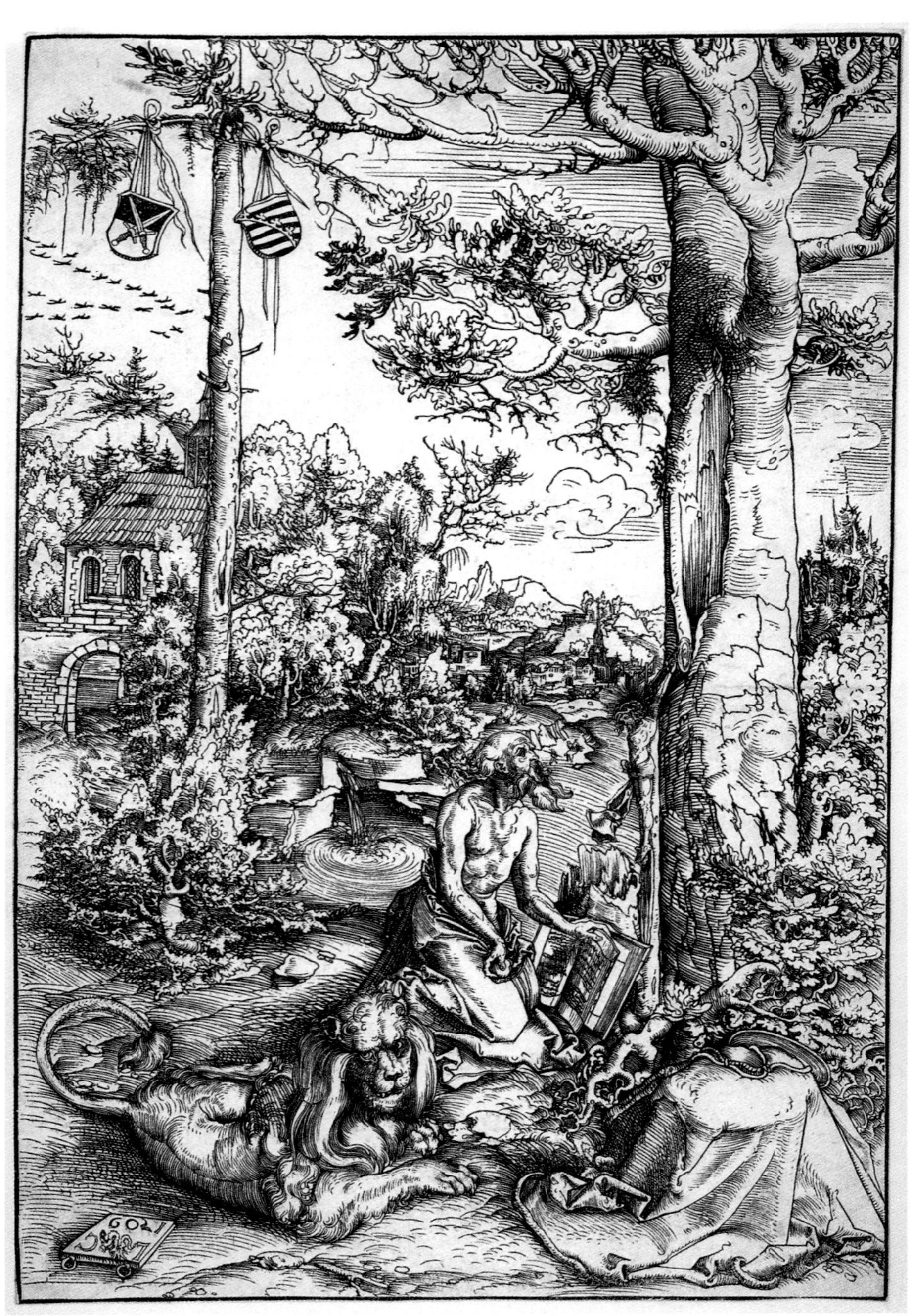

(fig. 30) and *Adam and Eve* (cat. 12) and reflected in a drawing now in the Getty (fig. 41). Other creatures also reflect well-established types. The two partridges are identical to those represented in many other of Cranach's paintings, such as the *Nymph of the Spring* in Liverpool (Walker Art Gallery; FR 259).[4] Although Cranach was renowned for the verisimilitude of his animals,[5] and made many detailed studies of dead and living birds and beasts, including cat. 9 and 6, he did not always follow these models in his paintings. His painted depictions of animals and humans suggest that he considered a degree of idealisation appropriate to this more finished form of representation. However, naturalistic details such as the roebuck gazing at its reflection show that studies made from life (such as cat. 6 verso) influenced his pictorial vision.

Unusually for Cranach, two compositional studies that can be connected to this painting have survived. Cranach's only known drawings of Adam and Eve (figs. 31 and 32) have been dated stylistically to around 1525,[6] and both represent early compositional ideas for the Courtauld panel. The Koenigs sheet (fig. 32), recently restituted to the Netherlands by the Ukrainian government, contains sketchy elements at top and bottom (the birds and the tree).[7] However, the greater part of this pen-and-ink study is fluently and confidently expressed. It depicts Eve seated on a kneeling stag at the right of an apple tree. She is in the process of handing an apple (placed right in the middle of the pictorial space) to Adam. He scratches his head, unsure if he should accept her gift. Before them, in the immediate foreground, a pair of partridges feed and scrape the ground. Elements of this composition – Adam's quizzical gesture, and the presence of the two birds – are found in the Courtauld painting, but (as will be discussed below) the significance of this drawing really lies in the fact that it connects Cranach's compositional thinking for Adam and Eve closely with his ideas for paintings of Apollo and Diana in the forest.

The Dresden drawing (fig. 31), which was lost in 1945, represents a more resolved stage in Cranach's thought processes for the composition which became the Courtauld *Adam and Eve*, and consequently is much more heavily worked. As in the Koenigs sketch, initial ideas were laid in with quick lines of ink, and then worked up with layers of wash. At this point the outlines of the figures, the animals and the most significant aspects of the landscape background were reinforced using dark ink. The basic composition is very close to the Courtauld painting. Adam and Eve's feet are in the same position as in the painting and, in an entrancing gesture, Eve's hair flows out on all sides of her body, as if it too is entrapping Adam. Eve pulls on a branch, as if to reach for another apple, while she feeds Adam directly with the fruit she has already plucked. The mere taste of the fruit of knowledge has already made Adam ashamed of his nakedness, and he covers his and Eve's genitals with a branch of the tree. A young stag approaches from the left, while a more mature beast (very close to the stag on which Eve sits in the Koenigs drawing) rests beside Eve. The foliage at both left and right has been deliberately cut (the drawing does not appear to have been trimmed), which further concentrates the viewer's attention on the main figures. This technique is also deployed in the Courtauld painting.

The Courtauld *Adam and Eve* is a static and carefully composed tableau. It is bereft of action – although sudden action in the past and present are implied – almost as if it were a still frame in the fast-moving cinematic narrative of man's downfall. The template represented by the Dresden drawing is refined still further. Cranach's revision of the composition on the panel is revealed by the x-radiograph (fig. 34) and the infra-red reflectogram (fig. 33). As Gunnar Heydenreich has described in his essay, the outlines of the composition were transferred to the white ground with which the panel had been prepared for painting using a black liquid medium applied with a pointed brush. The Tree of Knowledge, the figures of Adam and Eve and most of the animals in the foreground were blocked out very roughly at this stage (the stork, heron and horse were painted later, on top of the green meadow – see the

Fig. 31 Lucas Cranach the Elder,
Adam and Eve, around 1525–26
Pen and ink on paper, 20.8 × 15.8 cm
Dresden, Staatliche Kunstsammlungen,
Kupferstich-Kabinett (missing since 1945)

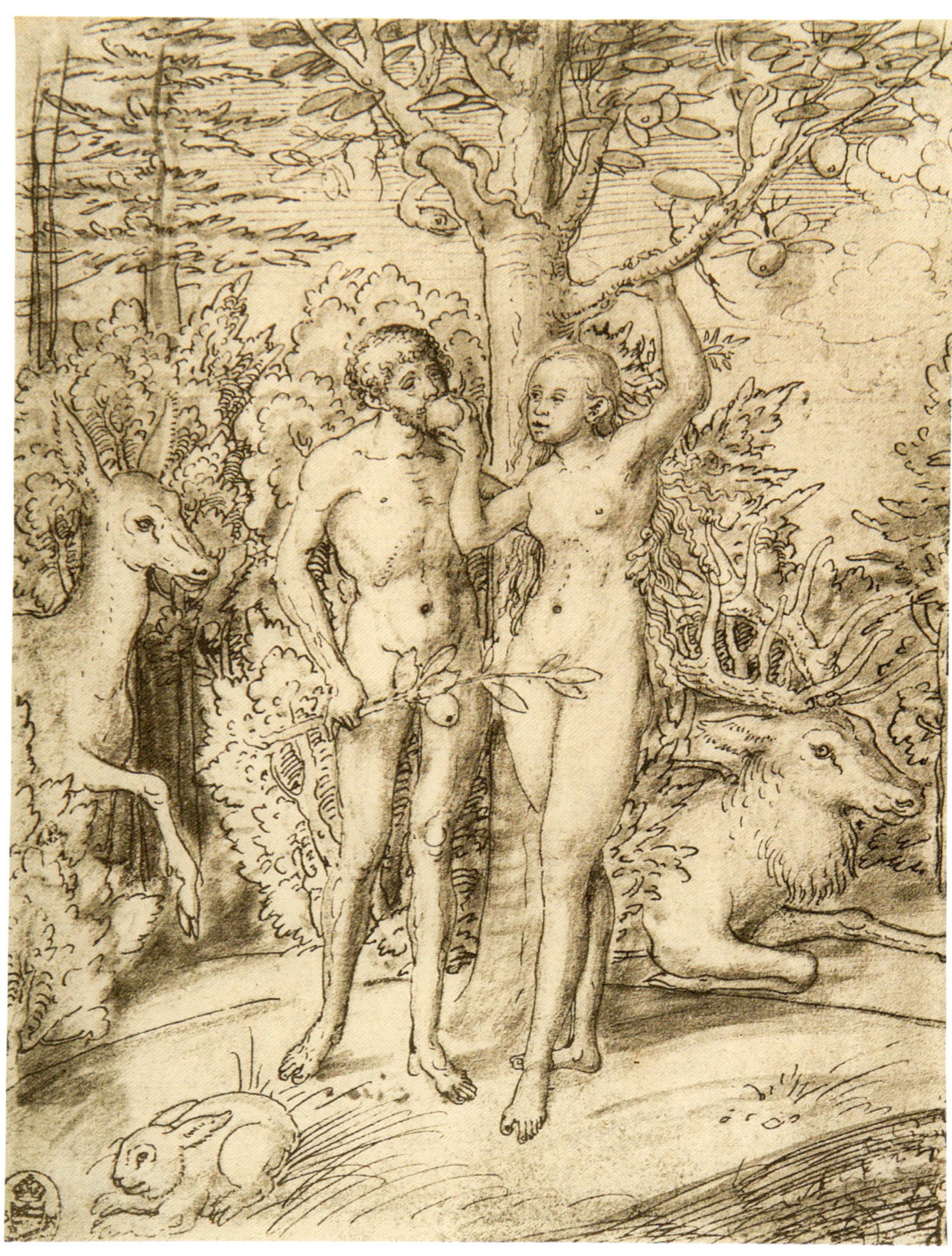

Fig. 32 Lucas Cranach the Elder, *Adam and Eve*, around 1525–26
Pen and brown ink on paper, 18.7 × 13.2 cm
Rotterdam, Museum Boijmans van Beuningen, on loan from the Instituut Collectie Nederland

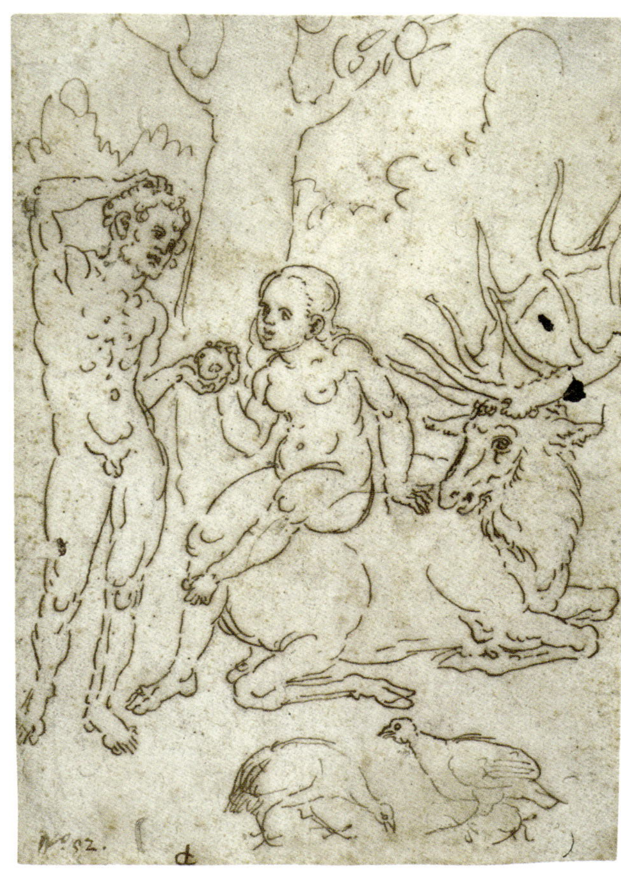

x-radiograph, fig. 34). The reflectogram reveals one interesting curiosity. The sheep which grazes quietly behind Adam appears to have been modelled fully in shades of grey, although it is partially covered by Adam's leg in the finished painting. However, Adam's basic pose seems not to have been changed. It is most likely that the sheep was added to the composition relatively late in the design stage, but that both it and Adam's position were fixed before painting began. A reserve was left for the figures and for the sky, but Cranach broke into this frequently, painting additional twigs, leaves and fruit late in the production of the painting. Numerous small alterations are also recorded both in the reflectogram and in the x-radiograph, such as the placement of the antlers of the huge stag seated at the left foreground: initially these extended further over Adam's body and genitals than they do in the completed painting. Cranach also changed his mind about the position of Adam's fingers as he scratches his forehead (see x-radiograph), and those of Eve as she prepares to pick another apple (see x-radiograph): however, both gestures seems always to have been intended in some form.

During the process of transferring the composition from paper to panel Cranach further refined the basic pictorial structure he had developed in the Dresden drawing. As we have seen, he returned to the question of Adam's agency in accepting the apple, addressed earlier in the Koenigs sheet (fig. 32). In the painting, Adam ponders what to do rather than meekly eating the fruit which his wife hands him. Compared to the Dresden drawing, the Courtauld painting has a more expansive vista, which includes the boundaries of Paradise, a row of trees perhaps referring to the Virgin Mary's *hortus conclusus*. Adam and Eve are surrounded by a large group of animals, like Cranach's woodcut of 1509 (cat. 12). At least three of the beasts in Cranach's painting – the crouching lion, the antlered stag and the sheep – are based on their representations in the print (see also essay by Gunnar Heydenreich). However, while the latter aims at artful randomness, nothing but precision and planning is revealed in the organisation of the animals in the 1526 painting. Each creature plays a distinct role in enhancing the meaning of the sacred story depicted.

Following Panofksy's influential analysis of the beasts in Dürer's 1504 engraving of *Adam and Eve* as representations of the Four Humours (see cat. 23), art historians have wished to interpret Cranach's depictions of Adam and Eve in the same light. However, as Schoen has demonstrated, Dürer's contemporaries rarely used his famous engraving as a model for their versions of Adam and Eve.[8] Instead, like Cranach, they drew upon long-established conventions

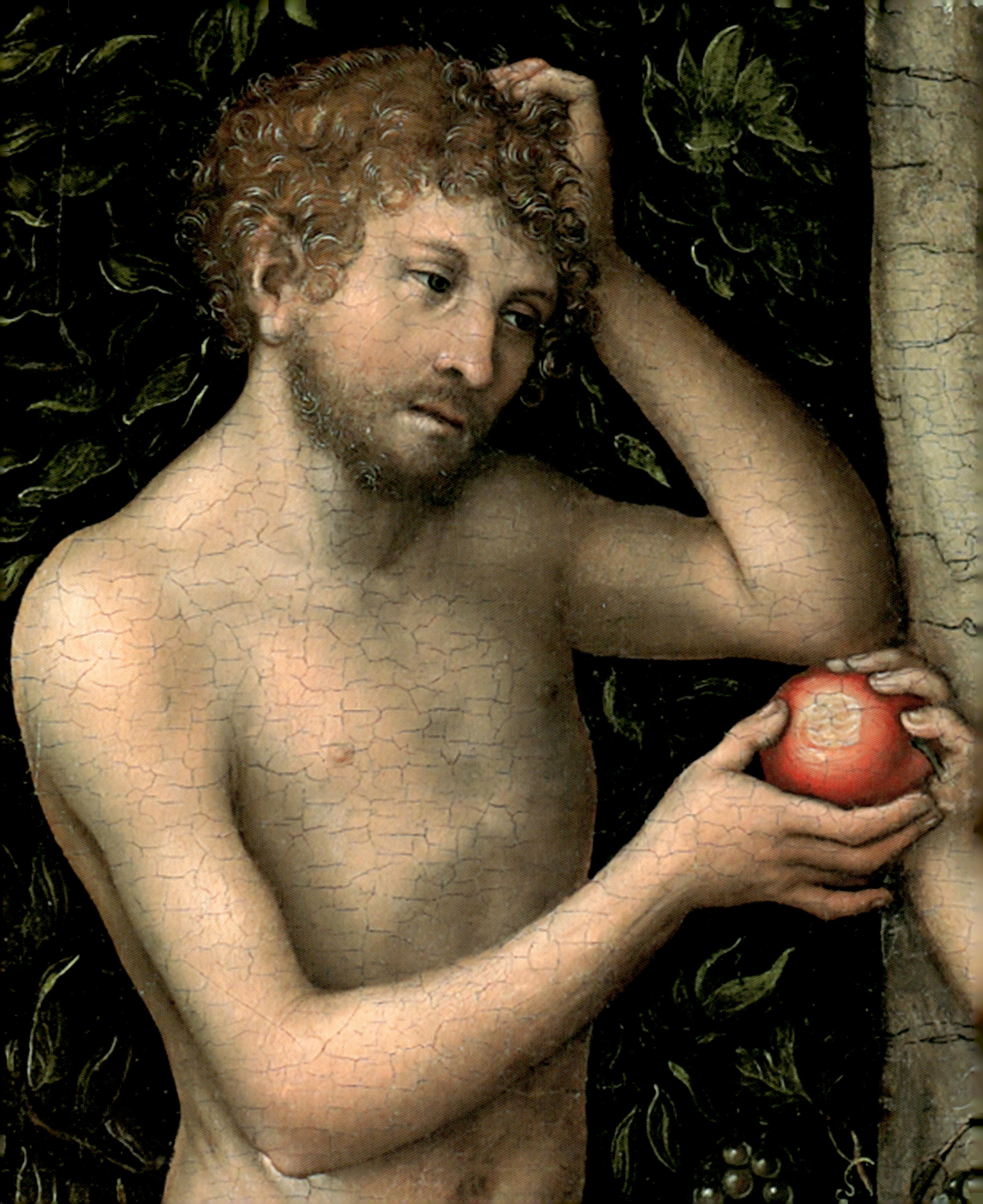

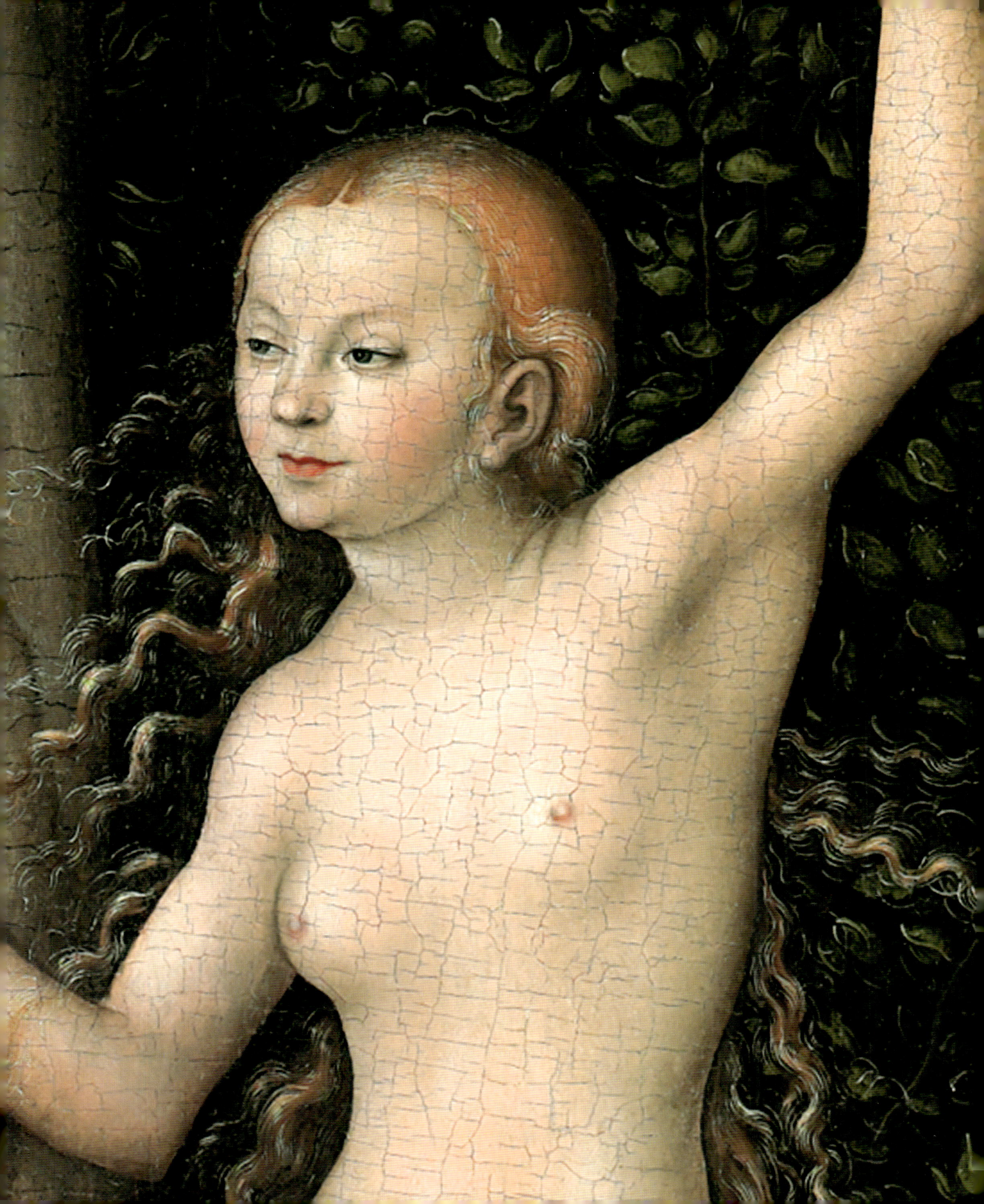

Fig. 33 Infra-red reflectogram of cat. 1
Tager Stonor Richardson photography

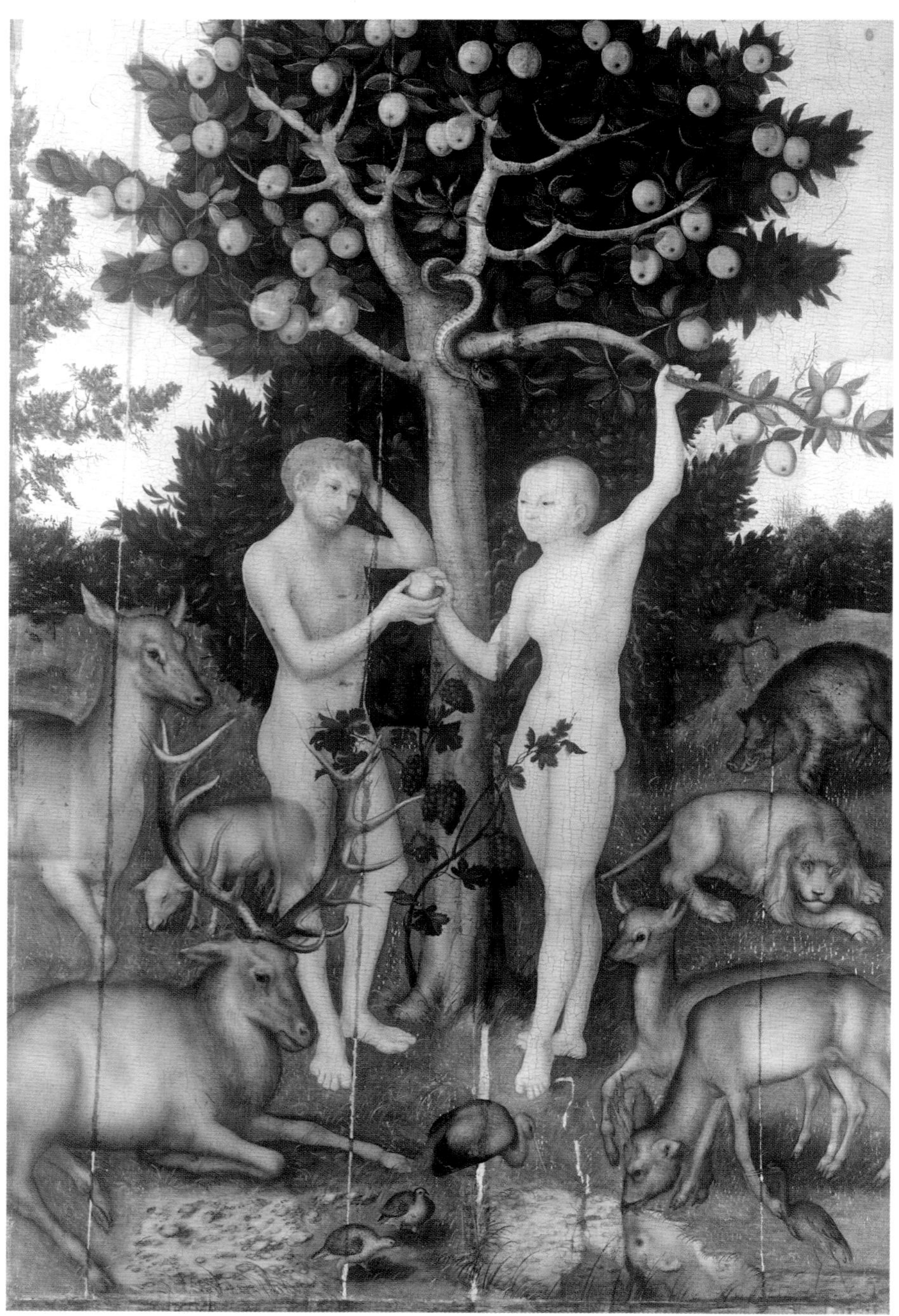

Fig. 34 X-radiograph of cat. 1
London, Courtauld Institute of Art Gallery

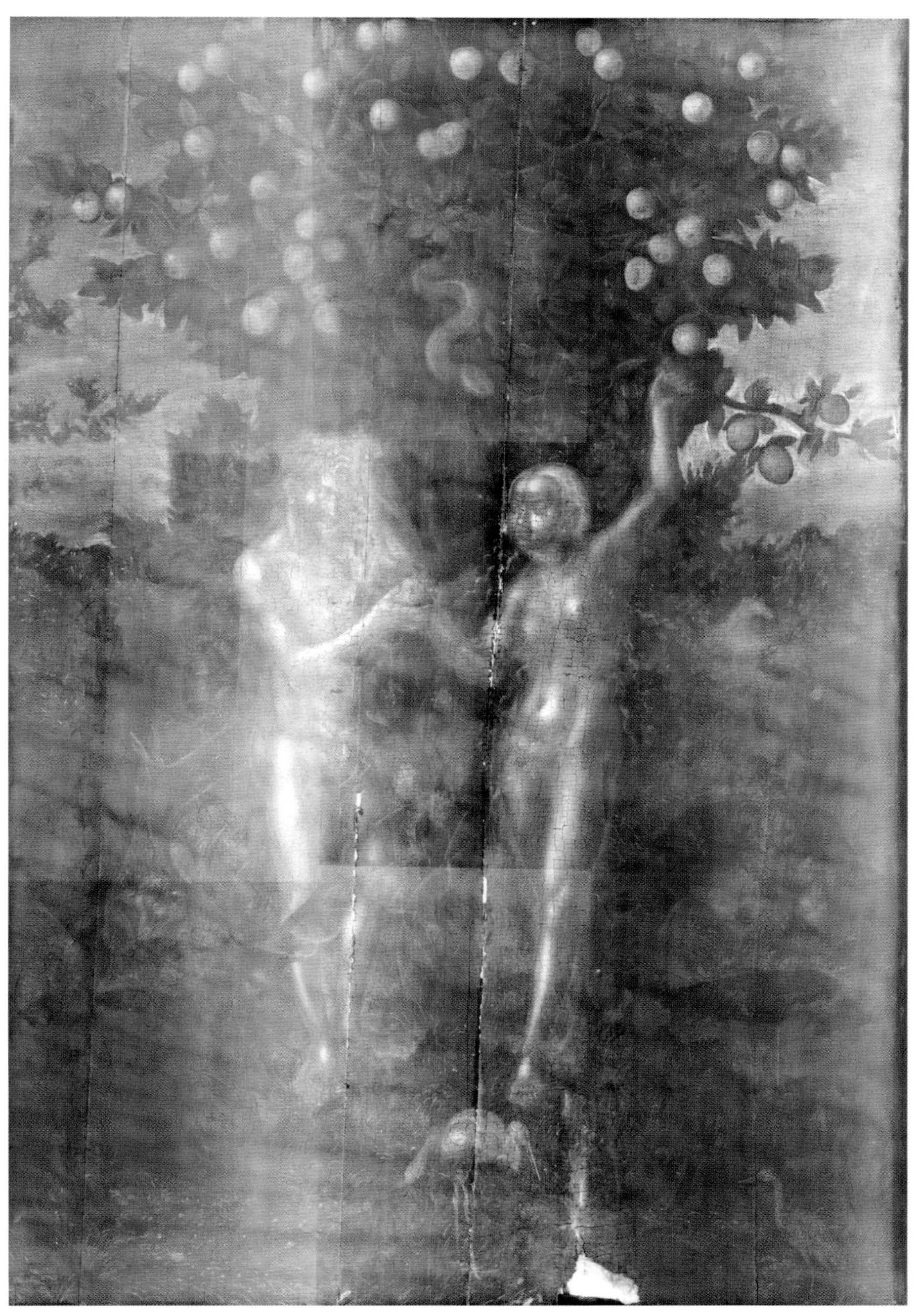

for the use of animals to convey aspects of Christian doctrine and to provide exemplars of Christian vices and virtues. The Bible abounds with examples of animal symbolism, and by the third century the *Physiologus* treatise had codified the basic Christian interpretation of the animal kingdom. This literature, augmented in subsequent centuries by bestiaries, and even hunting treatises such as Henri de Ferrières' fourteenth-century *Livre de chasse du Roy Modus*, underwent no significant changes during the Reformation.[9]

Most of Cranach's beasts bear moral meanings appropriate to Eden before the Fall. Many were used to evoke aspects of Christ, who would redeem mankind from the evil of Adam's choice. The most common symbol of Christ the redeemer was the stag, and each of the stags in *Adam and Eve* seems to refer to a different aspect of Christ's behaviour. The young antler-less stag (shown drinking from the pond at the lower right) could not defend himself, and thus was at the mercy of mankind, like the defenceless Christ when he first entered the world. However, Cranach's representation of the mature stag with antlers – which overlap Adam's body – probably refers to the resurrected Christ, and also to the righteous at the Second Coming, whom the theologian Aponius compared to stags raising their antlers.[10] The parched deer is a reference to Psalm 42, which compares the human thirsting after God to the stag in search of water.[11] The very species depicted is also relevant: roe deer were famed for their chastity and their devotion to one mate.[12] It is notable that the four deer in this painting are shown in couples: the stag and the hind together were used as emblems of Christian spouses.[13] Deer were also renowned for their enmity to serpents, the embodiment of sin. They were said to use their nostrils to drag snakes out of their lairs. According to Saint Augustine – a crucial figure for sixteenth-century theologians – the poison they ingested made them thirst for water: "The snakes are your sins; destroy the serpents of sin, and then you will more keenly long for the fountain of truth".[14]

Along with the deer, the sheep grazing contentedly behind Adam recalled the docility of true Christians, for whom "The Lord is my shepherd",[15] as well as Christ's sacrifice on the cross, represented by the mystery of the Eucharist.[16] This painting has pronounced Eucharistic references, for the grapes which shoot up from the Tree of Knowledge and cover Adam and Eve's genitalia allude to the bread and wine which Christ offered the disciples at the Last Supper as his body and blood, the New Testament between God and man which supplanted that of Adam.[17] Rather than a divider, this was a doctrinal unifier between Lutherans and Catholics. To the end of his life – in opposition to other Protestant reformers – Luther defended fervently the concept that Christ's body and blood could be present physically in the offerings on the Eucharistic table.[18] A stork stands directly under the grapes at the edge of a pond. This bird was associated by Christian iconographers with piety, purity and resurrection. A prudent creature, it had only one nest, which was used as a metaphor for the true Church, the only home for the faithful.[19] The heron, at the bottom right edge of the panel, shared these moral readings, as well as signifying one steadfast in the right path.[20]

The panel also depicts animals with more ambiguous allegorical meanings, including the pair of partridges next to the stork. The *Physiologus* described them as creatures prone to deceit and impurity. However, as a pair Cranach used them to represent the positive power of love – in contexts as diverse as images of Saint Jerome (fig. 15) and of the Nymph of the Spring – and this is probably their meaning here.[21] Most of the remaining creatures are clustered near Eve on the right-hand side of the painting. There is some evidence to support a reading of the boar as representing qualities opposite to those of the sheep (anger, brutality and lust) and as an embodiment of the Antichrist,[22] and the lion as an opponent of the stag and an embodiment of the devil.[23] The position is not clear-cut: just as Cranach's Eve deliberately recalls his depictions of the Virgin Mary (see in particular fig. 35, where Mary sits

Details of cat. 1

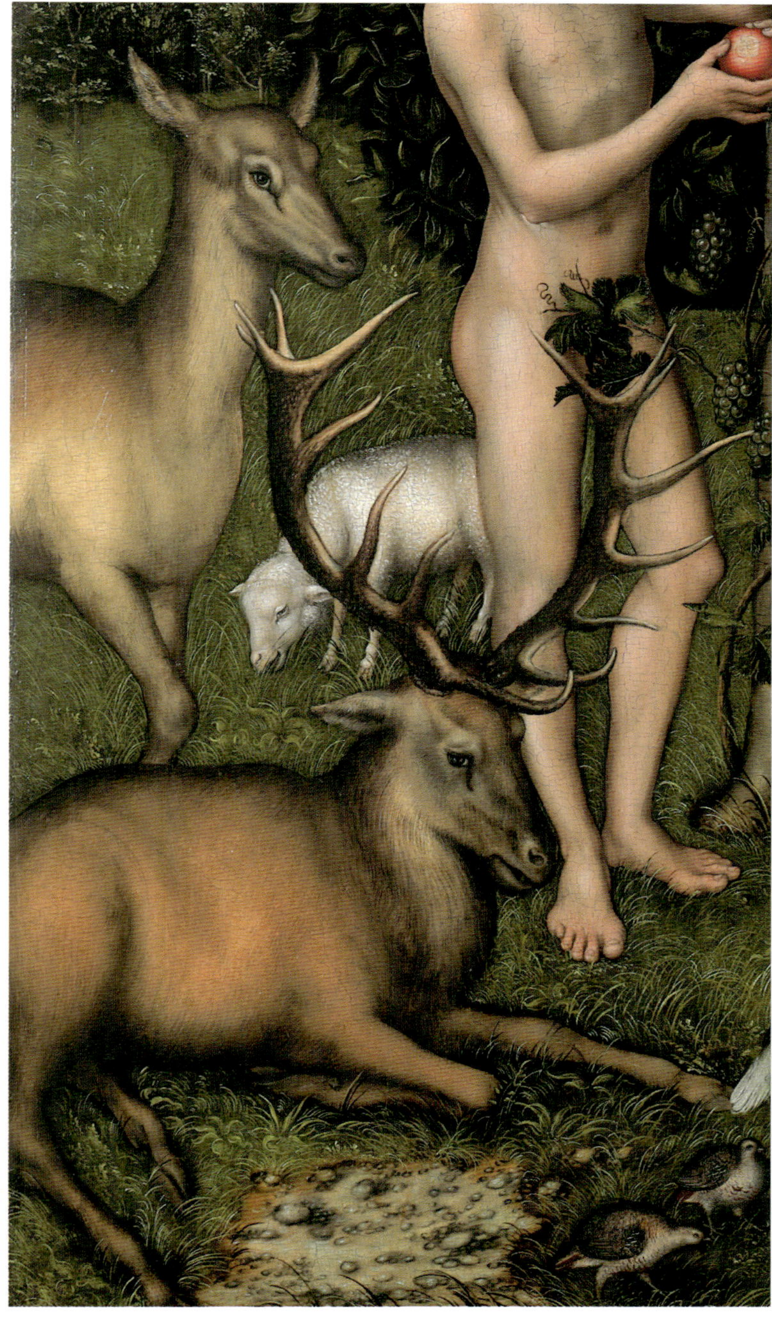

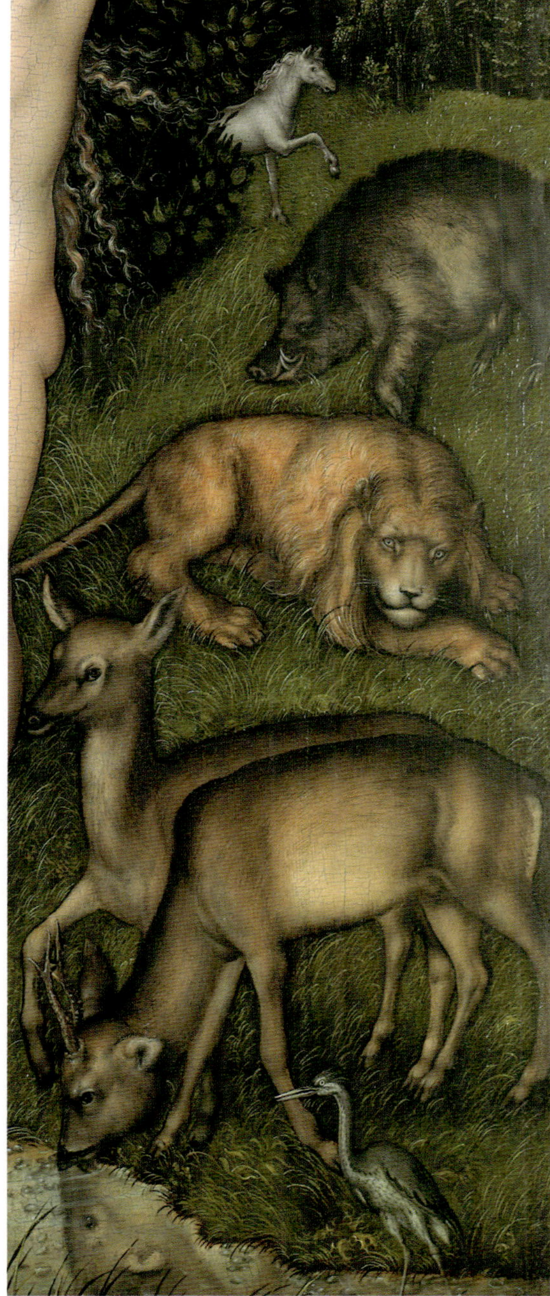

Fig. 35 Lucas Cranach the Elder, *The Virgin and Child under an Apple Tree*, around 1530
Oil on canvas (transferred from panel), 87 × 59 cm
St Petersburg, State Hermitage Museum

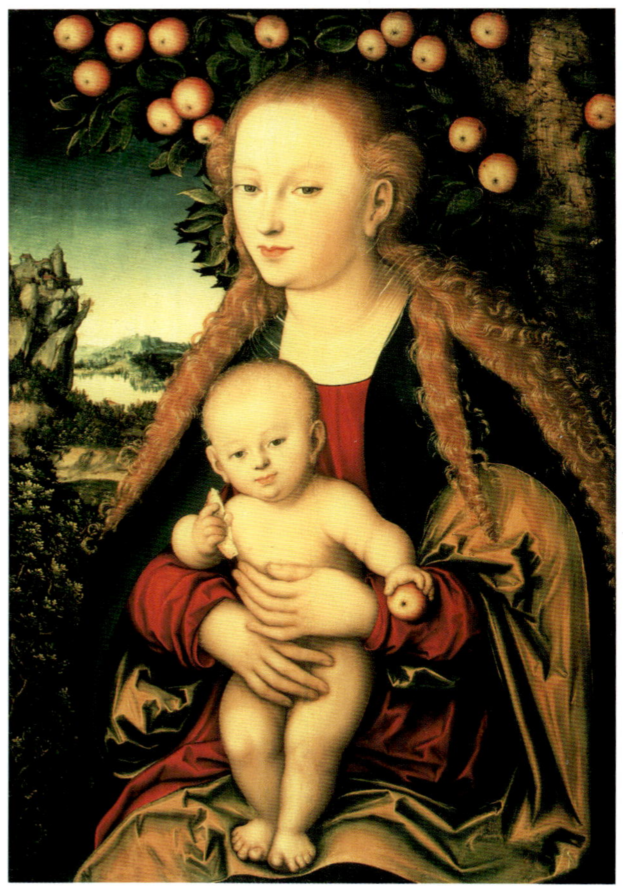

before an apple tree), the boar could be interpreted more positively as justice, independence and courage in the face of God's enemies, while the lion was also used to signify Christ, with whom it shared three natures, and naturally overcame evil (the devil).[24] However, Cranach's horse, another symbol of Christ,[25] which appears to be on the point of moving out of the pictorial space, suggests that the powers of good are about to abandon Eden with the imminent arrival of Original Sin. This apocalyptic feel is enhanced by the strange intensity of the light, crafted carefully to evoke the last remaining rays of evening light, after the sun has fallen.

For all this, Cranach's panel of 1526 is more than a simple vehicle for the conveyance of moral meanings. The exceptional beauty and skill with which the perfection of Eden is depicted imply strongly that the painting was made for a patron who would appreciate these elements as much as the Christian messages it contained (if interpreted properly). Both its dimensions and the finesse of its execution suggest that it was intended for a domestic setting. Its relatively unusual and complex iconography, intended to provoke discussion rather than provide definitive answers,[26] also supports the argument that it was specially commissioned. Who then might it have been made for? Sadly, the painting's secure history is unknown before the early twentieth century. However, the internal evidence of its iconography, and the thematic relationship it bears to the mythologies of primitive man which preoccupied Cranach during the late 1520s, suggest that its patron might have belonged to the Christian humanist circles at Wittenberg University. Cranach had close associations with such scholars, notably Philipp Melanchthon, and his interpretations of *Cupid complaining to Venus* (cat. 2) were made in tandem with the interest of Melanchthon and his students in the pseudo-Theocritus's nineteenth *Idyll*.[27] Interestingly, the National Gallery painting's representation of Venus, leaning on a branch of an apple tree, deliberately recalls Eve in the Courtauld panel (see essay by Susan Foister), and it has been argued that Cranach found in *Cupid complaining to Venus* a non-controversial means of creating a Christian image in a period when iconoclasm was a recurrent worry.[28] Might also the cross-referencing to Venus in the Courtauld *Adam and Eve* have protected Cranach from the potential accusation of idolatry?[29] Visual as well as iconographic features connect the two works. They share the same unusual deep-blue colouring of the sky and the distinctive quality of light at dusk, as if they capture the charms of the natural world just before its permanent destruction.

A similar nostalgic attitude towards unspoiled nature and its moral rectitude is expressed in two other mythologies by Cranach, *Apollo and Diana* (cat. 3) and *A Faun and his Family* (cat. 4). The survival of the Koenigs drawing of *Adam and Eve* (fig. 32) demonstrates that Cranach considered the Christian first couple before the Fall and the Greek goddess of chastity and her brother as closely related subjects. It must be remembered that sixteenth-century culture tended not to separate the sacred and the secular, and that there was a long Christian tradition of locating 'virtuous pagans' with Adam, Eve and other Old Testament worthies in Limbo, the first circle of Hell (whence they were rescued by the resurrected Christ). These shared characteristics have been used to suggest that these four paintings were made together in around 1526, the date of the Courtauld panel,[30] and even that they may have been produced as part of the same ensemble. This argument has much to recommend it visually and iconographically, and the panels are brought together for the first time in the exhibition this book accompanies in order to test this hypothesis. The technical examinations carried out recently by Yvonne Szafran for the Getty web-based Cranach research project have demonstrated very close connections between all four panels,[31] and in particular between *Apollo and Diana* and *A Faun and his Family*, which seem to belong together as a pair. The place of *Cupid complaining to Venus* in the group is less certain, because the panel was transferred to masonite in the early 1960s, but its almost identical dimensions, as well as the iconographic features mentioned above, make it very plausible that it originally belonged. The different scale of *Adam and Eve* does not argue necessarily against its inclusion in the group. Although no comparable domestic decorative schemes of paintings survive from sixteenth-century Germany, descriptions of such ensembles do; and similar surviving series from Northern and Central Italy often included elements of radically different dimensions.[32] Susan Foister (see essay) has suggested that these paintings, closely related in technique, quality and iconography, might have been made in connection with the marriage of the future Elector Johann Frederick the Magnanimous to Sibylla of Cleves in 1527. CMC

NOTES

1 Friedländer and Rosenberg (1978, p. 187) identify thirty-one paintings of this theme (FR 43–44a, 112–14, 191–99, 356, 357a–c, 431, 432), but over fifty are recorded in the Witt Library at the Courtauld Institute of Art.
2 For a summary, see Schoen 2001, pp. 197–203.
3 Cranach's first *Adam and Eve* in a forest dates from 1521 (Schleswig-Holsteinischen Landesmuseum; reproduced Bark 1994, p. 188, fig. 34), but the subject is not depicted by Cranach and his shop in large numbers until around 1525. See also Bonnet 1992, p. 260, who identifies three phases in Cranach's representations of *Adam and Eve*.
4 Reproduced in Friedländer and Rosenberg 1978, pl. 259.
5 Schuchardt 1851–71, I, p. 28.
6 Rosenberg 1960, nos. 39 and 48, pp. 22 and 24.
7 Elen 2004, no. 32.
8 Schoen 2001, p. 160.
9 For an introduction to this very extensive literature, see Hassig 1995 and Werness 2004.
10 Schoen 2001, p. 160.
11 Psalm 42: 1, "As the hart panteth after the water brooks, so panteth my soul after thee, O God".
12 Werness 2004, p. 131.
13 Charbonneau-Lassy 1940, p. 259.
14 Bath 1992, p. 211.
15 Psalm 23: 1.
16 Charbonneau-Lassay 1940, pp. 158–66.
17 Mark 26: 26–28.
18 MacCulloch 2003, p. 144.
19 Werness 2004, pp. 392–93.
20 Friedmann 1980, p. 224.
21 Friedmann 1980, p. 283. For the Nymph of the Spring in Cranach's oeuvre, see Koepplin and Falk 1974, II, pp. 631–41.
22 Charbonneau-Lassay 1940, pp. 173–75.
23 Schoen 2004, p. 160; Lebbrand 1989, pp. 151–53.
24 Charbonneau-Lassay 1940, p. 174; Werness 2004, p. 258. The lion is of course also the symbol of the Evangelist Mark.
25 Charbonneau-Lassay 1940, p. 211.
26 For what is perhaps an analogous example of a painting intended to provoke discussion, see Brinkmann 2007, pp. 36–47.
27 Pérez D'Ors 2007, pp. 88–89.
28 *Ibid.*, p. 98.
29 Kolind Poulsen 2002, p. 86.
30 Koepplin and Falk 1974, II, p. 500.
31 See www.getty.edu for this project, intended to go live as this catalogue goes to press.
32 Such as the Borgherini *camera* of 1515–18, for which see, most recently, B. Preyer, 'The Florentine *casa*', in Ajmar and Dennis 2006–07, pp. 42–44.

2 Lucas Cranach the Elder

Cupid complaining to Venus, probably 1526

Oil (identified as linseed) on wood (transferred to masonite board), 82 × 55 cm
Signed, at bottom right, with the winged serpent
Inscribed, at top right: *DVM PVER ALVEO[LO] F[VRATVR ME] LLA CVPIDO*
FVRANTI DIGITVM CV[SPIDE] F[IXIT] APIS
SIC ETIAM NOBIS BREVIS ET [PERI]TVRA VOLVPTAS
QUAM PETIMUS TRI[S]T[I] [M]IXTA DOLORE N[O]CET
(As the boy Cupid plundered honey from the hive, a bee pierced his finger with its spear; thus the brief and passing pleasure which we seek is mixed with sorrow and pain and does us harm.)
London, National Gallery, NG 6344

CRANACH'S TENDENCY TO VARY a composition and theme almost endlessly was one of his most salient characteristics as an artist. Together with *Adam and Eve*, *Cupid complaining to Venus* was among the subjects most often repeated within his workshop. There are at least twenty-seven versions of this allegory, of which the earliest that can be dated securely is inscribed 1527.[1]

Cupid, who has greedily pilfered honeycomb from a hive, has been attacked by the bees. As they swarm over his face and body and sting him, he complains to his mother Venus, the goddess of love, who holds up one hand as if to admonish him for this foolhardy action. The subject derives from a poem, 'The Honeythief', long believed to be by the third-century BC Greek poet Theocritus and to be the nineteenth of his *Idylls*.[2] It had a considerable literary and visual following in early sixteenth-century Germany, and the earliest depiction, a drawing by Dürer now in Vienna (fig. 22), dates from 1514. The poem was well known to humanists and theologians in Cranach's circle in Wittenberg, including Philip Melanchthon , Professor of Greek at the city's university, and his pupils. A number of Latin versions of the nineteenth *Idyll* survive from this milieu, including the inscription which the National Gallery painting bears. As Pablo Pérez D'Ors has discovered recently, this last was composed by one of Melanchthon's students, Georg Sabinus (1508–1560). It was first published in 1536, together with a similar poem by Sabinus's tutor, in Georg Rhau's *Enchiridion utriusque musicae practicae*.

Cranach's painting is on one level a witty warning of the effects of giving into temptation, and a visualisation of the inscription's admonition that transitory pleasure is followed by sorrow and pain. However, attraction is not represented solely by Cupid's foolish desire for honey, but also by the alluring figure of Venus, whose shapely naked body and face are turned towards the putative audience, offering them all that is on display. The temptation into which Cranach's Venus could lead the viewer is enhanced by the artist's deliberate use of Christian iconography. With her proper left hand, Venus grasps the branch of a heavily laden apple tree. It is the identical gesture used by Eve in the Courtauld painting (cat. 1) as she offers the fruit of the Tree of Knowledge to Adam. Strong similarities of technique and execution (see technical notes, below) further suggest that the two works must be very close in date. Although the National Gallery painting definitely represents Venus, the unmistakable references to Eve, the archetypal temptress and originator of Original Sin,

---

PROVENANCE

Sold from the Goldschmidt collection, Frankfurt am Main (Rudolf Leptke Kunst Auktions Haus, Berlin, 27 April 1909, lot 48); understood to have been chosen by Mrs Patricia Lochridge Hartwell, an American war correspondent, in 1945 from premises in Germany controlled by American armed forces and taken by her to the USA; apparently sold by Mrs Hartwell to Messrs A. and E. Silberman, New York, between March and June 1962, from whom purchased by the National Gallery, 1963

SELECTED LITERATURE

Friedländer and Rosenberg 1978, no. 246L, p. 119; Levey 1964; Smith 1985, p. 92, pl. 38; Leemann 1984; White and Pilc 1993, p. 88; Campbell, Foister and Roy 1997, p. 29, pl. 11; Kolind Poulsen 2002, pp. 85–86; Bomford 2002–03, p. 35, figs. 55 and 56; Foister 2003, pp. 120–23; Kolind Poulsen 2003; Pérez D'Ors 2007

BRIEF TECHNICAL NOTES

The panel was transferred to masonite (a synthetic board made from compacted wood fibres) in June 1962 by Thorp Brothers of New York. The original panel seems to have consisted of two vertical boards. A fine layer of canvas between the paint and the board was probably applied during the transfer. Despite some losses, notably to Venus's right heel, through the inscription at top right, and in the top left corner, the condition of the paint surfaceis good for a transferred panel. The x-radiograph shows

would have further emphasised the image's potential didactic message, and – it has been argued – in a manner immune to the potential reproaches of iconoclasts.[3]

Cupid complaining to Venus was a particular response to Cranach's circumstances in Wittenberg. Cranach cannot be categorised as a 'Lutheran' painter, and this painting is far from being Lutheran. However, the multiplicity of possible readings it offers bears witness to the impact of Lutheran theology upon Cranach's pictorial language, in particular the 'constant choice' between good and evil it demanded of its adherents.[4] This openness to a variety of interpretations was also a reflection of the other (often interrelated) components of Cranach's clientèle – the Saxon court and Wittenberg University, renowned for theological and humanist studies. The painting therefore was receptive to a number of explanations from these different quarters. For example, the stag standing in the wooded glade at the left could recall the favourite court pastime of hunting (see cat. 17, 18). However, simultaneously this motif might also refer to the origins of the German people in the forest, as recounted by the Roman historian Tacitus, and much discussed by humanist scholars.[5] In addition, since the stag could symbolise both Adam and Christ's temptation and sacrifice, it could further emphasise the dangers of giving in to short-lived desire.

The National Gallery painting is not simply a warning of the dangers of temptation. Like Adam and Eve, it is closely connected to a whole group of paintings Cranach made of the primitive history of man in the late 1520s and early 1530s, including *Apollo and Diana* (cat. 3), *A Faun and his Family* (cat. 4) and *The Silver Age* (including fig. 20). As Susan Foister has argued (see essay), these were inspired by a growing interest in the tales of early humanity told by the Greek poet Hesiod and subsequently by the Latin authors Virgil and Ovid. These evoked a 'Golden Age' followed by ages of silver, bronze and iron, where the development of human 'civilisation' was matched by the rise of conflict and warfare. The 'Golden Age' provided a pagan analogue to the existing Christian belief of the perfection of Eden and humanity before the Fall. Thus in *Cupid complaining to Venus* the goddess of love is not yet an active temptress. Like Eve she is an idealisation of female beauty, who stands in an unspoiled idyll. This may be on the cusp of change and degeneration, but that depends on the viewer. It is on this interpreter that the future of Venus and her son Cupid hangs. CMC

that the painting was worked up in a very similar fashion to the Courtauld *Adam and Eve*. Red lines were detected under the paint surface in certain areas (including Venus's hat). These appear to be freehand and in a liquid medium, and seem to have formed a simple linear underdrawing of the main parts of the composition. The painting was surface-cleaned in 1963.

NOTES

1. Pérez D'Ors 2007, p. 89.
2. Holden 1974, p. 116; Gow 1988, I, p. 146.
3. Pérez d'Ors 2007.
4. Kolind Poulsen 2002, p. 86.
5. Foister 2003, p. 127.

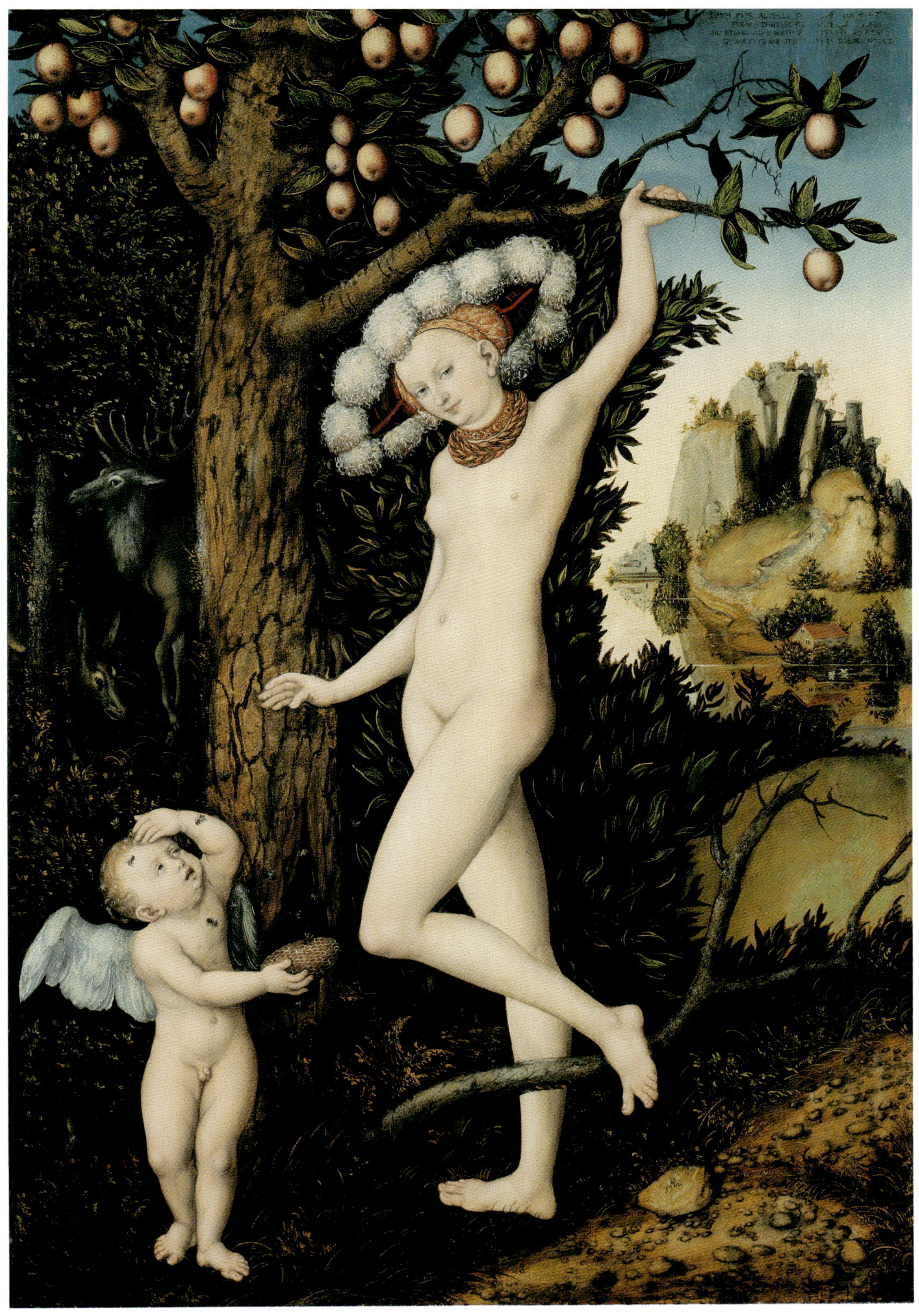

3 Lucas Cranach the Elder

Apollo and Diana, probably 1526

Oil on beech, 84.6 × 57.2 cm
Signed with Cranach's monogram of the black winged serpent at the lower left
Her Majesty the Queen, Royal Collection 407294

THE PANEL DEPICTS the twin children of Leto, Apollo and Diana (or Artemis), deities admired for their physical and moral beauty and associated respectively with music and with archery, chastity and hunting. The scene is set at the edge of a mixed forest of conifers and deciduous trees, with vistas opening to a mountainous landscape behind, populated with occasional turrets, including a palace (perhaps Torgau?) and a church tower. The placid lake at the right, with its swimming swans in the manner of Memling (compare to cat. 2), forms a deliberate contrast to the untamed world of the forest, where Apollo (wearing only a quiver with a billowing sash that covers his genitals) prepares to loose an arrow at an unseen target. To his right, his naked sister Diana sits on an antlered stag. Her proper right leg is crossed over her left, and she clasps her right foot with a gesture Cranach adapted from the antique sculpture of the *Spinario*, or boy removing a thorn, a motif much copied in the sixteenth century. The turquoise sky deepens in colour towards the top edge of the painting, probably in allusion to Diana's domain of night as goddess of the moon.

Although *Apollo and Diana* probably dates from around 1526, like cat. 1, 2 and 4, it is much inspired by the production of Cranach and his contemporaries in the first years of the sixteenth century. The wooded landscape recalls Cranach's work in the early sixteenth century as a member of the Danube School of artists (compare to cat. 16), and both Apollo and Diana's bodies are echoed by the shapes of the trees and landscape in front of which they are placed. The painting has clear antecedents in Dürer and Jacopo de' Barbari's related engravings of the same subject, made around 1503 (see cat. 22). Cranach's figure of Apollo, his body depicted as tautly as his fully drawn bow, is taken from Jacopo, while the idea of placing a seated Diana next to a stag was used by both artists. Comparison of Cranach's painting with these engravings, which (as Sabine Heiser has demonstrated) he knew by 1503, makes his iconographic sources very obvious; however, it must be emphasised that Cranach's *Apollo and Diana* is a new composition, not simply an amalgamation of these earlier interpretations. It was one which he replicated on several occasions: two further autograph paintings of the subject survive.[1]

The absence of positive attributes for the deities accounts for the painting's identification as *Adam and Eve* until the mid twentieth century, and in 1911 Cust attempted to connect it with a panel of this subject by Cranach which was included in the sale of Charles I's collection at Somerset House.[2] Although the telling absence of a fruit tree makes it clear that the Royal Collection painting cannot represent Adam and Eve, the confusion is not surprising since the two subjects appear to have been closely associated in Cranach's mind in the years he was working on these panels. Visual as well as iconographic comparisons support a blurring of the sacred/secular boundaries between these paintings – which certainly were far less strict in sixteenth-century Europe than art historians have liked to believe – and Cranach's other depictions of mankind's early history, whether told by Christian or pagan sources (including

PROVENANCE
Friedrich Campe, Nuremberg; from whom bought by Prince Albert on the advice of Ludwig Grüner, 1844 or 1846

SELECTED LITERATURE
Cust 1911, p. 49; Bishop 1937, pp. 95–96; London 1946–47, no. 140, p. 60; Manchester 1961, no. 86, p. 36; Koepplin and Falk 1974, II, p. 500; London 1977, no. 47, p. 25; Millar 1977, pp. 192–93, pl. 43; Friedländer and Rosenberg 1978, no. 271A, pp. 122–23; Lloyd 1991, no. 83, p. 222; Grimm and Brockhoff 1994, no. 173b, p. 350; Roberts 2002, no. 3, p. 73; Heiser in Berlin 2002, p. 65; Koepplin 2003, pp. 146–47

BRIEF TECHNICAL NOTES
The support is a beechwood panel with a vertical grain, composed of two vertical planks (the join is approximately 33 cm from the left edge). The panel has been cradled and thinned. It was treated by Drown between 1949 and 1951, when the cradle was removed and the thinned panel adhered to plywood. Subsequent restoration in 1991 removed the varnish and much old and discoloured retouching.

cat. 1, 2 and 4 and fig. 20). For instance, Cranach uses the same typology of female beauty (long, curling blond hair framing an oval face, and a slim body with small, pert breasts) for his representations of Eve before the Fall, Diana, the Virgin Mary and other women in a state of perfection.

Apollo and Diana has been connected in particular with the J. Paul Getty Museum's *A Faun and his Family* (cat. 4). The paintings are on the same beech support, of almost identical dimensions, and their primeval narratives are arranged in a similar fashion, the figure group being surrounded by foliage and the landscape opening up into a view of a lake and mountains. Their subjects also bear close comparison. Strong technical and visual similarities make it likely that they were made as a pair – perhaps also, as has been argued for cat. 1, as part of a larger ensemble which included *Adam and Eve* and *Cupid complaining to Venus*. As Koepplin and Falk elaborated over thirty years ago, mythological subjects such as Apollo and Diana were often interpreted according to Christian and humanist precepts in the circles in which Cranach moved in Vienna and Wittemberg. Apollo, god of the sun and the Greek epitome of male perfection – cultured, intelligent, and beautiful – was described in terms similar to Christ, whom he could figure in allegorical representations.[3] The virgin Diana, embodiment of purity, could also be seen as a forerunner or even a pagan analogue of Mary, the mother of Christ unstained by sin.

These hypotheses are supported by a drawing by Cranach from the Koenigs collection (fig. 32). The Koenigs sheet depicts Eve seated on a stag in the same pose as Diana in the present painting, handing an apple to Adam, who stands to her left. It is generally said to be a preparatory drawing for the Courtauld *Adam and Eve* (cat. 1), but it seems also to represent an intermediary stage between this and the Royal Collection painting. Other depictions by Cranach of Adam and Eve have an even closer relationship with the present *Apollo and Diana*, especially fig. 29 (Münster). It is difficult to establish the relative order of their production, and indeed Cranach may well have painted them at the same time. However, the existence of the Koenigs drawing, and the secure 1526 date of the Courtauld *Adam and Eve*, suggest that Cranach conceived of the Fall of Man in a wooded landscape first, and realised swiftly that this format could be applied to other narratives of temptation, beauty and primitive man.

CMC

NOTES

1 Berlin, Gëmaldegalerie, inv. 564 (FR 271); Brussels, Musée des Beaux-Arts, inv. 779 (FR 270).

2 See Cust 1911, p. 49. It is described in the sale catalogue of Charles I's collection as: "Done by Lucas Chronich. Item. The picture of a naked standing Adam and Eve, where by in a bush lying a great stag, with long horns, Adam is eating the apple: intire little figures; bought from Germany, by my Lord Marquiss of Hamilton. 1 ft. 7 in. by 1 ft. 1½ in." This panel was sold at Christie's, London, 20 March 1959, lot 54. Its present location is unknown to the author.

3 Panofsky 1955, p. 87.

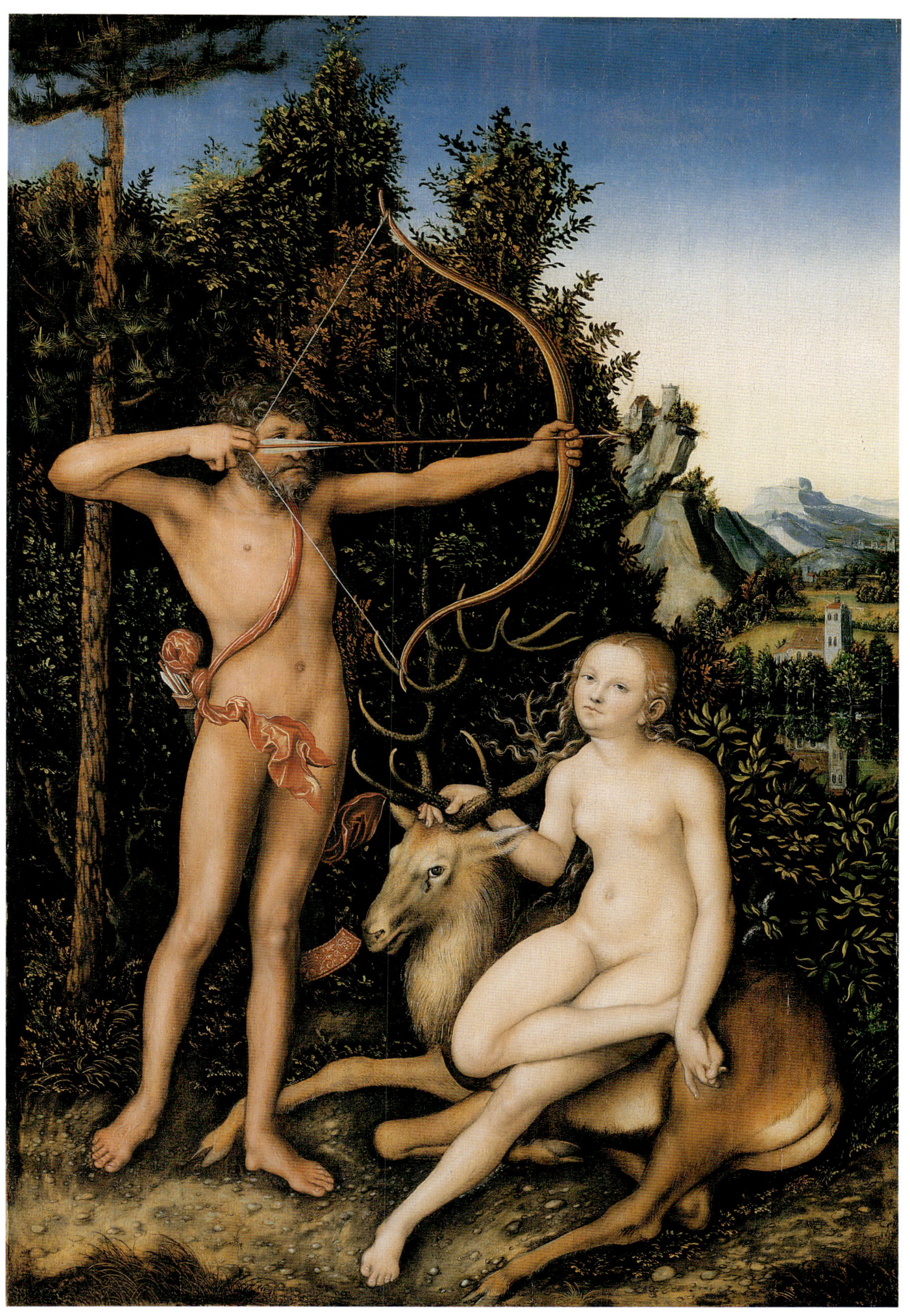

4 Lucas Cranach the Elder

A Faun and His Family with a Slain Lion, about 1526

Signed with the winged serpent on a small block, centre left
Oil on panel, 82.9 × 56.2 cm
Los Angeles, J. Paul Getty Museum, 2003.100

IN *A FAUN AND HIS FAMILY WITH A SLAIN LION*, painted in the detailed and polished style of his best works from the late 1520s, Cranach presents a refined interpretation of a popular subject usually portrayed in prints. Intended for erudite patrons at the Wittenberg court, Cranach's elegant composition blended influences from many different sources, including antique literature, Germanic folklore and contemporary commentary in a highly original portrayal of wildness.

In a pebbly clearing, the faun sits regally on a hewn block, holding his wooden staff across his lap. The elongated contours of his left ear (its pointed tip was previously obscured by overpaint, now removed), along with the fine hair covering his body, are the primary physical clues to his identity. At his feet lies the corpse of the male lion he has just slain, bleeding copiously from its nose and mouth and a wound on its head. The faun gazes thoughtfully at his gracefully proportioned female companion and their children, one of whom reaches towards his father. Even without primitive attributes, their nudity defines their place in this realm. Beyond the leafy confines of the faun's domain rises a rocky mountain topped by a castle. At the centre, a lake reflects the towers of a city as well as the delicate hues of the sky.

In this lyrical work, Cranach evoked the spirit and way of life of a mythical figure that had long captured the imagination, rather than a specific episode from a literary source. Cranach combined elements both of the late medieval 'wild man' extolled in poetry and represented on decorative objects and of the elevated discourse of ancient poets such as Lucretius and Hesiod about the earliest ages of mankind that captivated Cranach and his contemporaries in Wittenberg (see essay by Susan Foister). The carcass of the magnificent lion, for example, one of the beasts whose ferocity was second only to the forest dweller, denotes his legendary strength and valour. This brutal element, painted with great delicacy and precision, contrasts with the serenity of the family group itself. The faun and his stone block seat recalls Tacitus's description of the primitive early inhabitants of Germania, who had not learned how to utilize quarry-stone. Classical writers, as well as contemporary Wittenberg intellectuals such as Conrad Celtis and Hans Sachs, portrayed primitive man as master of his natural environment and protector of his family, living a simple, almost paradisiacal, existence free of the conflicts of the civilised world. The idyllic life of the wild family in a region separate from, but adjacent to, civilisation is neatly expressed through Cranach's characteristically structured screen of foliage, which serves as a foil for the figures and offers a window onto an expansive landscape. The subject of early, uncorrupt man offered a profane counterpart to Cranach's sacred themes of the same period, such as *Adam and Eve* (cat. 1) and *Adam and Eve in the Garden of Eden* (cat. 5). The resemblance of the faun with his dead lion to the myth of Hercules, and the sensual nude female to the type of Venus or Charity, particularly in Cranach's oeuvre, is part of the

PROVENANCE
Possibly Maximilian I, Elector and Duke of Bavaria, from about 1598; with Spink & Son Ltd, London, by 1948;[6] from whom acquired by Sir Robert Bland Bird, 2nd Bart (London and Solihull, Warwickshire), 1952; by inheritance to Pamela Stephanie Helen Bird, Viscountess de Mauduit, Paris, in 1960; with Dr. Otto Wertheimer, Paris, by 1963; by whom sold to Dr. h.c. Max Schmidheiny, Zurich, 1963; by descent to Dr. Thomas Schmidheiny, Zurich, 1993; sold through Hall & Knight, Ltd, London, to the J. Paul Getty Museum, 2003

BRIEF TECHNICAL NOTES
The painting is in excellent condition. The panel is composed of three vertically joined planks, and has an original rebate on all four edges. The joins of the planks have been reinforced with fibrous material on the reverse, which is coated with at least two layers of paint, possibly original. Some underdrawing, notably in the figures, is visible with infra-red reflectography and with the naked eye.

multivalence of the artist's treatment of mythological themes in this period.

The Los Angeles panel is Cranach's earliest painting of wild folk. Fauns or wild men (their ears covered by bushy curls) with their mates and children appear in his graphic work of the early 1520s, including the woodcut frontispieces for the sermons of his friend Martin Luther (1523). For the present painting Cranach eschewed the important models of satyr families introduced in prints shortly after 1500 by Jacopo de' Barbari, his friend Albrecht Dürer and Albrecht Altdorfer. Cranach's domestic scene relates most directly to the wild family portrayed by the French illuminator Jean Bourdichon (about 1500), which feature an intimate glimpse of the family outside their rustic home, with the buildings of civilisation in the distance. Dürer's influence, however, was never far away. The balanced placement of figures around a central element in *A Faun and his Family*, with a screen of foliage behind and a distant hilltop edifice, owes much to Dürer's seminal *Adam and Eve* (1505; cat. 23).

Cranach's lively, descriptive brushwork is one of the most remarkable features of this work. Liquid touches animate the characteristic textured foliage, while graphic brushstrokes delineate the lion's mane and the fine strands of the female faun's hair, attesting to Cranach's technical skill and long career as a draughtsman. *A Faun and his Family* was intended for close inspection, rewarding viewers with minutely executed details such as the *Landsknecht* running down the distant road.

Cranach painted two later versions of the *Faun and his Family*, which vary in composition – the small *Faun and his Family with a Slain Lion* (about 1530; Donaueschingen, S.D. Fürst zu Fürstenberg), with its tighter figure group, and a painting possibly executed with the assistance of his son Hans (private collection).[1] The Getty painting retains its original unpainted rebated edges, indicating that the panel has not been trimmed. Like *Apollo and Diana* (cat. 3), with which it shares a standard-size panel, *A Faun and his Family* surely belonged to a group of gallery paintings of mythological subjects.[2]

Unfortunately, there is no evidence that this work was part of the great collection of German Renaissance paintings formed by John, Lord Lumley at the end of the sixteenth century.[3] However, a painting attributed to Cranach in the 1598 inventory of Maximilian I of Bavaria, identified as *Hercules and Venus* "with a child in her right arm and leading another by the hand", may be the Getty panel or the Donaueschingen version.[4] The description of another Cranach painting in the same collection corresponds with the Royal Collection *Apollo and Diana* (cat. 3), raising the possibility that Cranach's mythological subjects, like Dürer's prints, *Apollo and Diana* and *The Satyr's Family*, were perceived as complementary, if not as a pair.[5] The present exhibition provides the opportunity to consider whether the Los Angeles and London paintings, alike in size and delicacy of execution and exhibited together for the first time, might have been pendants. ATW

SELECTED LITERATURE
Waterhouse 1953, p. 306; Birmingham 1953, p. 29, no. 145; Manchester 1961, no. 84, p. 36; Levy and White 1961, p. 487; Pieper 1962, pp. 3–4; Koepplin and Falk 1974, I, p. 38, II, no. 500, pp. 600–01; Friedländer and Rosenberg 1978, no. 267, p. 122; Glaser 1980, I, p. 250; Bierende 2002, p. 423; Schade 2003, pp. 129, 159

NOTES

1 Koepplin and Falk 1974, nos. 502 and 501, respectively, pp. 601–02.

2 For Cranach's use of standard-size panels see Heydenreich 2003.

3 The reference to the Lumley collection appears to be anecdotal: see note 6.

4 Glaser 1980, I, p. 250.

5 Hollstein 1959, nos. 64 and 65; Koepplin and Falk (1974, II, pp. 600, 602) were not aware of the paintings in Maximilian I's collection.

6 Seen at C. Marshal Spink's by E.K. Waterhouse, 22 December 1948: he noted that the painting was "said to have been in the possession of the Lumley family". Ellis Kirkham Waterhouse Notebooks and Research Files, 1901–1987 (most of them *c.* 1924– *c.* 1979), Getty Research Institute, Research Library, accession no. 870204: Notebook 29, p. 32.

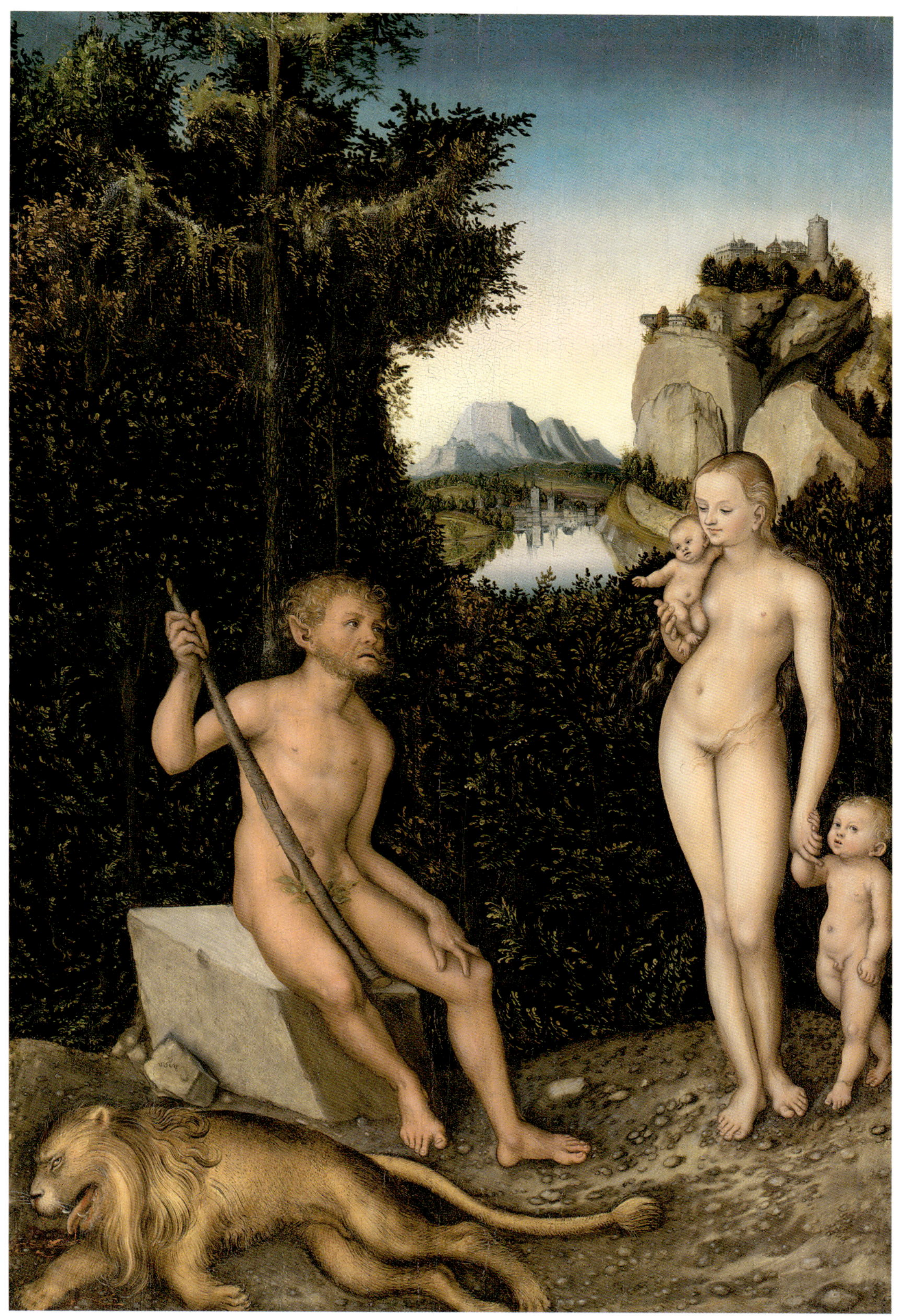

5

Lucas Cranach the Elder

Adam and Eve in the Garden of Eden, 1530

Oil on panel (limewood), 80 × 118 cm
Signed with the winged serpent at lower right and dated *1530*
Dresden, Staatsliche Kunstsammlungen, Gemäldegalerie Alte Meister, 1908 A

ALTHOUGH CRANACH AND HIS SHOP made over fifty representations of Adam and Eve, this is one of only two surviving depictions of the Garden of Eden. Both panels, the present work and fig. 37 (Vienna), date from 1530, and are very close although not identical. The internal and narrative organisation of each is quite distinct, and there is no reason to suppose that one was made as a replica of the other. Rather it seems that they were produced side by side in Cranach's studio. At the same time he was also working on a series of evocations of the Greek poet Hesiod's Golden Age (see fig. 21). In terms of both iconography and style these bear very close connections with the Garden of Eden pictures.

The Dresden painting is divided into two levels, which could be read entirely separately. The top half of the panel places the various episodes of man's Creation and Fall within the integrated landscape setting of the Garden of Eden, from Adam's creation to Adam and Eve's expulsion from Paradise by a winged angel (Genesis 2: 7, 21–23; 3: 6–7, 23–24), while the bottom section depicts the animal and bird life of Paradise. At the centre of the composition, God the Father instructs Adam and Eve in their duties, and shows them the world over which he has set Adam in authority. This figural group, who are depicted on a disproportionately large scale, link the two registers of the painting – the history of Adam and Eve and the imperfect world they create and the unchanging perfection of Paradise. This manner of representation (which is also seen in the Courtauld *Adam and Eve*, cat. 1) derives from the tradition of manuscript illumination (see essay by Stephanie Buck), and Cranach's wide experience as a book-illustrator (see cat. 19, 20). The division of the pictorial space into parallel planes of activity also recalls Netherlandish tapestry of the late fifteenth century, such as the *Hunt of the Unicorn* cycle, woven between 1495 and 1505 (New York, Metropolitan Museum).[1]

The foreground is dominated by depictions of the beasts over which God gave Adam dominion (Genesis 2: 16–20). Like Adam and Eve, most of the animals are in pairs, and, since this is Paradise, the hunters and hunted rest and graze harmoniously in each others' company. The whole range of animal life is represented, from everyday domestic beasts like cattle, sheep and chickens to more exotic species such as apes, peacocks and even the fabled unicorn. The animals have more than a decorative function. Some, including the deer and the lions, are very frequently found in Cranach's depictions of Adam and Eve (see cat. 1 for discussion of their potential meanings), while others like the fox and the he-goat are more unusual.[2]

Almost every creature which Cranach has depicted had a potential symbolic meaning in fifteenth- and sixteenth-century European culture. That he intended them to be interpreted in this way is clear by the important supplementary narrative role which some of them play. Directly

PROVENANCE
Freiherr von Freisen, Schloß Schleinitz; from whom purchased, 1928

SELECTED LITERATURE
Posse 1930, p. 500; Dresden 1937, p. 13; Aragon and Cocteau 1957, p. 22, 141–42; Weimar 1972, p. 72; Friedländer and Rosenberg 1978, no. 202, p. 109; Dresden 1992, p. 159; Torgau 2004, I, no. 184; Marx and Mössinger 2005–06, no. 1, pp. 200–07

BRIEF TECHNICAL NOTES
The panel is composed of five horizontal planks. The back, which has been planed, is covered with a reddish varnish. The paint surface is in good condition, although there are some losses along the panel joins. Some abrasion is evident in the figures of Adam and Eve and in the sky. The panel was restored before entering the collection in 1928, in 1955 (while in the Soviet Union) and in 1973. Examination with infra-red reflectography has detected some underdrawing in a fluid medium in the peacock's feathers and in the unicorn.

underneath the main figure of Eve Cranach has painted a he-goat, who is about to head-butt the stag sitting peaceably beside him. It seems that the goat, a common symbol of the devil and of licentiousness, is an animal *doppelgänger* of Eve, while the stag represents Adam and, ultimately, his descendant Christ, who will redeem the sin of humanity. In a similar fashion the hare, which stands for unrestrained lust, has been carefully placed beside the vignette of Eve offering the fruit of the Tree of Knowledge to Adam at top right.

Discussion of this painting, and of the closely related panel in Vienna, has tended to focus on its Lutheran qualities. The prime importance given to God's instruction of Adam and Eve has been argued to reflect the influence of Reformed thought and its emphasis on teaching the faithful. In particular, it has been connected convincingly to the series of sermons which Luther delivered on the Book of Genesis in Wittenberg between March 1523 and September 1524, which were first published in 1527, and to Cranach's 1529 representation of *The Fall and Salvation of Man* (see fig. 36). However, *Adam and Eve in the Garden of Eden* must also be viewed in the context of long-established traditions of Catholic representation and devotion. As Hanne Kolind Poulsen has argued, the impact of Luther's conceptions of images on Cranach was actually to increase, not limit, the potential ways in which his paintings, prints and drawings could be seen and used.[3] No one means of interpretation excluded any others. For instance, there is nothing in this panel to preclude its use by a Catholic. Nor needed the painting to be used in a strictly devotional context. There was nothing to stop a sixteenth-century viewer from taking pleasure in its beautiful and idealised landscape – even if such a scrutiny was bound to heighten the contrast between the world he inhabited and Cranach's idealised vision of Paradise before the Fall. CMC

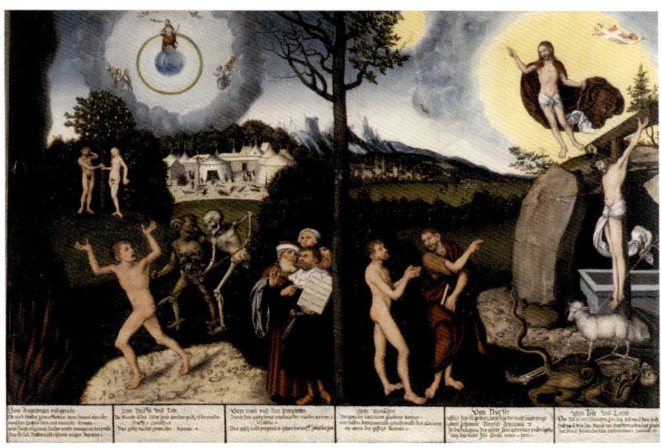

Fig. 36 Lucas Cranach the Elder, *The Fall and Salvation of Man*, 1529
Oil on limewood, 80 × 115 cm
Gotha, Stiftung Schloss Friedenstein, Schlossmuseum

NOTES

1 See Campbell 2002, no. 5, pp. 70–79.
2 See Werness 2004, p. 184.
3 Kolind Poulsen 2002, p. 86.

Fig. 37 Lucas Cranach the Elder,
Adam and Eve in the Garden of Eden, 1530
Oil on limewood, 81 × 114 cm
Vienna, Kunsthistorisches Museum

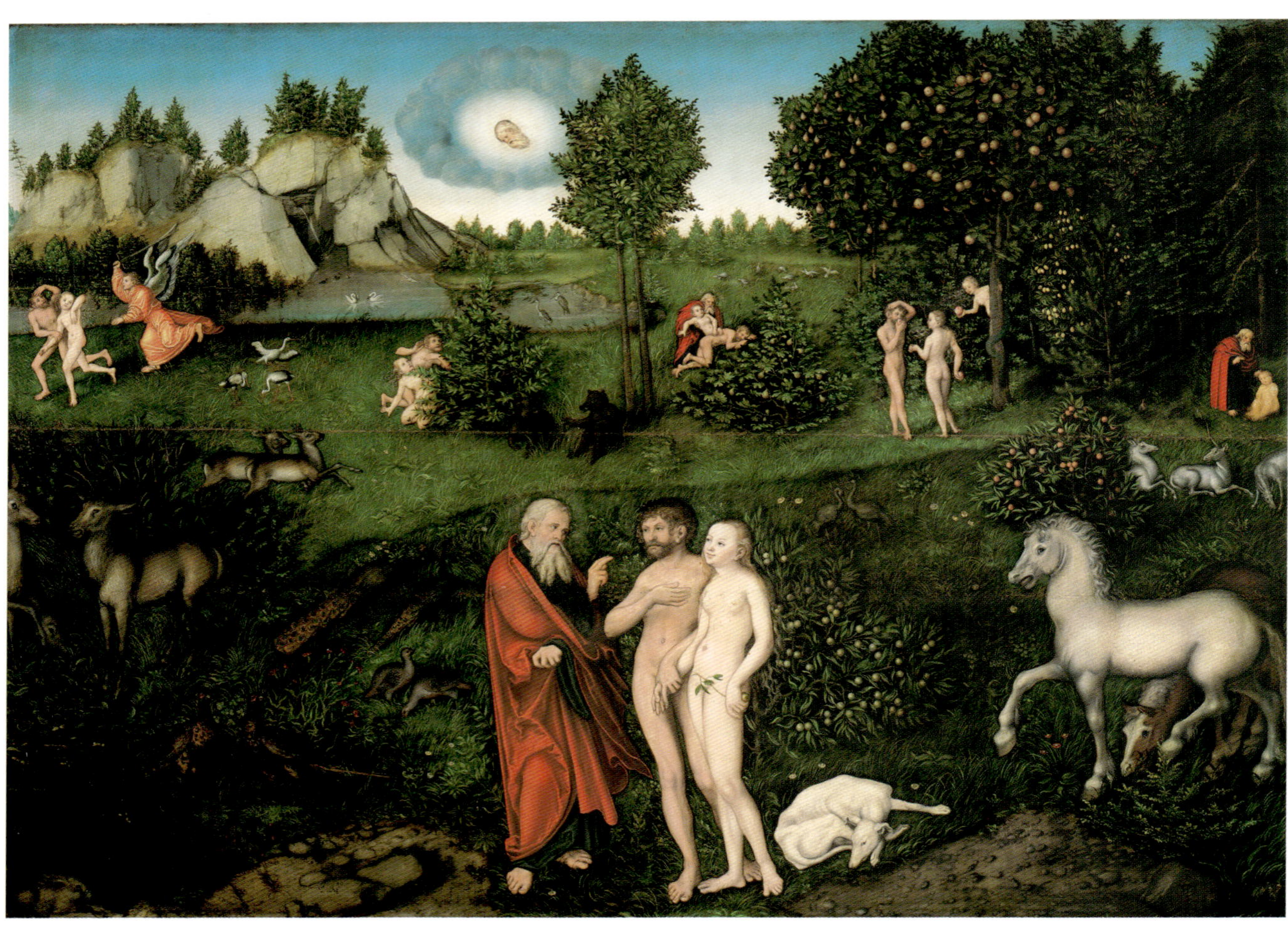

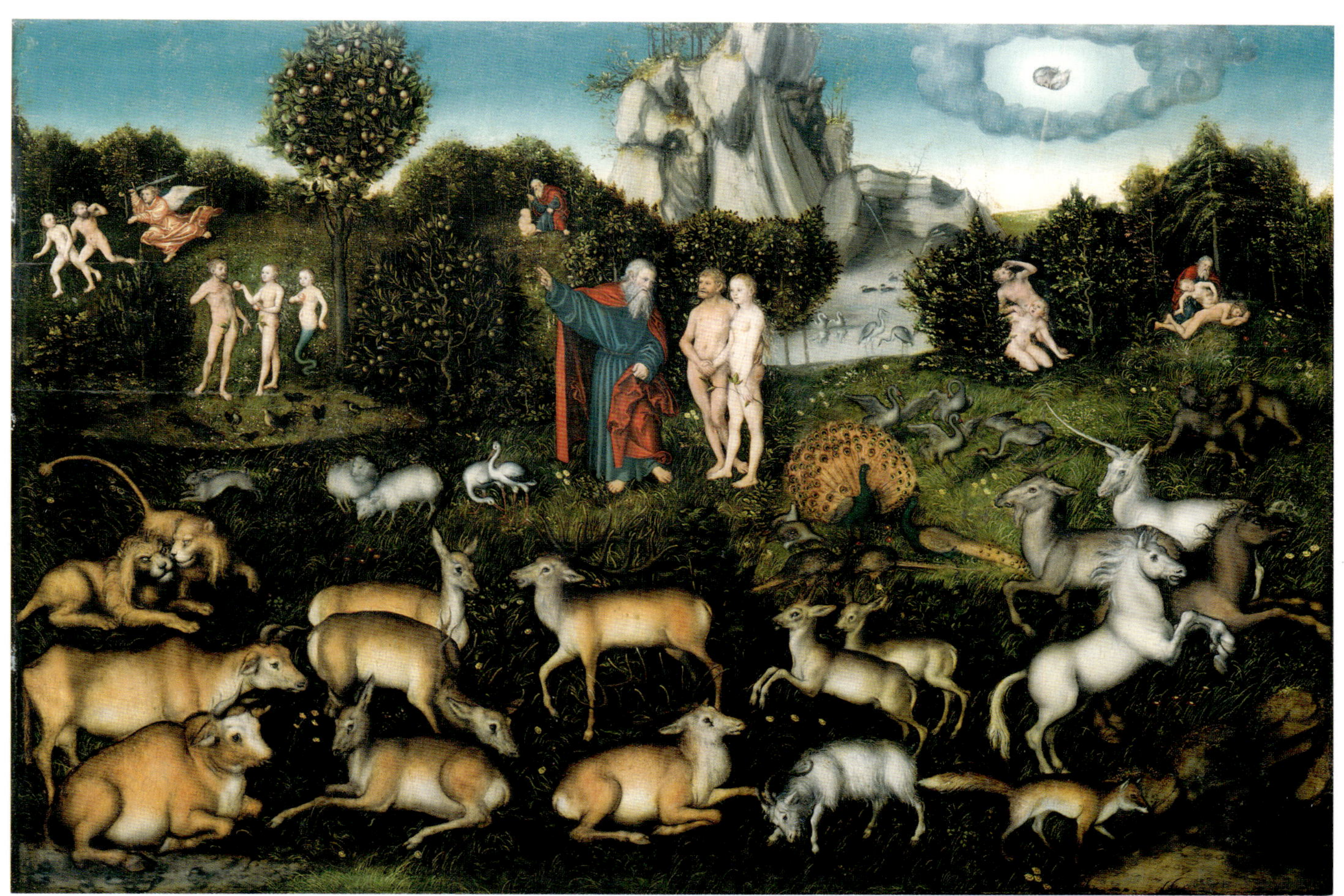

6 Lucas Cranach the Elder

RECTO: *A Dead Hind, with a Study of its Head*
VERSO: *Stags fighting, Herd of Hinds, Stag and Hinds, Study of Foliage*

c. 1525–30

RECTO: Pen and brush, dark brown and grey ink, water and body colours, heightened with white, over traces of preliminary drawing in black chalk or charcoal, on laid paper; false Dürer monogram in the lower right corner
VERSO: Pen and dark brown ink, over preliminary drawing in black chalk or charcoal; inscribed by a later hand: *albrechtis darer*
20.0 × 28.4 cm
Paris, Musée du Louvre, Département des Arts Graphiques, R.F. 3894

"I cannot ignore ... that everybody praises you for painting with marvellous rapidity, so that you surpass not only Nicomachus or Marcia but all painters. In my opinion you acquired this rapidity through continuous study and steadfast diligence. Pliny writes that Apelles never spent a day, no matter how busy it was, without drawing at least one line in order to exercise his art .... As far as I can see, you spend not a single day, hardly an hour, in idleness; your brush is always busy .... Whenever the princes take you hunting, you take a panel with you, which you complete amidst the hunt, or you draw Frederick rousing a stag, or Johann chasing a boar."[1]

IN DESCRIBING CRANACH as an assiduous artist who worked rapidly, even in the midst of a hunt, this famous encomium by the humanist Christoph Scheurl, published in 1509, helps to elucidate this exceptional drawing, which, unlike any other, unites two extremes of Cranach's draughtsmanship – mimetic painterly precision and the utmost sketchiness. The recto demonstrates the artist's ability to portray a dead animal with tactile accuracy, in the description not only of the soft fur but also of the bones and muscles. Cranach chose to isolate the hind and render it in profile with all four legs outstretched, thus making use of the entire sheet of paper. The remaining top right corner was used for another study of the hind's head in the same scale, this time seen from above. An accurate mimetic effect is achieved by an astonishing economy of means. Cranach broadly brushed on the brown and reddish water and body colours, having indicated the hind's contours with fine discontinuous pen lines and, in a few places around the neck and front leg, having described the thick hair with densely applied flexible dashes of various lengths. This genuine interest in the exploration of a dead animal's appearance recalls Albrecht Dürer's earlier animal studies in watercolour,[2] and resulted in the drawing's attribution to the famous Nuremberg master, indicated by the false monogram in the lower right corner. Typical of Cranach, however, and essentially different from Dürer, is the stylised flatness, noticeable both in the organisation of the sheet and in the placement of the hind legs, which adds elegance to the work where Dürer's analytical mind would have sought scientific accuracy.[3]

This characteristic is particularly apparent when this drawing is compared with the painted depiction of a dead hind in the foreground of Lucas Cranach's panel of *The Hunt of Frederick the Wise* (Vienna, Kunsthistorisches Museum), dated 1529,[4] where the animal's body is far more voluminous and lacks the Louvre drawing's elegance. The panel, however, indicates the watercolour's probable function as a pattern for paintings, also suggested by the numerous splatters of colour and ink dispersed across the sheet.

The verso presents Cranach as the rapid draughtsman so highly praised by Scheurl. The draughtsman excels in

PROVENANCE
Acquired in 1909 (Lugt 1886a)

SELECTED LITERATURE
Demonts 1911, p. 19, fig. 3; Paris 1936, no. 31, p. 18; Girshausen 1937, no. 67, p. 50; Berlin 1937, no. 199, pl. 134; Demonts 1937–38, I, no. 89, pl. 29; Thöne 1939, pls. 44–45; Rosenberg 1960, nos. 61, 62, p. 26; Paris 1965, no. 47, p. 24, pl. XIII; Koepplin and Falk 1974, I, no. 147, p. 246; Paris 1991, no. 113, p. 121; Koepplin in Basle and Berlin 1997–98, p. 251; Koepplin in Washington 1999, p. 201

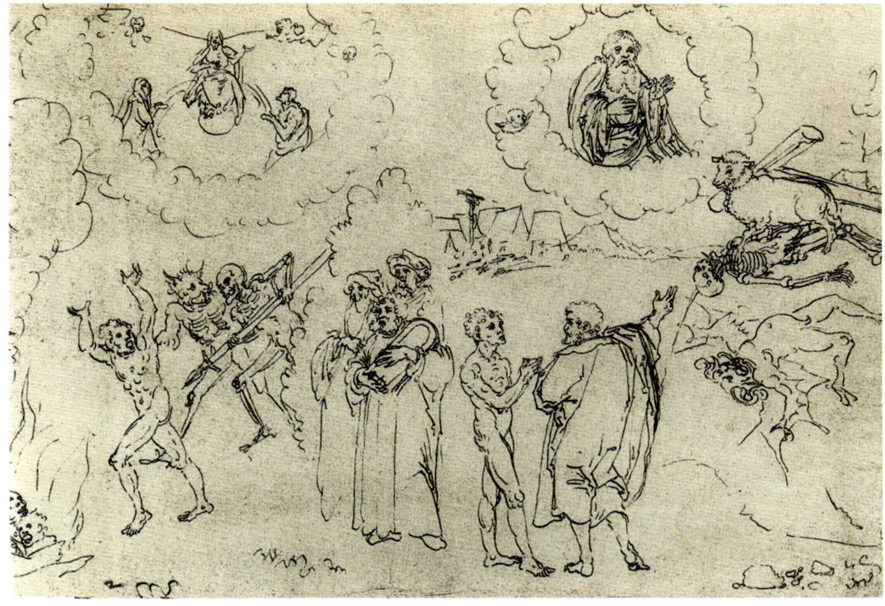

Fig. 38 Lucas Cranach the Elder, *The Fall and Salvation of Man*, 1529
Pen and brown ink on paper, 19.8 × 28.5 cm
Dresden, Staatliche Kunstsammlungen, Kupferstich-Kabinett
(missing since 1945)

fresh and direct observation: hasty pen strokes capture stags and hinds in their natural behaviour in the rutting season. The sketch's composition is built up from the bottom, where two stags are fighting whilst a herd of hinds grazes above them. The objective of the fight is revealed at the top, where a stag and a hind are mating. Mere scribbles indicate bushes, both setting the scene apart and cleverly expressing the excitement of this pairing.

Stylistically this sketch corresponds closely with Cranach's pen-and-ink drawings of around 1525–30, for example the *Adam and Eve* from the Koenigs Collection (fig. 32)[5] and the signed *Allegory of the New and Old Testament* (formerly Dresden, Kupferstich-Kabinett; fig. 38), dateable to around 1529,[6] which both exhibit a similar graphic handwriting that relies on open contours composed of short, arched strokes and quick scribbles to indicate bodies and plants. There is no need to suppose that the recto and verso of the Paris drawing were executed at different dates, as *Two Dead Bullfinches*, signed and dated 1530 (missing since World War II; fig. 39),[7] showed the same combination of brush and pen drawing. Among the surviving drawings the *Dead Hind* serves as a starting point for discussion of the undated animal studies less securely attributed to Cranach, executed in both water-colour and in pen and ink. SB

NOTES

1 Schuchardt 1851–71, I, pp. 32–33.
2 See Falk and Koepplin 1974, p. 201, and Washington 1999, p. 201.
3 A similar tendency can be observed in Hans Holbein the Younger's studies of a lamb and a bat (Basle, Kupferstichkabinett) of *c.* 1523; see Müller 1996, nos. 148–49, pp. 98–99, colour pls. 9–10.
4 Friedländer and Rosenberg 1978, no. 281, p. 125.
5 Rosenberg 1960, nos. 39 and 48, pp. 22 and 24.
6 Rosenberg 1960, no. 52, pp. 24–25. The drawing belongs within the context of Cranach's most programmatic Protestant composition, *The Fall and Salvation of Man*, known in different versions, the earliest dated 1529; see Friedländer and Rosenberg 1978, no. 221, p. 113; for a summary of the vast literature see Badstübner *et al.* 1994, nos. 28–47, pp. 29–40.
7 Rosenberg 1960, no. 68.

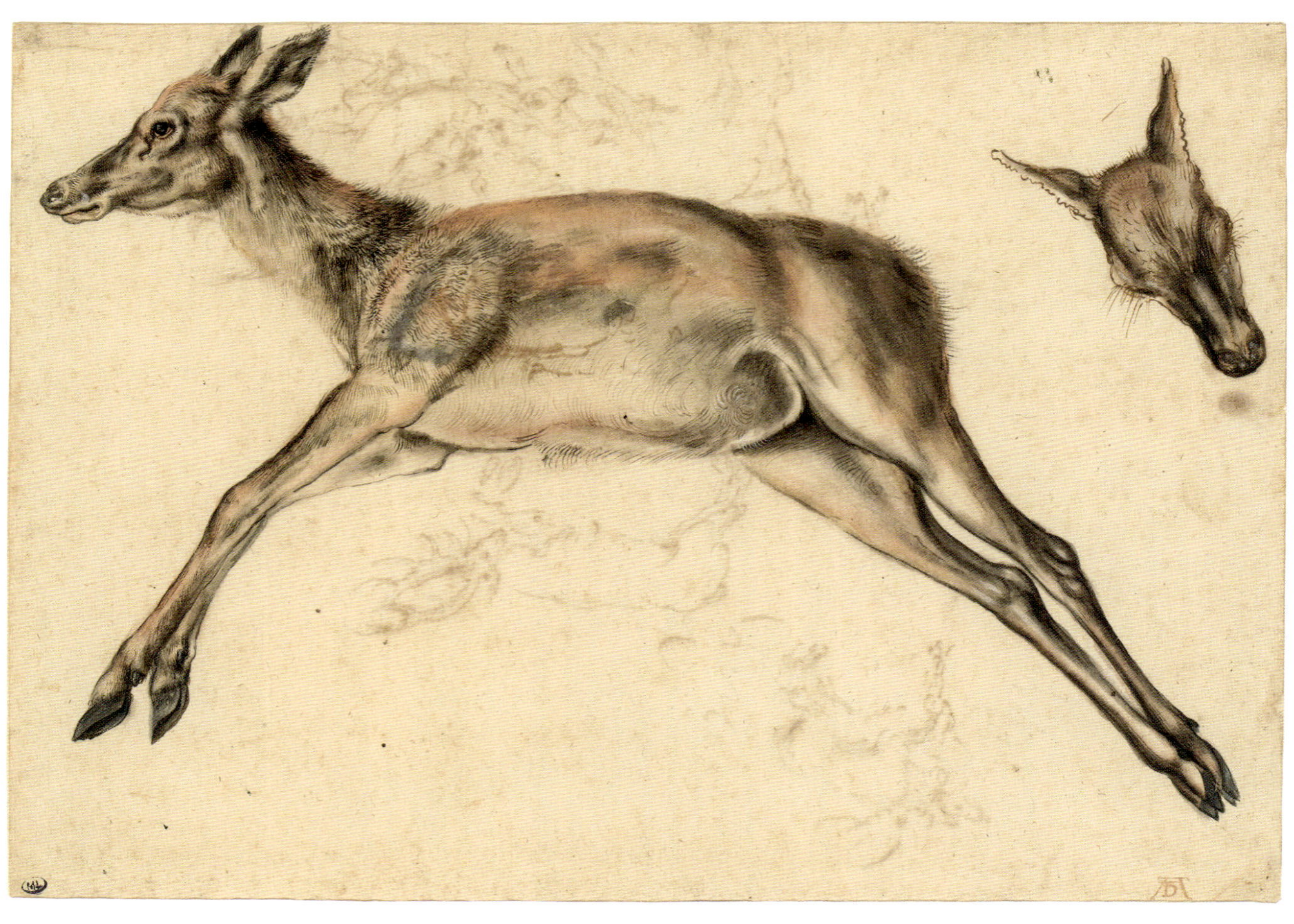

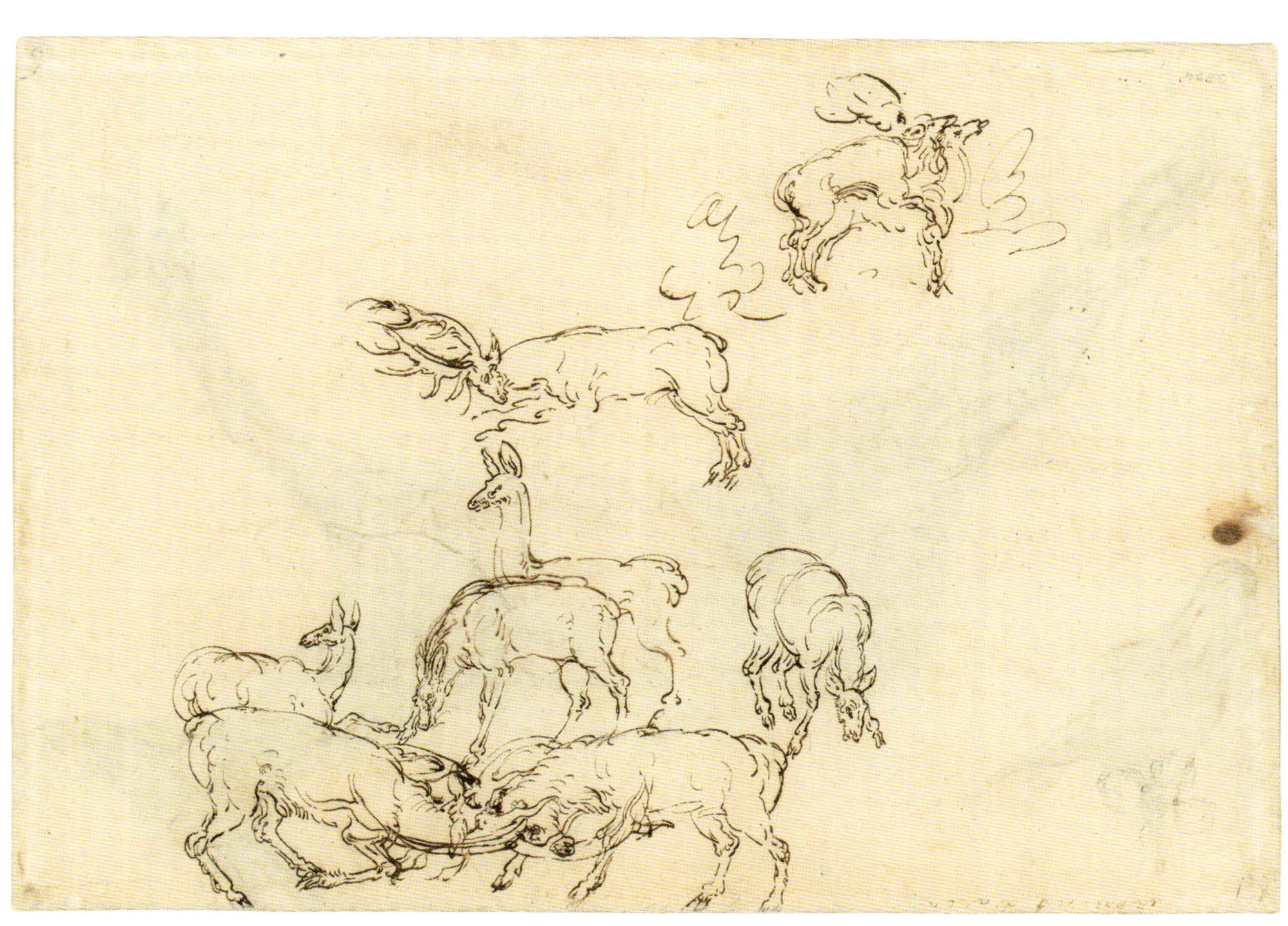

7

Lucas Cranach the Elder

Wild Boars and Hunting Hounds, *c.* 1525–30

Pen and dark brown ink over preliminary drawing, probably charcoal, on laid paper; border added later in brown ink; erased, false Dürer monogram on the lower border
15.0 × 24.1 cm
Watermark: high crown (variant of Piccard 1961, IX, 81ff., and variant of Briquet 4971 or 4988)
Berlin, Staatliche Museen zu Berlin Preussischer Kulturbesitz, Kupferstichkabinett, KdZ 386

IN STYLE AND FUNCTION, this drawing of wild boar and hounds has an important position within Cranach's oeuvre of animal studies. More elaborate in execution than the sketchy verso of the Louvre sheet with stags and hinds (cat. 6), it demonstrates a rare alacrity in the confident handling of the pen – otherwise less evident in Cranach's painterly depictions of animals executed in watercolour. As Koepplin rightly stressed, this drawing reveals the typical characteristics of a study sheet, combining several motifs of a hunt. These could have been isolated from the sheet without difficulty when re-using them as patterns for paintings.

Cranach began by roughly sketching the animals in a dry black medium, probably charcoal, that could be wiped off after the permanent ink drawing was added. An attacking hound jumping to the right beneath the free-standing wild boar was left incomplete, as was another indistinguishable animal in the upper left corner. The head of a wild boar was commenced in darker brown ink, but also left unfinished. The remaining three boars are depicted in various poses, though any daring application of foreshortening is omitted, even in the boar being attacked by a pack of hounds – angrily turning his heavy body but unable to extricate himself as one of the dogs tears his hind leg and another sinks its teeth firmly into his back. Above this foremost group a smaller boar is captured in mid flight, in contrast to the more static animal to the right. Similar in pose to the wild boar in the Courtauld's *Adam and Eve*, this figure also proved a suitable pattern for compositions not depicting a hunt.

Despite the isolation of the separate themes, the underlying motif of the hunt is clearly perceptible. Cranach stresses the nervous excitement of all the animals ingeniously by adding rows of sharp strokes on the wild boars' backs to depict their erect stiff bristles – an indication of his close observation and the precision of his pen.

Accurate dating of this work poses problems for scholars, evident in Rosenberg's ambiguous designation "*c.* 1510/20; however a later date is not impossible". Similarly, Koepplin suggested a date of *c.* 1506–07 but also considered a later period, closer to the hunting paintings that first appear in 1529. The early dating corresponds with the probable time of execution of Cranach's woodcuts of a stag and a boar hunt (cat. 17, 18); however, no particular stylistic similarities support this date. On the other hand the loose arcs, especially visible in the hastily drawn hounds, are compatible with those found in drawings more firmly situated within Cranach's later oeuvre (such as fig. 39).[1] The drawings in the Prayerbook of Maximilian I dated 1515 (figs. 12, 19), although comparable in motif, are unhelpful because their function was quite different.[2]

While other aspects remain so unreliable, the watermark may be taken into consideration. Although not identical to an example found on a dated document, it fits well into category IX of Piccard's handbook of dated watermarks, exclusively traceable to papers used after 1529 and as late as the mid-sixteenth century. This provides a strong indication that the Berlin drawing was not executed before 1525, but rather in close proximity to the Louvre drawing (cat. 6). SB

PROVENANCE
Neville collection; D. Goldsmid collection (Lugt 1962); Suermondt collection (Lugt 415); acquired in 1879

SELECTED LITERATURE
Lippmann 1895, p. 7; Berlin 1910, no. 202, p. VI; Bock 1921, p. 20, pl. 26; Berlin 1937, no. 198; Girshausen 1937, no. 66, p. 50; Thöne 1939, p. 13; Rosenberg 1960, no. 60; Berlin 1967, no. 66, pp. 70–71; Steigerwald 1973, no. 53, p. 48; Schade 1972, no. 17, p. 38; Schade 1974, p. 48, pl. 165; Stockholm 1988, p. 62, fig. 47; Koepplin in Basle and Berlin 1997–98, no. 17.2, pp. 251–52; Koepplin in Washington 1999, no. 88, pp. 201–02

NOTES
1 This pen-and-ink drawing, now lost, is datable to around 1529: Rosenberg 1960, no. 52, pp. 24–25.
2 For a discussion of the possible functions of the drawings in the Prayerbook see Buck 2006.

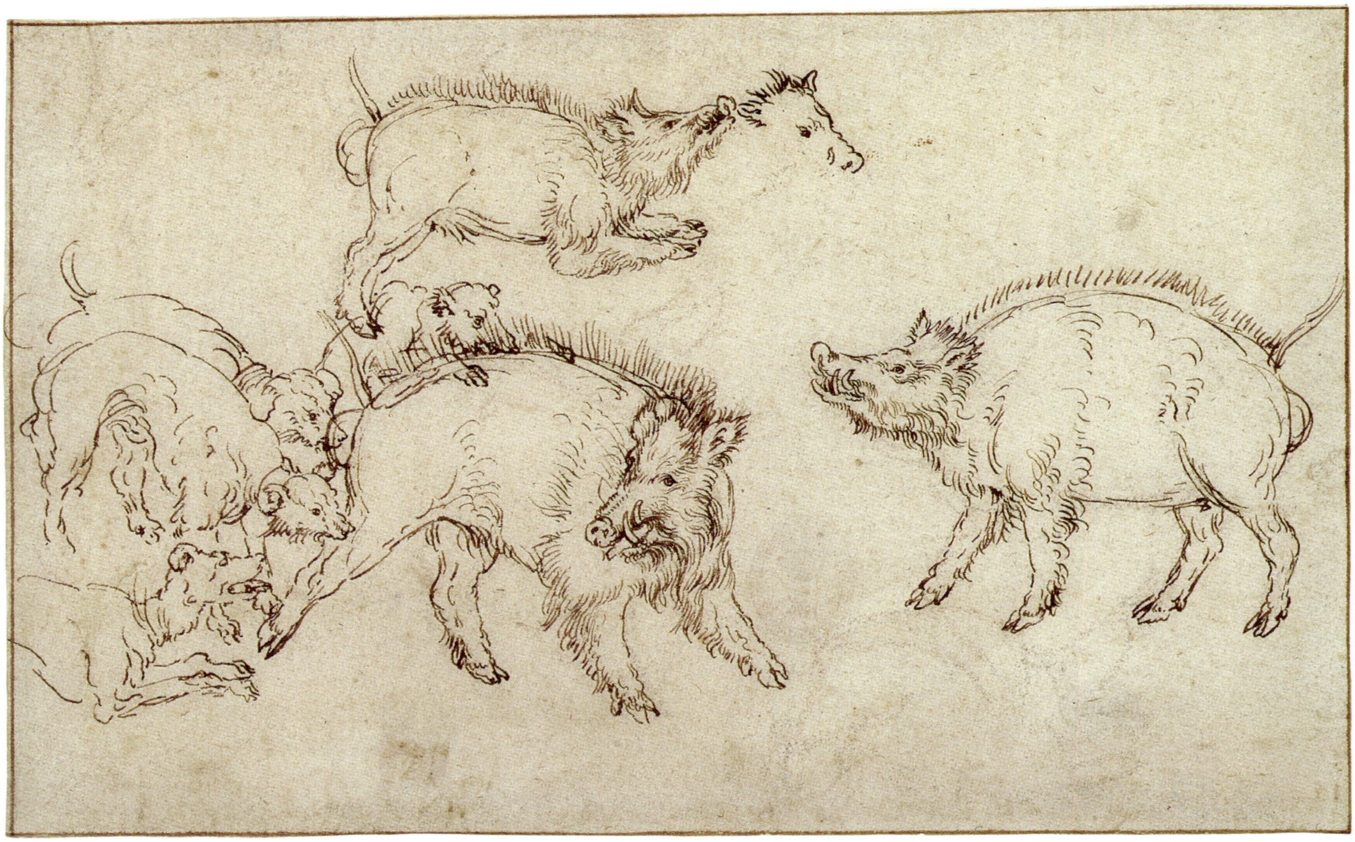

8

Lucas Cranach the Elder

Young Stag, *c.* 1525–30

Brush and water and body colours, heightened with white, over preliminary drawing in chalk or charcoal, on laid paper
47.9 × 37.7 cm (upper left corner added)
Watermark: Gothic P (not corresponding to anything in Piccard or Briquet)
Dresden, Kupferstich-Kabinett, C 1960-32

THIS DEPICTION OF A YOUNG STAG, finely executed in watercolours on a remarkably large single sheet of paper, has the appearance of a finished work of art. Unmistakable signs of workshop use, such as splatters of ink or colour, characteristic of other animal studies by Cranach (cat. 6, 10), are not apparent. Scheurl asserted in 1509 that the dukes of Saxony enjoyed Cranach's depictions of the hunt as much as the hunt itself.[1] Although the idea that watercolours of animals were considered attractive collector's items therefore cannot be excluded, there is no real support for it. The *Young Stag* is not signed and lacks an inscription, unlike *The Fall and Salvation of Man* (formerly Dresden, Kupferstich-Kabinett), a rapid pen-and-ink drawing Cranach dedicated to the Duchess of Mecklenburg and Saxony.[2] It is more likely that, like Cranach's other animal studies, the *Young Stag* was used in the workshop as a model for paintings. As elaborate patterns, however, such sheets could have given patrons the opportunity to choose the details of commissioned panel paintings, such as the Courtauld's *Adam and Eve*. With this in mind, it is worth noting that the drinking roebuck in the lower right corner of the panel is smaller in size than the stag of the drawing.

This sheet belongs to a group of watercolours that have been in the possession of the Dresden prints and drawings collection since the eighteenth century. Only in 1961–62, however, did Werner Schade first identify it – together with a larger group of Dresden watercolours, including *Two Dead Partridges* (cat. 9) – as the work of Lucas Cranach the Elder. Schade stresses the masterly quality of the *Young Stag*, apparent in the precise contours of the figure and the strict attention to the decorative effect of the remaining areas of blank paper. This last observation points to a characteristic also evident in the Louvre drawing of a *Dead Hind* (cat. 6), in which the placement of the animal on the picture plane demonstrates a similarly strong tendency to make the best use of the paper and, at the same time, achieve a decorative effect. A closer examination of the working process provides further clues: like those of the Louvre drawing, the contours were sketched in a dry, black medium, probably charcoal, followed by layers of colour that, despite the deft application of brushstrokes, respect the clear contour lines. The complex build-up of the luminous eye and its placement in its socket, as well as the depiction of bones and muscles, are also comparable to the Louvre sheet. Lastly, the subtle observation of the shy animal's behaviour is consistent with Cranach's skill as a painter of animals. The stag is rendered in an attentive pose, seemingly eavesdropping. Cranach underscores its alertness by the unconventional depiction of light from the right, which casts a shadow of the stag's hoofs to its left. Although the *Young Stag* is executed exclusively with a brush, and thus lacks the clear linear structure characteristic of Cranach's securely attributed animal watercolours, such as *Two Dead Bullfinches*, signed and dated 1530 (fig. 39),[3] the sheet may reasonably be ascribed to him, and dated to approximately the same period as his other animal watercolours. SB

PROVENANCE
Alter Besitz; probably acquired before 1756

SELECTED LITERATURE
Schade 1961–62, pp. 40–41; Schade 1963, no. 80, pp. 34–35, pl. 33; Schade 1972, no. 15, p. 38; Washington, New York and San Francisco 1978–79, no. 580, p. 249

NOTES
1 Schuchardt 1851–71, I, p. 33.
2 Woermann 1896, II, no. 66, p. 22, pl. 20; Rosenberg 1960, no. 52, pp. 24–25: *Der durchlauchtigen hochgeborenen Fürstin und Frawen Katharina geborene Herzogin von Meckelburgk und Herzogin zu Sachsen und meiner gnädigen Frawen.*
3 Rosenberg 1960, no. 68.

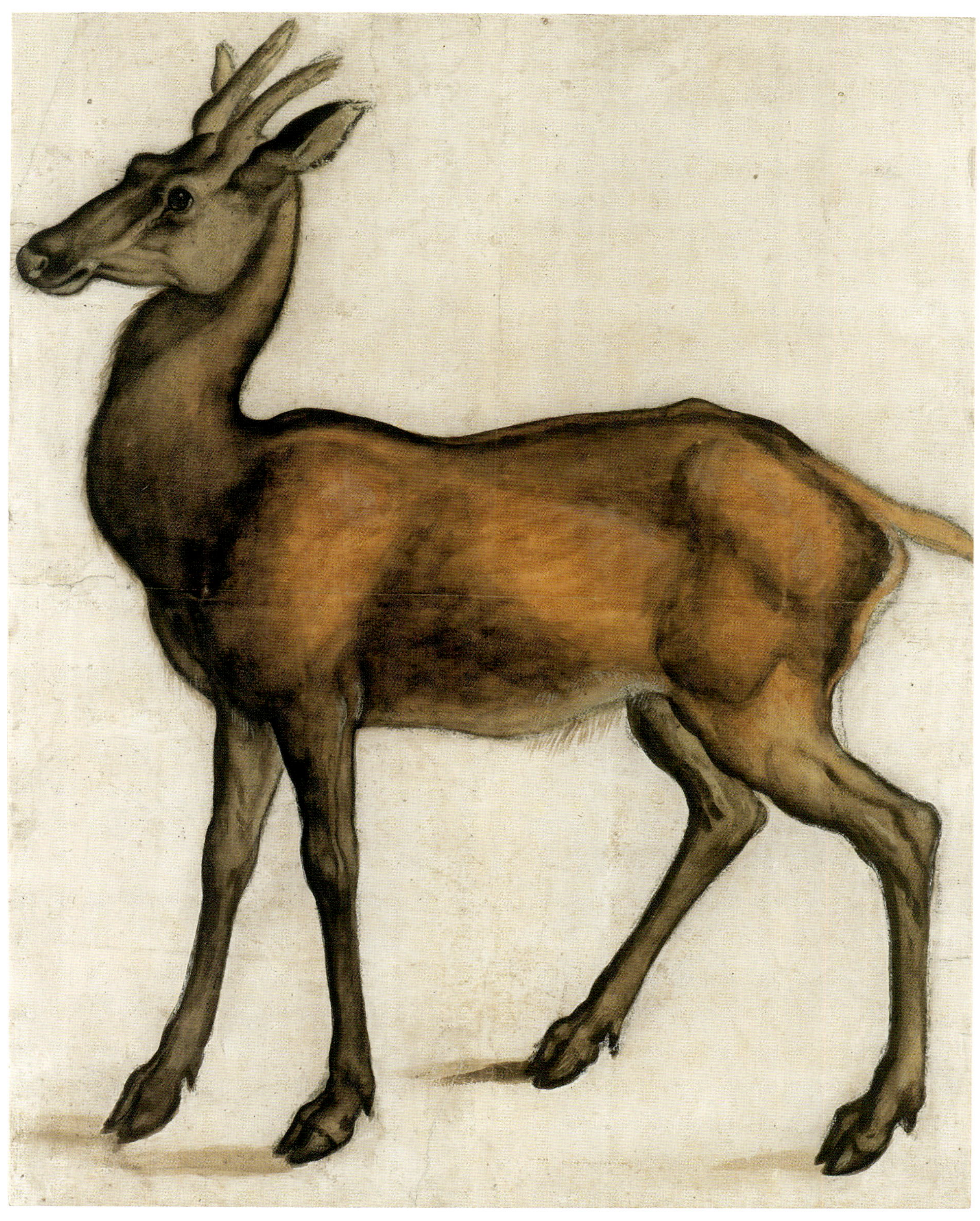

9

Lucas Cranach the Elder

Two Dead Partridges, *c.* 1530–35

Brush and water and body colours, heightened with white, on laid paper
41.2 × 24.5 cm
Dresden, Kupferstich-Kabinett, C 1195

THIS NEARLY LIFE-SIZE DEPICTION of two dead partridges is executed exclusively in brush without the aid of a preliminary charcoal or chalk sketch, thus lending a strong painterly quality to the work. The colour is applied in loose, breezy layers, allowing the paper to become part of the overall picture, particularly along the contours where the brush 'dried out'. Even the final rendering of the plumage, with curly arcs and deft daubs, is rather summary (and different from that of *Two Dead Bullfinches*, signed and dated 1530; fig. 39). This, however, does not detract from the work's strong mimetic impact. On the contrary, the technique and rich tonality of browns and greys evoke three-dimensionality and tactile surface, imbuing the work with an astonishingly modern appearance. This may explain the attribution of this watercolour in the Dresden Kupferstich-Kabinett's inventory of 1865 to the seventeenth-century Netherlandish still-life painter Jan Weenix.[1]

Since Werner Schade first attributed this and another closely related watercolour of four dead partridges nailed to a wall to Lucas Cranach or his eldest son Hans,[2] these works have been unanimously accepted as significant contributions to the early development of animal still-life painting. The genre had been established earlier at the court of Saxony by Jacopo de' Barbari, Cranach's predecessor as painter to the dukes, who mediated an Italian tradition of still lifes (going back to ancient wall-painting) otherwise not known in Northern Europe. A panel painting of a dead

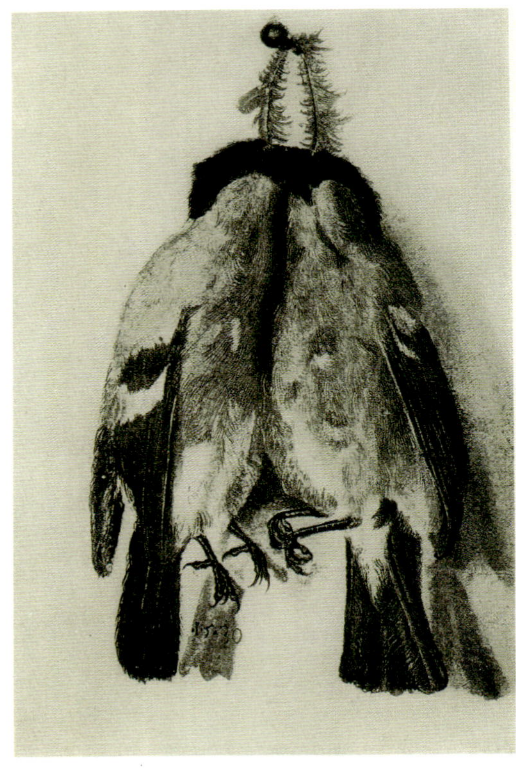

Fig. 39 Lucas Cranach the Elder,
Two Dead Bullfinches, 1530
Pen and brush with water and body colours,
21.6 × 14.3 cm
Dresden, Staatliche Kunstsammlungen,
Kupferstich-Kabinett (missing since 1945)

PROVENANCE
Alter Besitz; probably acquired before 1756; later attributed to Jan Weenix

SELECTED LITERATURE
Schade 1961–62, p. 34, fig. 7; Schade 1963, no. 78, p. 34; Schade 1977, p. 50; Koreny 1985, p. 50; Erichsen and Grimm in Grimm, Erichsen and Brockhoff 1994, no. 184, pp. 358–59, fig. p. 360; Schnitzer in Warsaw 1997, no. III 2, p. 97

partridge and an iron glove dated 1504 in the Alte Pinakothek in Munich and a drawing of a partridge executed in pen and ink and brush and watercolour in the British Museum, London,[3] document this tradition and leave no doubt about Cranach's indebtedness to it. The painterly interpretation of this subject in the medium of watercolour is, however, Cranach's personal contribution, as it abandons the focus on minute detail characteristic of Jacopo de' Barbari's style, rooted in the earlier tradition of fifteenth-century coloured pen-and-ink drawing.

As Schade pointed out, the partridges were used as early as 1532 by Cranach's workshop as props in several paintings, mostly of *Hercules and Omphale*. The inclusion of these birds in a depiction of the classical Greek hero's subjugation to the attractive Lydian queen and subsequent lampooning by her maids seems to have been deemed appropriate because partridges both symbolised true love and embodied sinful lust.[4] Not only did Lucas Cranach the Elder use this pattern but so did his son, Hans, shortly before his death in 1537 in Bologna – the birthplace of Jacopo de' Barbari. One of Hans Cranach's two surviving signed paintings depicts *Hercules and Omphale* and includes two similar partridges (fig. 40). Yet the birds in this painting or in the other fourteen versions Koreny lists do not correspond exactly to those of the watercolours.[5] These functioned as workshop models but were not traced or otherwise copied precisely. Although these two surviving watercolours of partridges were certainly not the only such drawings in the studio, their lack of clear contour makes it unlikely that either these or others similar now lost were meant to function in this manner.[6] This is an indication of the level of skill and degree of professionalism in the Cranach workshop.

The freedom of execution evident in the Dresden sheet of partridges militates against an attribution of the work to Hans Cranach, whose documented paintings reveal a more tidy technique and a neat surface structure.[7] Shortcomings in the depiction of the bird hanging to the left, described by Schade, such as the shaggy plumage at the neck and the flatness of the left wing, may be attributed instead to the working mode and rapid technique of Lucas Cranach the Elder, documented in Christoph Scheurl's encomium of the artist (see cat. 6). SB

NOTES

1 Probably Jan Baptist Weenix (1621–1663) and not his son Jan Weenix II (1642–1719) is referred to.
2 Dresden, Kupferstich-Kabinett, C 1193.
3 Munich, Alte Pinakothek, and London, British Museum, inv. 5264-23.1928-3-10-103; see Koreny 1985, no. 6, pp. 44–47.
4 See Grate 1961, pp. 34–36. For the symbolism see Dittrich 2004, pp. 379–89.
5 Koreny 1985, no. 8, note 8.
6 Scheurl's account of Cranach's paintings of "hares, pheasants, peacocks, partridges, ducks, quails and fieldfares" hanging from a wall (Schuchardt 1851–71, I, p. 31) suggests that he did numerous similar depictions.
7 Compare to cat. 7, here tentatively ascribed to Hans Cranach.

Fig. 40 Hans Cranach,
Hercules and Omphale, 1537
Oil on panel, 57.5 × 85 cm
Madrid, Museo Thyssen-Bornemisza

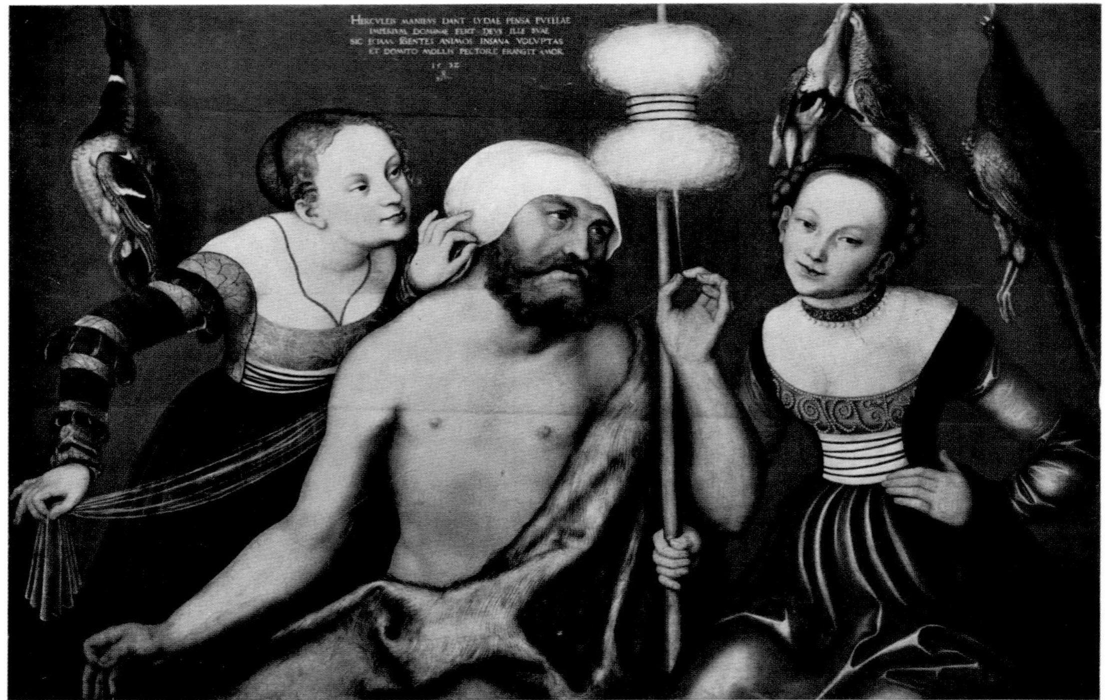

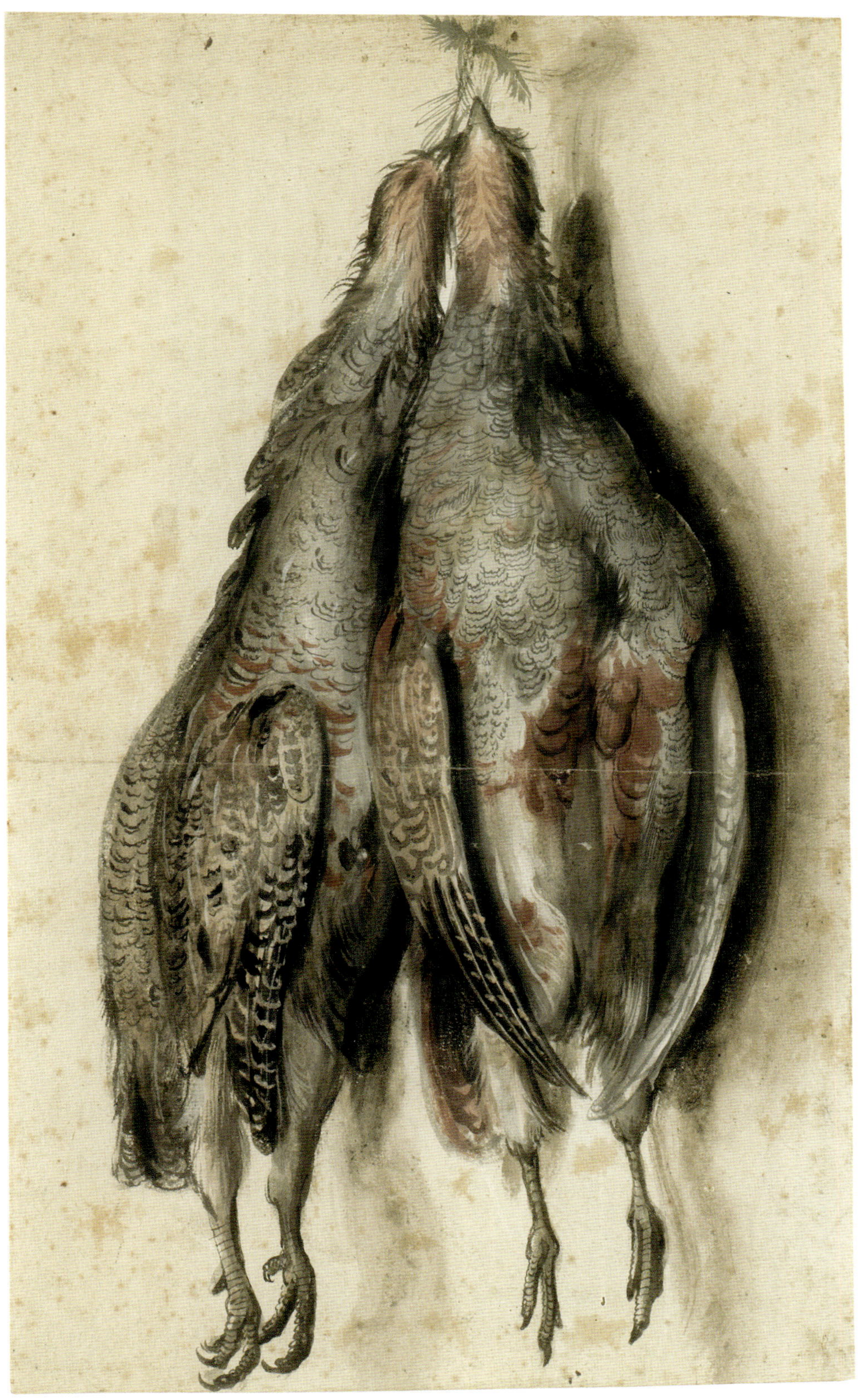

10

Lucas Cranach the Elder

RECTO: *Study of a Stag*
VERSO: *Study of Goats*
c. 1520–30?

RECTO: brush and watercolour, heightened with white, over traces of preliminary drawing in black chalk or charcoal, on laid paper
VERSO: brush and watercolour, over preliminary drawing in black chalk
13.5 × 16.6 cm
Los Angeles, The J. Paul Getty Museum, 84.GC.36

THIS MODERATELY SCALED SHEET is the only one associated with Cranach and his workshop which depicts animals on both recto and verso in watercolour. The execution is exceedingly rapid, especially in the grazing goats on the verso. There the watercolour is broadly brushed on over a preliminary sketch in black chalk, which is unusual for Cranach. Characteristically, however, he evokes the tactility of the fur with fine pen or brush lines (cat. 6, 9). Though the build-up of the stag on the recto is more complex, the final heavy brushstrokes describing the animal's thick winter pelt are deftly applied, lending a sketchy quality to the drawing: this is especially evident in the unusually imprecise rendering of the antlers, the most characteristic feature of a stag, the one which normally defines each animal's individuality. Three tones of colour are used to describe the fur – a dark brown, erratically applied with a brush that 'dries out', a lighter grey that depicts some of the smaller branches of the antlers, and a yellow, used for the stag's rump. Although the radical looseness of the technique and sketchy depiction of the animal find no equivalent in Cranach's small oeuvre of watercolours, this work can be compared with *Two Dead Partridges* (cat. 9); like *A Dead Hind* (cat. 6), that drawing is also characterised by a freely applied undercoat of paint, although the final modelling is more detailed and less sketchy than on the present sheet.

Similar in technique and in the way the animals are presented in profile, the depictions on recto and verso nonetheless show substantial differences. The stag is isolated on the sheet, and, typically for Cranach, it is placed in a manner that uses all the space available; the shadows cast by the hoofs align with the lower edge of the sheet. Despite the abbreviated rendering of the eye, it is clear that the animal is looking at the viewer, as it is depicted doing in many paintings by Cranach, such as the Courtauld's *Adam and Eve*. In fact, the stag is one of the animals most often included in Cranach's pictures, both as prey in depictions of the hunt (cat. 17, 18) and, outside a narrative context, in isolation, charged with symbolic meaning (cat. 1, 3, 12, 20).[1] Probably the closest likeness to this stag elsewhere in his work can be found in the one standing in the lower right corner of Cranach's *Golden Age* (fig. 21).[2]

Thus this drawing was probably a useful workshop pattern. Such a function is also suggested by the condition of the paper, which is spattered with ink and colour and

PROVENANCE
S. Rosenthal, Berne; L.V. Randall, Montreal; sale, Sotheby's, London, 6 July 1967, lot 2; private collection, New Jersey; acquired in 1984

SELECTED LITERATURE
Girshausen 1937, no. 68, p. 76; Montreal 1953, no. 101; Rosenberg 1960, no. 63, p. 26–27; Goldner 1988, no. 128, p. 284

NOTES
1 For the symbolism see Dittrich 2004, pp. 411–21.
2 Friedländer and Rosenberg 1978, no. 261, p. 121.
3 See Dittrich 2004, pp. 571–81.

shows traces of red chalk unrelated to the figure of the stag.

On the other hand, the depiction of goats on the verso, also heavily splashed with colour, is unusual, as the animals are integrated in a narrative context. The main goat grazing on a meadow is comparatively small in scale. As it is followed by a second animal, with its head sharply cropped, a herd is suggested. No goat is depicted in any of Cranach's paintings, despite the fact that many symbolic meanings were attached to the species. Probably the best-established image was the he-goat, which referred to the devil.[3] However, this drawing shows a female animal with a distended udder. Rather than intended to provide a motif for a painting it seems to have been purely the result of observation, capturing a scene in nature for its own sake. As such it is unique in Cranach's oeuvre. This fact, combined with the radical sketchiness of the work, makes its dating highly problematic. As a casual study, perhaps done in a sketchbook, it might date from the same period as the rest of the animal studies. SB

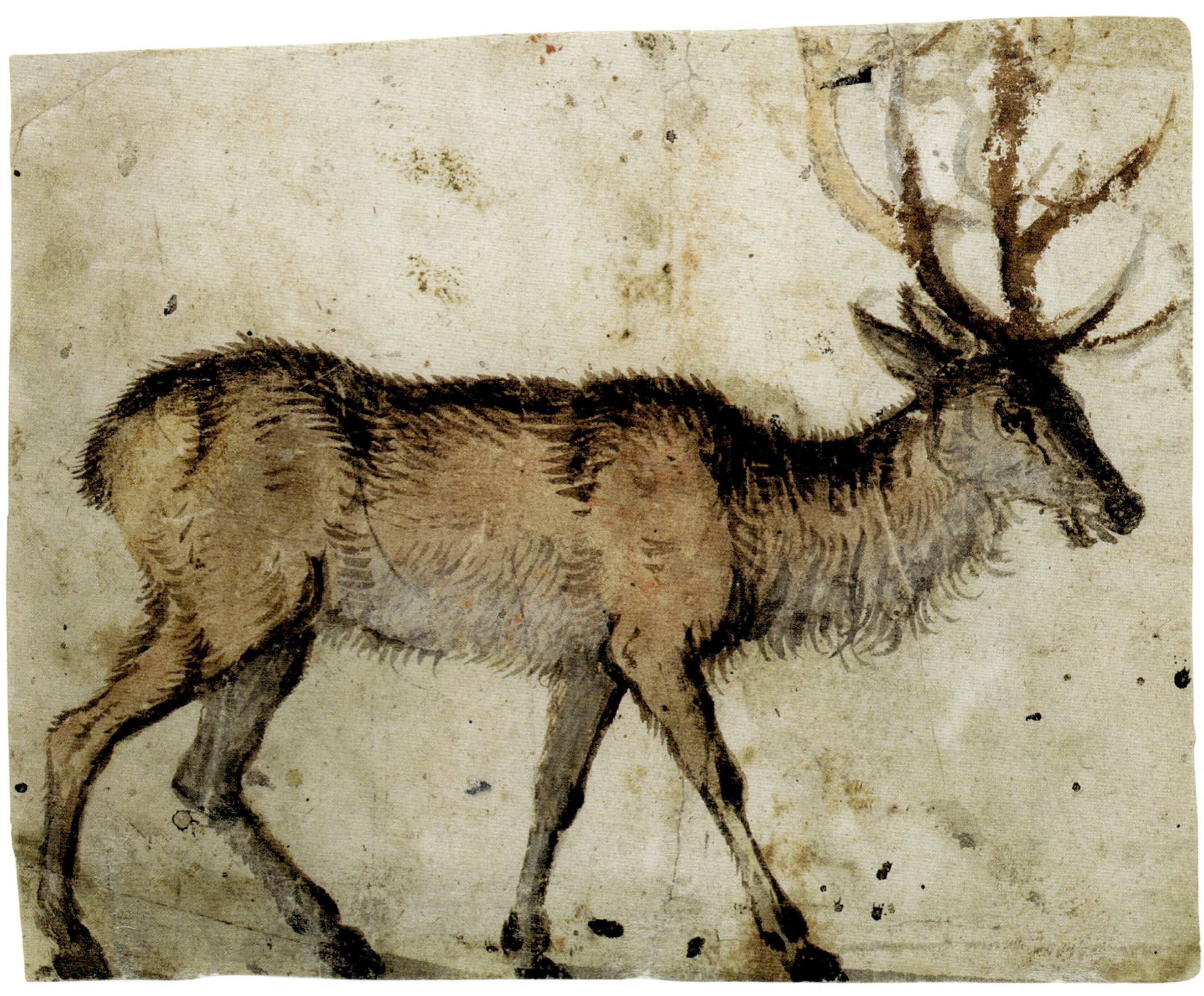

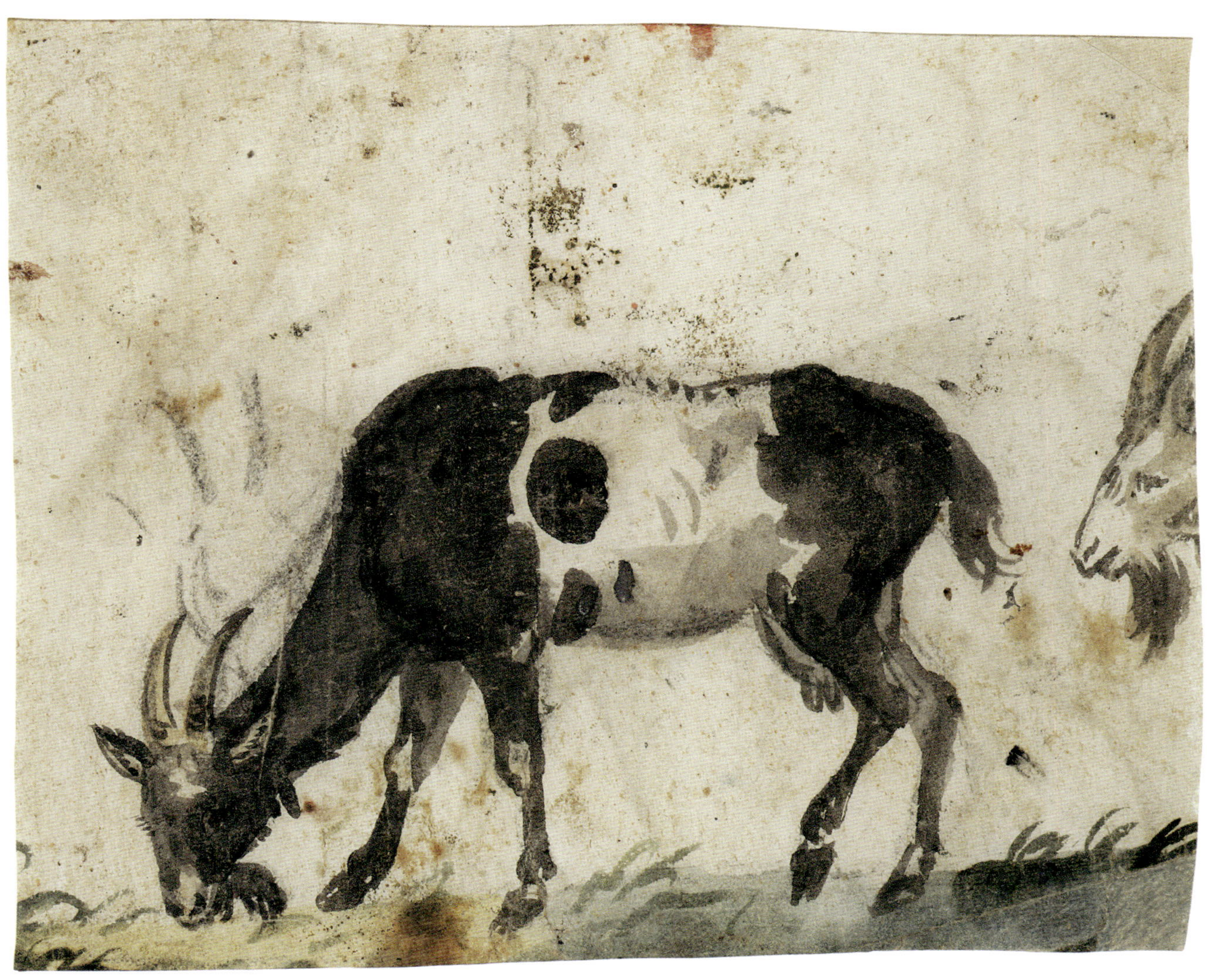

11 Workshop of Lucas Cranach the Elder (?Hans Cranach, *c.*1513–1537)
Spotted Wild Boar, *c.* 1535

Pen and brush, brown and grey ink, water and body colour, heightened with white, on laid paper
16.4 × 24.1 cm
Dresden, Kupferstich-Kabinett, C 2174

LIKE RED DEER, wild boars were favoured hunting game at the court of Saxony. This is documented not only in Christoph Scheurl's encomium of Lucas Cranach dated 1509, in which Johann of Saxony is mentioned as chasing a wild boar,[1] but also in various depictions executed by Cranach's workshop, such as the woodcut of a *Boar Hunt* of *c.* 1506 (cat. 17) and the Berlin drawing with wild boars and hounds (cat. 7), both by Cranach the Elder, as well as the later hunting paintings commonly attributed to his son Lucas. Although these pictures are largely devoted to the stag hunt, they include wild boars being chased in the background.[2] Such animals were appreciated by the court as trophies, which may explain the interest in the individual depiction of various specimens with clearly distinguishable furs. In addition to this portrayal of a spotted wild boar, two other drawings of similar size and technique were in the Dresden Kupferstich-Kabinett, one showing a greyish animal,[3] the other a black one.[4] As Schade (1971) suggested, the drawings might have been commissioned in connection with a commission from the court. However, there is no documentation showing that Cranach's workshop ever received such an order. The animal in the Courtauld *Adam and Eve* is, however, similar in size to the wild boars in the three drawings. It therefore seems likely that the boar in *Adam and Eve* was modelled on drawings such as those in Dresden, even if they were executed later and depict different specimens.

The attribution of this sheet to Lucas Cranach the Elder has long been accepted. Yet closer comparisons to other animal studies by Cranach, such as *Two Dead Bullfinches*, signed and dated 1530 (fig. 39)[5] or the Louvre's *Dead Hind* (cat. 6), challenge this attribution. Despite the shadows, cast by all four legs and executed in a peculiar yellowish green otherwise not found in the drawing, the lighting is indecisive, fails to impart three-dimensional modelling, and flattens the body. This is exacerbated by the compact, even application of a layer of greyish paint that lacks the vitality of Cranach's technique in comparable studies, such as the *Dead Hind* (cat. 6). A more detailed linear structure, added in pen and brush strokes to indicate the fur, does not merge with the underlying paint, and appears schematic, unable to communicate the tactile qualities of fur as Cranach's authentic watercolours typically can. Moreover, the construction of the animal's eye with a simple black dot for the pupil and a single white highlight does not parallel the luminous quality of the eyes in the *Young Stag* or the *Dead Hind* (cat. 8, 6), and a closer look at the mouth reveals three ornamental arched strokes that do not convincingly abbreviate the structure of the snout. Overall, the graphic structure speaks of a rather hesitant artist who places neat, ornamental patterns above close observation of nature.

These characteristics can also be found in the only two securely attributed paintings by Hans Cranach, both dated 1537.[6] The partridges on *Hercules and Omphale* (fig. 40) reveal a similar build-up of the surface, with white, gently arched strokes indicating short feathers, neatly distributed on the surface – very like the strokes which indicate the fur of the wild boar. Owing to the lack of comparative material, an attribution to Hans Cranach cannot be substantiated, but may be considered a possibility. An attribution of the sheet to the Cranach workshop seems entirely justified. SB

PROVENANCE
Alter Besitz; probably acquired before 1756

SELECTED LITERATURE
Schuchardt 1851–71, III, no. 40, p. 149; Woermann 1896–98, II, no. 70, p. 23, pl. 22; Glaser 1921, p. 50, pl. 21; Girshausen 1937, no. 69, pp. 51–52; Berlin 1937, no. 195, fig. p. 135; Thöne 1939, pl. 42; Berlin 1958, no. F138; Rosenberg 1960, no. 64, p. 27; Schade 1961–62, p. 29; Schade 1963, no. 74, p. 33; Schade in Dresden 1971, no. 122, p. 111; Schade 1972, no. 16, p. 45; Koepplin and Falk 1974, no. 141, p. 244, fig. 103; Friedrich in Washington, New York and San Francisco 1978–79, no. 578, p. 249

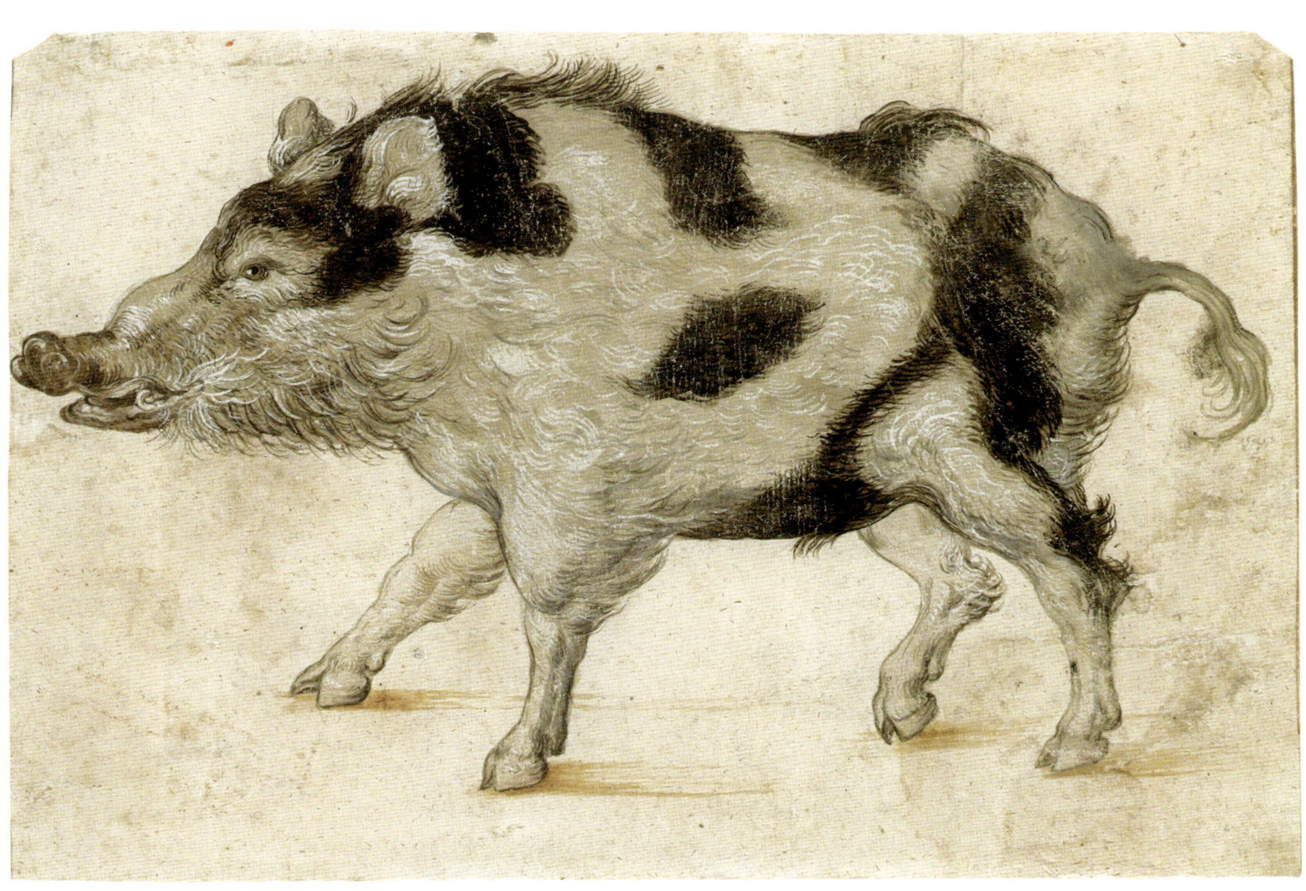

NOTES

1 Schuchardt 1851–71, I, p. 33.
2 See, for example, the paintings in Madrid, Museo del Prado, of 1544 and in Cleveland, Cleveland Museum of Art, of 1540; Friedländer and Rosenberg 1978, nos. 411–12, p. 152.
3 Dresden, Kupferstich-Kabinett, C2176, 14.2 × 22.9 cm; Rosenberg 1960, no. 66, p. 27.
4 Missing since World War II; 17.2 × 25.8 cm; Rosenberg 1960, no. 65, p. 27.
5 Rosenberg 1960, no. 68, p. 27.
6 *A Portrait of a Bearded Man* and *Hercules at the Court of Omphale*, both preserved in Madrid, Thyssen-Bornemisza Collection; see Isolde Lübbeke, *The Thyssen-Bornemisza Collection. Early German Paintings 1350–1550*, London 1991, nos. 40–41, pp. 178–89.

12 Lucas Cranach the Elder

Adam and Eve, 1509

Inscribed in a cartouche on the tree: *LC* with the bat-winged serpent, and dated: *1509*.
The coats of arms of Saxony and the Elector Frederick hang from the left branch.
Woodcut, 33 × 22.7 cm (cut to the border)
London, The British Museum, Department of Prints and Drawings, 1895-1-22-245

THIS FINE WOODCUT is one of a number of prints (including cat. 14–18) of high quality which Cranach executed between 1506 and 1509 under the legal protection of his patron, Elector Frederick of Saxony, and which bear the Elector's coats of arms.

At the centre left of the composition stands the Tree of Knowledge, with branches bearing plump apples and fig leaves (compare to Dürer's *Adam and Eve*; cat. 23). Cranach has chosen to depict the absolute split-second before the Fall, and Adam sits in the lea of the trunk, raising the forbidden fruit towards his mouth. Eve encircles him protectively with one arm, while reaching with her unoccupied hand to pluck a second apple from the tree. The serpent hovers on the branch above her, its forked tongue flickering from its mouth.

The print is notable for its depiction of a multitude of birds and beasts, over whom God had given Adam dominion (Genesis 1: 26). These crowd round the first couple to the extent that they almost submerge them: for example, Eve's hair appears to merge with a stallion's curly mane. In accordance with Isaiah's description of animals' natural urges being tamed by love in Paradise (Isaiah 11: 6–7), a lion lies contentedly beside a stag, normally its prey.

This woodcut has little in common with Cranach's early paintings of Adam and Eve (such as figs. 6 and 9), although they are of broadly similar date. Instead it is more closely connected with the depictions of this subject from the 1520s and 1530s, especially the Courtauld *Adam and Eve* (cat. 1) and the two 1530 paintings of the Garden of Eden (cat. 5 and fig. 37). The 1509 woodcut seems to have been one of the most important starting points for the Courtauld painting. It adopts many specific details from the earlier print, such as Eve's corkscrew curls which billow out behind her, the seated stag in the left foreground, and the grazing sheep at the far right edge. However, this animal is reversed in the painting, and is given a position of greater prominence immediately to Adam's left. The lion, who looks out towards the viewer from the centre right of the woodcut, also appears in mirror image in cat. 1. The ultimate source for Cranach's lion is reflected in a drawing of 1509 or earlier now in the J. Paul Getty Museum (fig. 41), from which the beast in another 1509 woodcut, *The Penitence of Saint Jerome* (fig. 30), also derives.

Dürer's engraving of 1504 (cat. 23) is regularly cited as a precedent for Cranach's interpretations of Adam and Eve, and this is certainly true of Cranach's early paintings of the subject (including figs. 5 and 9). However, it does not appear to have influenced the iconography of this print enormously. Although certain small details, including Eve's hair, probably derive from it, key elements of Cranach's woodcut and its ultimate meaning are quite at variance with Dürer's engraving. For instance, Cranach's buxom Eve is emphatically female, in contrast to Dürer's more androgynous form. Such differences are highly significant. While Dürer strives to transform Adam and Eve into idealised, God-like figures, Cranach emphasises their humanity, and thus also the inevitability of their fall from grace. CMC

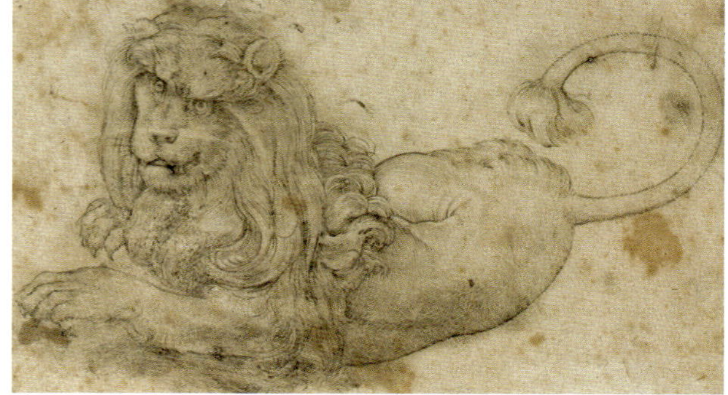

Fig. 41 ? Lucas Cranach,
Study of a Lion, 1509
Pen and brown ink, 5.08 × 10.16 cm
Los Angeles, J. Paul Getty Museum

PROVENANCE
Presented by William Mitchell (1820–1908), 1895

SELECTED LITERATURE
Hollstein 1959, no. 1, p. 10; Panofsky 1969, p. 28; Koepplin and Falk 1974, II, no. 573, p. 658; Falk 1980, no. 1 (279), p. 319; Schade 1980, pp. 34–35, pl. 47; Schäfer 1994, no. 2.5, p. 98; Bark 1994, p. 76; Schoen 2001, p. 204

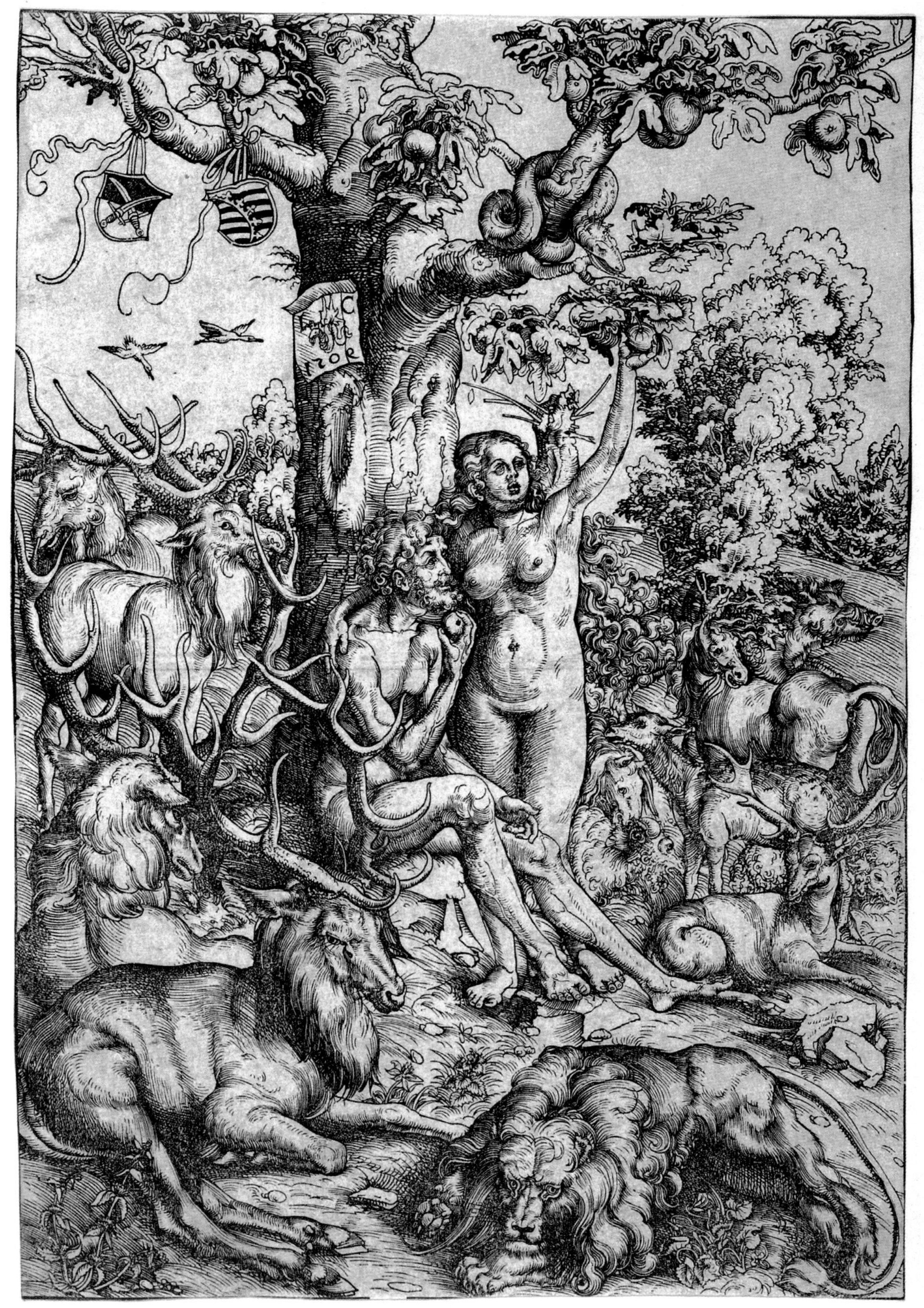

13 Lucas Cranach the Elder

The Fall of Man, mid 1520s, perhaps 1523

Woodcut, 27.9 × 22.1 cm (cut to the border)
London, The British Museum, 1927-5-8-12

THIS LITTLE-KNOWN WOODCUT is the most conventional of Cranach's depictions of Adam and Eve in its insistence upon Eve's evil agency and dominant role in the Fall of Man (compare to Baldung, cat. 25). It is also probably the most Lutheran, in its conviction that the Fall of Man was inevitable and that neither Adam nor Eve could have prevented it, even had they wished to do so.[1] Eve is depicted passing the apple to Adam, who raises his empty hand as if to remonstrate futilely with her. Although Adam has not yet eaten the fruit, two details of the print make it certain that he will, and that evil consequences will ensue. He is already ashamed of his nakedness, and a low branch of the Tree of Knowledge helpfully conceals his modesty. At the far left, a winged avenging angel enters the scene. He bears a scourge (in what must be a deliberate reference to Christ's flagellation), with which he will expel Adam and Eve from Paradise. The tree with dead foliage behind him is another reference to the misery that awaits the couple outside Eden.

The serpent is identified with Eve to an extent unusual in Cranach's work. It is not twisted round a branch of the tree, but leans against its trunk, a position normally reserved for Eve, and whispers suggestively into her left ear. Although the serpent is clearly identified by its snake's tail, its upper half is a full-sized woman's torso. Not only is it on the same scale as Eve, but it also resembles her closely. Both figures share the same large breasts, slightly protruding stomach and wind-swept curling hair. It is as if the serpent is almost Eve's mirror image.

The print is unsigned and undated. Max Geisberg dated it to 1523, but gave no reason for this. However, the woodcut has parallels with Cranach's book illustrations of the mid 1520s, and in particular the frontispiece with three stags and a hind (cat. 20), which was probably designed in 1525 and was first used for the title page of Luther's German *Mass and Order of Service*. The half-woman half-serpent recalls the snake-tailed grotesque in the top right of this title border. Stylistically, the simple shading, which makes use of different widths of parallel lines and has no cross-hatching at all, also conforms with a date in the mid 1520s. The deliberate cropping of the image at the left and right is another characteristic of Cranach's work at this period (see essay by Stephanie Buck), particularly evident in the Courtauld *Adam and Eve* (cat. 1). CMC

SELECTED LITERATURE
Schuchardt 1851–71, III, no. 1a, pp. 212–13; Geisberg 1923–29, XIII, no. 538; Hollstein 1959, no. 2, p. 11

NOTE
1 MacCullough 2003, p. 151.

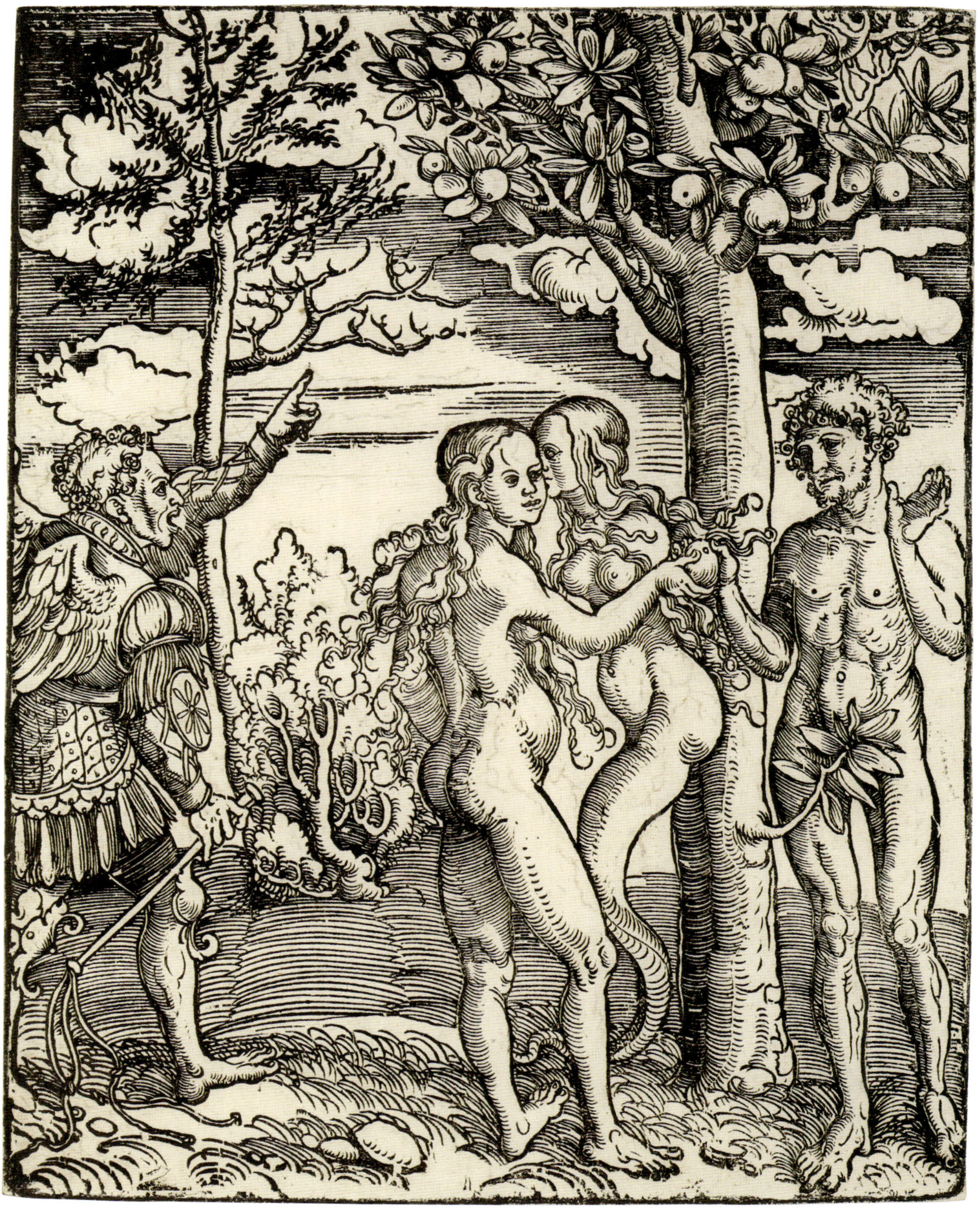

14, 15 Lucas Cranach the Elder (around 1472–1553)

Venus and Cupid, probably 1509

Signed and dated in the block: *L* [winged serpent monogram] *C 1506*

CAT. 14
Woodcut, 1st state (before the change to Venus's right shoulder).
The grey and brownish-red washes found on the tree, Venus's arm and her left shoulder are of some age, and may be original.
27.8 × 19.2 cm
Stuck down to mount, so no watermark can be seen.
Oxford, Ashmolean Museum, WA 1863.2733

CAT. 15
Woodcut, chiaroscuro, 1st state
27.6 × 18.8 cm (to border); 27.9 × 19.1 cm (sheet)
London, British Museum, Department of Prints and Drawings, 1895-1-22-268

Venus and Cupid is among the very first of Cranach's monumental and classicised single-figure female nudes. The clouds around Venus's feet indicate that she has just descended to earth from the heavens (in a charming conceit, the cloud next to her foot assumes the shape of a conch shell, on which she had landed from her watery birth).[1] The swirling shawl she holds also suggests recent rapid movement. To her left stands her winged son Cupid, whom she attempts to restrain from shooting an arrow from his bow. She stands under a barren tree, from which are hung Elector Frederick's coats of arms, and a shield bearing Cranach's emblem of the winged serpent and the date 1506, the year following his arrival in Saxony.

Despite this date, the print seems to have been made three years later, during the artist's immensely productive period as a printmaker under the sponsorship of Frederick the Wise. The most convincing evidence for this is provided by the heraldry. Cranach was only granted the winged serpent as his coat of arms in 1508. Moreover his depiction of the Elector's arms (both of Saxony and the Wettin dynasty) on *Venus and Cupid* is quite different to that found on his prints of 1505–07. Here, the upper part of the armorial shield bearing the two swords is black. This is absent from Cranach's prints before *The Judgement of Paris* (1508).[2] Although it is not absolutely clear why Cranach should have falsified the date of *Venus and Cupid* deliberately, he may have wished to claim the invention of the chiaroscuro woodcut – a technical innovation enabling printing in colour – from other German printmakers, in particular Hans Burgkmair.[3]

Stylistic and iconographic analysis supports this hypothesis. The cotton-wool clouds next to Venus and the treatment of the landscape resemble closely Cranach's work of 1509. In addition, 1509 is the date inscribed on Cranach's life-size painting of an unclothed *Venus* accompanied by Cupid (St Petersburg, State Hermitage Museum, FR 22).[4] It is most likely that these related versions of the same subject were made simultaneously. Perhaps Cranach conceived the woodcut as a means of diffusing more widely his conception of the female nude. Some art historians have interpreted Cranach's 1509 *Venus*es as a key example of his receptiveness to Dürer, to the extent of reducing them almost to adaptations of Dürer's depiction of Eve (which was also expressed in painted and print form: see fig. 5 and cat. 23). Rather, these works suggest Cranach's desire to lay claim to the territory of the female nude. In particular, the subject of Venus and Cupid held great significance for the artist (see cat. 2), and he returned to it on many occasions. This explains his eagerness to perfect his first interpretation of it. Several states exist of the woodcut, both in colours and in black and white. There are also impressions simply

---

CAT. 14
PROVENANCE
Sir Joshua Reynolds (1723–1792; Lugt 2304 on verso); bequeathed by Francis Douce (1757–1834) to the University of Oxford, 1834; transferred from the Bodleian Library to the Ashmolean Museum, 1863

CAT. 15
PROVENANCE
Presented by William Mitchell, 1895

SELECTED LITERATURE
Schuchardt 1851–71, II, no. 117, pp. 272–73; Bartsch 1866, no. 113, p. 291; Dodgson 1903–11, vol. 2, no. 62, 62a; Geisberg 1923–39, X, no. 616, ill. 25; Jahn 1955, plate 44 and 45 (2nd state); Hollstein 1959, no. 105, p. 81; Koepplin and Falk 1974, II, cat. 555, pp. 644–50; Falk 1980, no. 113, p. 406; Landau and Parshall 1994, pp. 191–97

pulled from the line block, as well as those printed in chiaroscuro, including cat. 15.

Cranach's depiction of Venus accompanied by a Cupid with uncovered eyes, as a manifestation of 'pure' love, was influenced directly by the newest innovations in German humanist thought, as well as recalling a long-established tradition representing Venus as a planetary goddess. The first German visualisation of the 'antique' type of Venus had appeared recently, in Hans von Kulmbach's illustration of the gods in their correct classical form for Konrad Celtis's *Four Books of Love* (Nuremberg, 1502).[5] An idea of the interpretations to which Cranach's woodcut was open is suggested by the Latin and German verses appended to later impressions of the print's second state.[6] The Latin advised the viewer to follow an ordered and godly married life, while the main section of the German text warned against the arrow of love which Venus's son and messenger could plunge easily into the heart. Such potential multiplicities of message are very characteristic of Cranach. They were further developed in his work of the 1520s and 1530s, including cat. 1 and 2. CMC

NOTES

1 Landau and Parshall 1994, p. 192.
2 Koepplin and Falk 1974, II, pp. 644–45; Stogdon 1991–92, no. 23.
3 Landau and Parshall 1994, p. 197; Bartrum 1995, p. 133.
4 Friedländer and Rosenberg 1978, no. 22, p. 72, pl. 22.
5 Koepplin and Falk 1974, II, p. 645.
6 Hollstein 1959, no. 105.

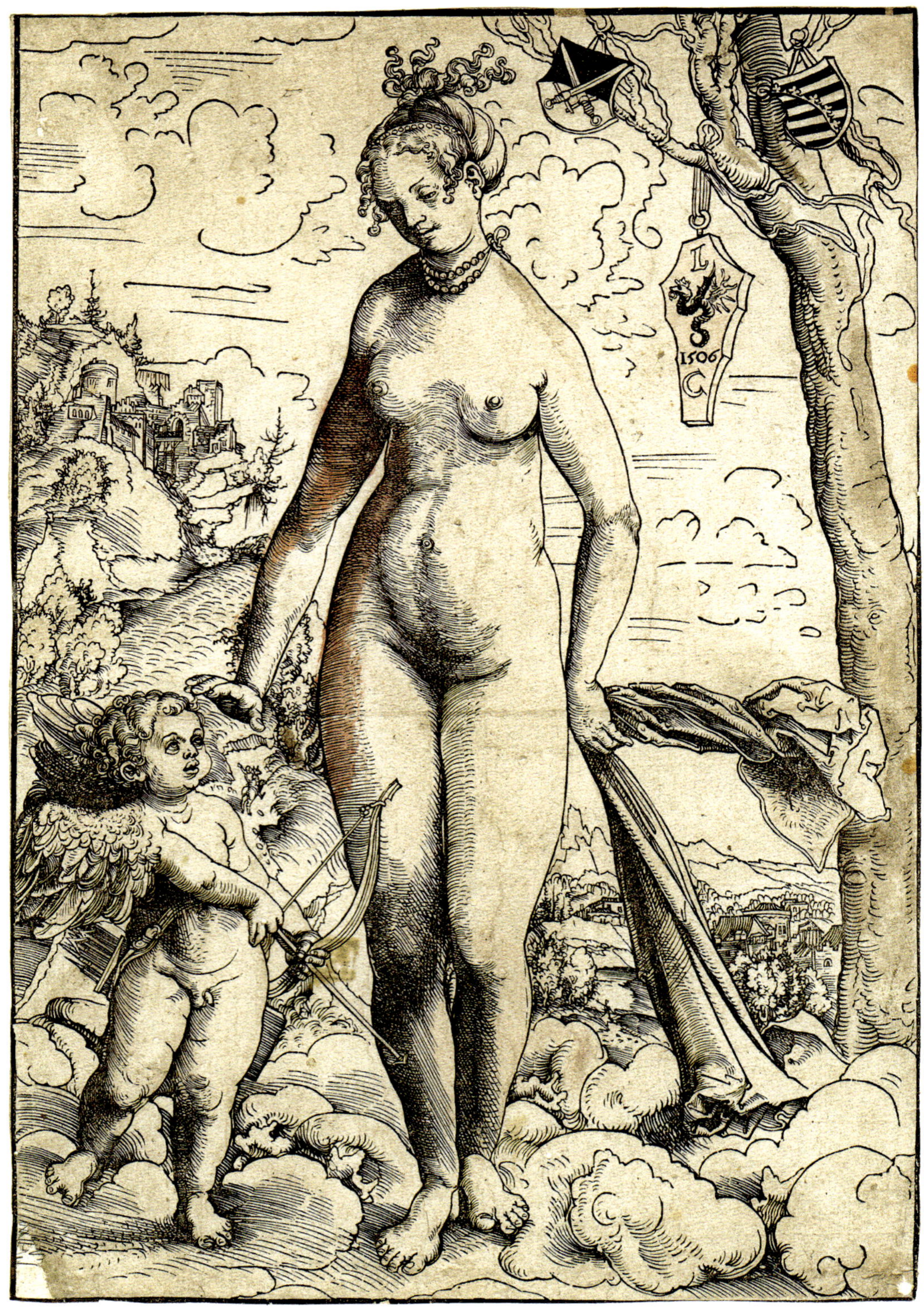
L
1506
C

CAT. 15

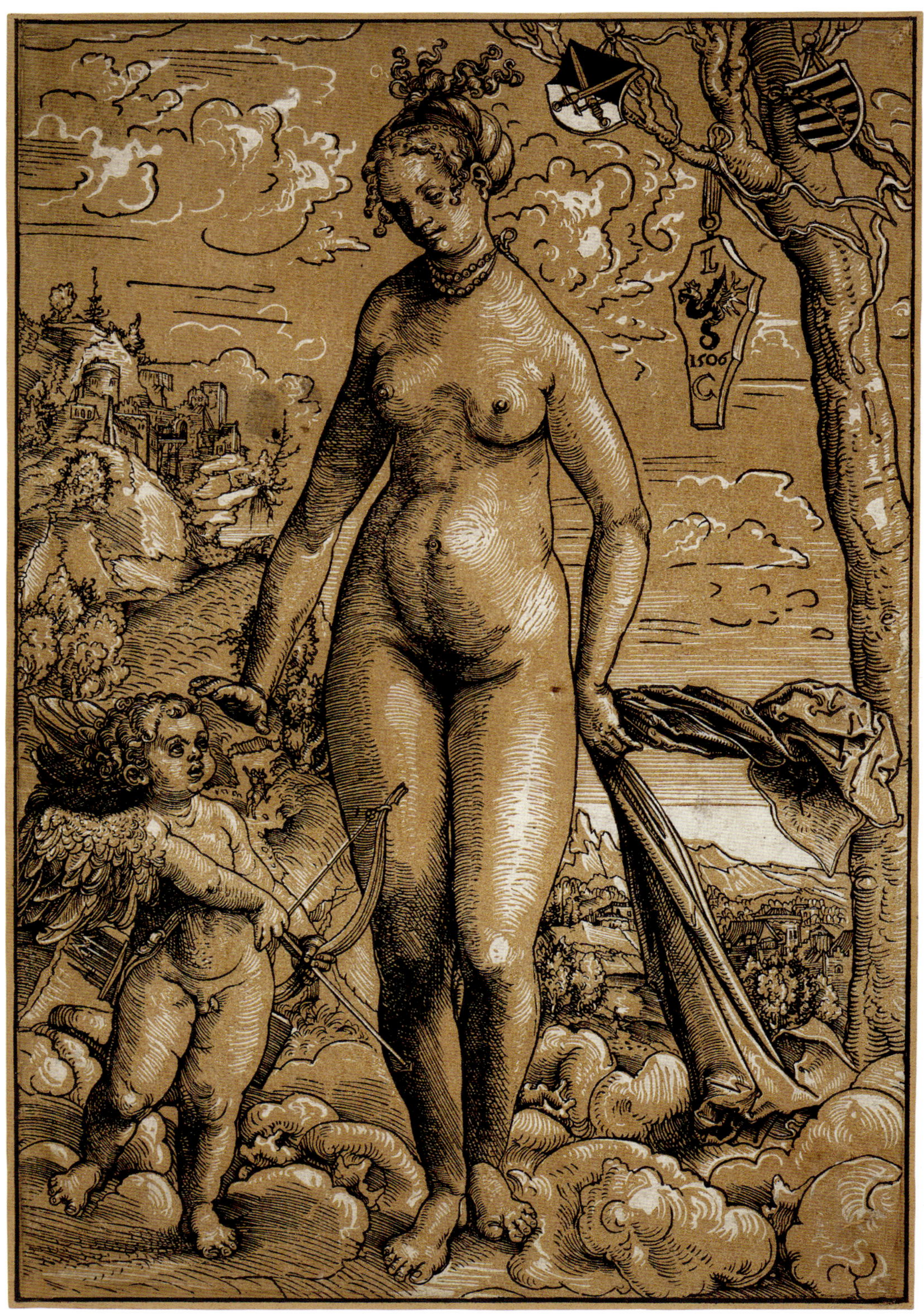

16 Lucas Cranach the Elder
The Penance of St John Chrysostom, 1509

Engraving on paper
26 × 20.2 cm (sheet size)
Signed with initials, date and the winged serpent on block at the front right of the pictorial space: *LC/1509*
Stuck down to mount, so no watermark can be seen.
Oxford, Ashmolean Museum, WA 1863.2662

CRANACH'S ENGRAVING DEPICTS a probably apocryphal incident from the life of Saint John Chrysostom. John had renounced the world for the life of a hermit. However, one day he found an emperor's daughter, who had been collecting flowers, sheltering from a storm in the mouth of his cave. The saint was unable to control his lust and afterwards, fearing that he would be tempted again, he threw the innocent girl off a cliff. Filled with remorse for his evil deed, he took to his haunches like a beast.

Miraculously, the girl was uninjured by her fall. She gave birth to a child and lived contentedly in the wilderness. Several years later, another child of the emperor expressed a desire to be baptised by Saint John. The saint confessed his crime but, while the emperor was searching for his daughter's body, he found her alive and well, and with her baby. The story is not found in any of the early accounts of Saint John Chrysostom's life, but by the later Middle Ages it appeared in many popular versions of the lives of the saints. The details of the narrative vary, but Cranach was probably familiar with the version in the *Leben der Heiligen* (Lives of the Saints) published in Augsburg by Günter Zainer in 1471, and in further editions.

This print is an early example of Cranach's interest in man's primitive history – whether Christian or pagan – and of the harmonious world of unspoilt nature, expressed most clearly in paintings of the late 1520s and 1530s, including *A Faun and His Family* (cat. 4) and *Adam and Eve* (cat. 1). The emperor's daughter rests under a rock (an allusion to Saint John's attempt to kill her), while her baby sleeps against her leg. Both her flowing hair and her curvaceous, womanly body recall closely Cranach's depiction of Eve (compare to cat. 12) of the same year. Like Adam and Eve in Eden, they live peaceably with wild beasts – two stags and a cock pheasant. The beauties of nature also surround them: two irises, symbols of purity often associated with the Virgin Mary, grow at the mother's side, while in the foreground an oak sapling springs from a dead stump, symbolising the emperor's daughter's miraculous survival, and perhaps also the Resurrection. The perfect harmony of nature and man is emphasised by the great precision and delicacy with which the mother and child and their environment are portrayed. In contrast, Saint John is depicted in a deliberately rougher and less highly worked manner. Through his brutish actions, he has regressed to the life of a beast, and is shown scrabbling in the dirt on his hands and knees in the background. Even his fingers have turned into claws.

Cranach made very few engravings, and this is his earliest surviving print in this medium. However, the exceptionally fine detail, the natural flow of the lines, and the masterly shading and contrast between light and dark, suggest that he had previous experience of this precise and difficult art form. He must also have had the opportunity to study Dürer's and Jacopo de' Barbari's engravings. The style recalls Jacopo's work, particularly his so-called *Saint Sebastian*, while a similar approach to a primitive subject-matter is seen in his *Apollo and Diana* (cat. 22). The arrangement of the woman's legs is indebted to Dürer's *Sea Monster*, while the placement of the mother and child under the lee of a rock was surely influenced by Dürer's earlier engraving of the same subject of St John Chrysostom. CMC

PROVENANCE
Bequeathed by Francis Douce (1757–1834) to the University of Oxford; transferred from the Bodleian Library to the Ashmolean Museum, 1863

SELECTED LITERATURE
Bartsch 1866, no. 1, p. 276; Jahn 1955, pp. 204–05; Hollstein 1959, no. 1, p. 2; Falk 1980, no. 1, p. 313; Andersson and Talbot 1983, no. 122, p. 226; Cohn 1995; Strehle and Kunz, 1998, no. 1, pp. 52–55

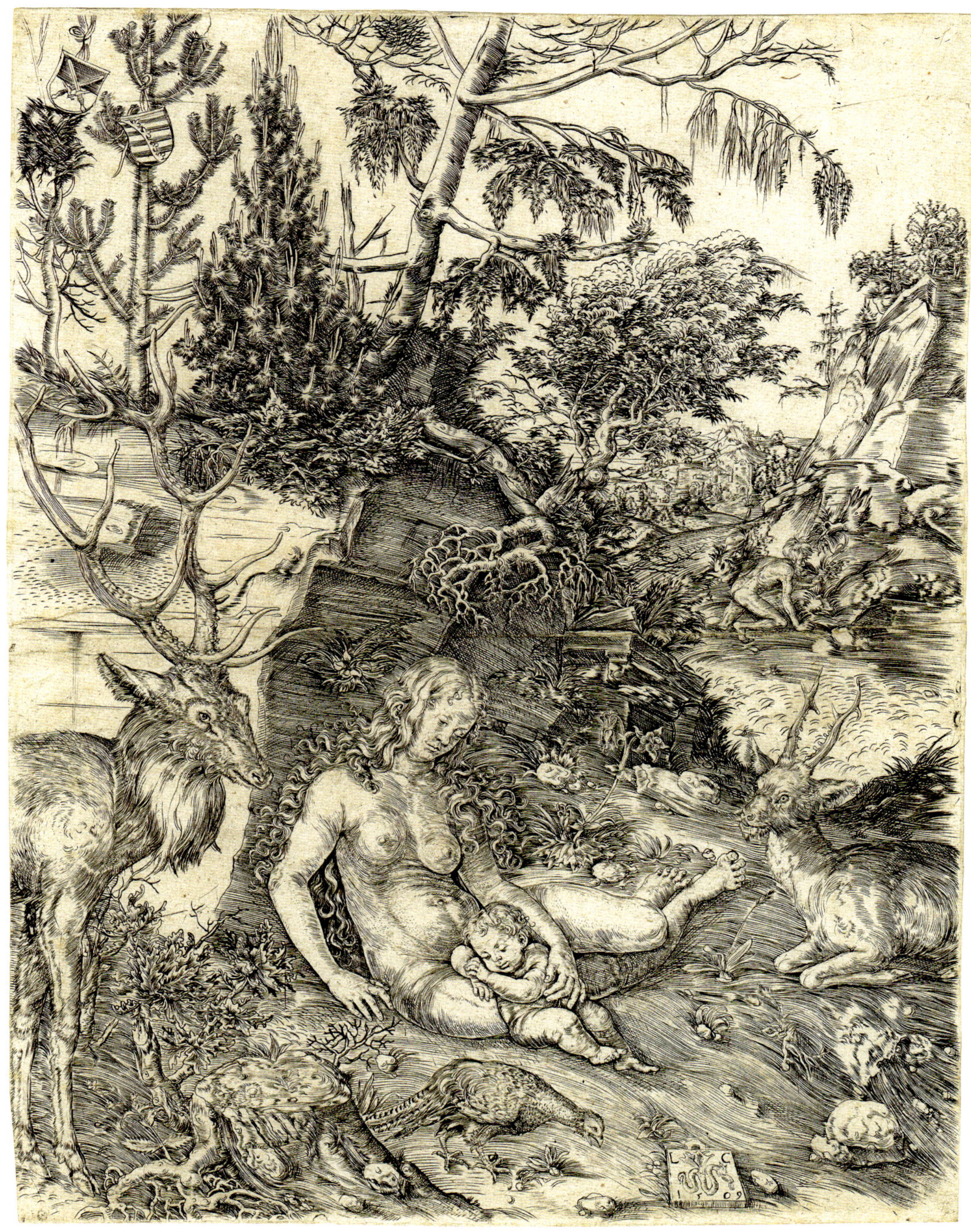

17 Lucas Cranach the Elder (around 1472–1553)
The Boar Hunt, probably 1506

Woodcut, 1st state
Signed with initials *LC* at lower right.
Bears the Electoral and Saxon coats of arms, at top right
(the Electoral coat of arms is sable in base).
18.1 × 12.6 cm
Stuck down to mount, so no watermark can be seen.
Oxford, The Ashmolean Museum, Department of Western Art, WA 1863.2739

IN DENSE FOREST, a mounted huntsman watches his dogs bring a bristling, tusked boar to bay at close quarters. He is in the act of plunging his hunting sword into the side of his prey. Despite the success of the hunt, the huntsman and his pack's escape from the wounded animal is not certain. Massed vertical ranks of trees seem to close in claustrophobically upon him. This enhances the impression of the huntsman's – and the viewer's – hazardous proximity to the cornered boar. The danger of the moment is further conveyed by the compression of the narrative into the bottom right quadrant of the print. Like *The Stag Hunt* (cat. 18), this small-scale woodcut was made at the start of Cranach's long career as court painter to the Saxon Elector Frederick the Wise, and the hunter is dressed almost identically to his peers in the larger print. Throughout his career Cranach was an active recycler of successful artistic motifs, and he used a boar like that depicted here as a model for subsequent representations of this animal, not least in the Courtauld *Adam and Eve* (cat. 1).

Cranach is said to have accompanied his master on hunting expeditions (see cat. 18), and this vignette further attests to his familiarity with the chase at the Saxon court.[1] The huntsman has oak leaves twined round his hat, for boar hunting was reserved for the cold months from November to February, when the beasts were sleek and fat, and could scent the acorns they particularly craved. The wild boar was extremely fierce when hunted, and specially trained and selected hounds called alaunts (often of mixed breed) were used to tackle cornered animals near the end, to save the less hardy greyhounds. Cranach's shaggy, sturdy dogs, depicted plunging their teeth into the boar's left flank,[2] resemble alaunts. They also wear the large collars typically reserved for them (when not hunting, they were used as watchdogs).

Although not quite as prestigious as stags, boars were favoured prey, perhaps because of the extreme danger involved in hunting them, and boar hunts formed part of the most important tapestry cycles of the fifteenth and sixteenth centuries, including the Devonshire *Hunts* (London, Victoria and Albert Museum) and *The Hunts of Maximilian* (Paris, Musée du Louvre).[3] A drawing by Cranach (cat. 7) shows that he had ample opportunity to study them in action during the hunt, as well as dead or from memory. Scheurl recounts (see cat. 6) that a painting – more probably a watercolour – of a wild boar made by Cranach so terrified a hunting hound that it ran away. In 1508, Cranach presented a watercolour of a boar killed by Frederick the Wise (perhaps the same object?) to the Emperor Maximilian during his visit to the Low Countries. CMC

PROVENANCE
Bequeathed by Francis Douce (1757–1834) to the University of Oxford, 1834; transferred from the Bodleian Library to the Ashmolean Museum, 1863

SELECTED LITERATURE
Bartsch 1866, no. 118, p. 292; Hollstein 1959, no. 113, p. 90; Jahn 1955, pp. 390–91; Falk 1980, no. 118, p. 411

NOTES
1 On at least one occasion (in 1524) Cranach was given a boar from the Elector's hunt. See Schade 1980, p. 412.
2 One theory held that boars were invincible on their right sides. See Werness 2004, p. 49.
3 See Digby 1971; Campbell 2002, nos. 37–40, pp. 329–38.

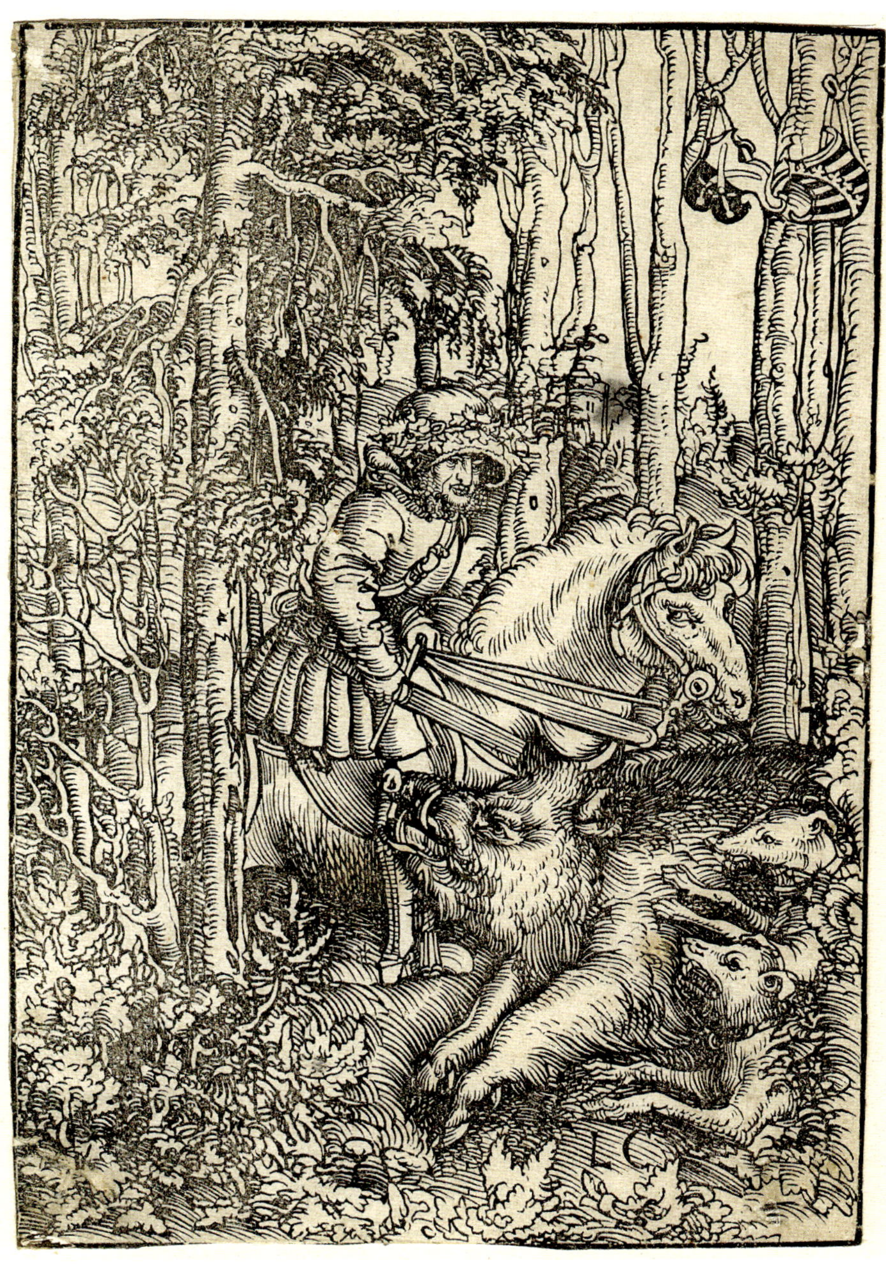

18 Lucas Cranach the Elder

The Stag Hunt, 1st state, around 1506

Woodcut, two blocks pasted together in the middle
37.2 × 51.0 cm (sheet size)
Signed with intertwined initials *LC*, at lower right. Bears the Electoral (at left) and Saxon coats of arms (at right) (the Electoral coat of arms is sable in base).
Stuck down to mount, so no watermark can be seen.
Oxford, Ashmolean Museum, Department of Western Art, WA 1863.2742

CRANACH MADE THE DEPICTION of hunting, and the wild beasts which were the hunter's prey, into one of his particular specialities. In 1508, two years at most after the date of this print, the humanist Christian Scheurl delivered an encomium of Cranach (published the following year in Wittenberg; see cat. 6). Comparing the Saxon court artist in typical early sixteenth-century terms to the almost legendary ancient Greek painters Apelles and Zeuxis, he claimed that Cranach outdid even their famed illusionistic abilities. According to Scheurl, birds attempted to land on the antlers of stags which Cranach had painted on the walls of the Elector's castle at Coburg, while hounds barked at Cranach's picture of a deer.[1]

During Cranach's lifetime hunting and jousting were the most important and prestigious leisure activities at the courts of Europe and among members of the élite. Wittenberg was no exception: Elector Frederick was a passionate hunter, and Scheurl reports that Cranach accompanied his master on hunting expeditions, bringing with him a "drawing panel (*Zeichentafel*)" so that he could record the events of the hunt immediately. It is telling that Cranach's very earliest work as the Elector's court painter includes this print and four woodcuts of tournaments.[2] Hunting subjects remained an important part of Cranach's repertoire until his death, particularly those representing specific hunts (including fig. 3).

The Stag Hunt stands out among Cranach's oeuvre at this date for its size and also for its production using two blocks. The large dimensions allowed the artist to depict the elements of the chase with particular clarity. The castle complex seen in the left background is probably Frederick the Wise's favourite seat, the hunting lodge at Lochau (known as Annaberg since 1572), the place where he died in May 1525. The moors round Lochau were famous for the quantity of wild creatures they supported, and many hunting visits there by Frederick and his court are documented. The continuous narrative moves round the pictorial space in a circular fashion, starting at the top left, where the hunting dogs are released from their kennels. They quickly pick up the scent of three stags, which they chase with increasing ferocity. Archers with crossbows are placed beside the river to direct the chase of the dogs and their quarry towards the high nobles on horseback. Once the stag has been forced to land, it is harried by the dogs and foot soldiers towards the group of knights at the bottom left. One (perhaps the Elector?) delivers the *coup de grace* to the stag with his sword. The violence of the hunt is underlined by the dog which lies dead at the bottom left corner. The convincingly accurate manner of depiction finds a parallel in *The Hunts of Maximilian*, a remarkable set of twelve tapestries made in Brussels in the early 1530s probably for Mary of Hungary.[3]

The print's precise function is unclear. Although the coats of arms unambiguously state Cranach's position as an Electoral servant, it was not necessarily made specifically for Frederick the Wise. However, it could have been used by him as a diplomatic gift, like Cranach's "*Tuchlein*" (linen painting) – sadly lost – of a stag hunt sent by the Elector to the Pfalzgraf Friedrich in 1522, which included his brother John the Steadfast and his son among the participants. Cranach's woodcut was certainly known in such courtly contexts outside Wittenberg. Its influence can be seen in a minature made in 1512 for the Emperor Maximilian and in Loy Gering's bronze relief for the Hauptsaal (principal room) of the Castle at Grünau.
CMC

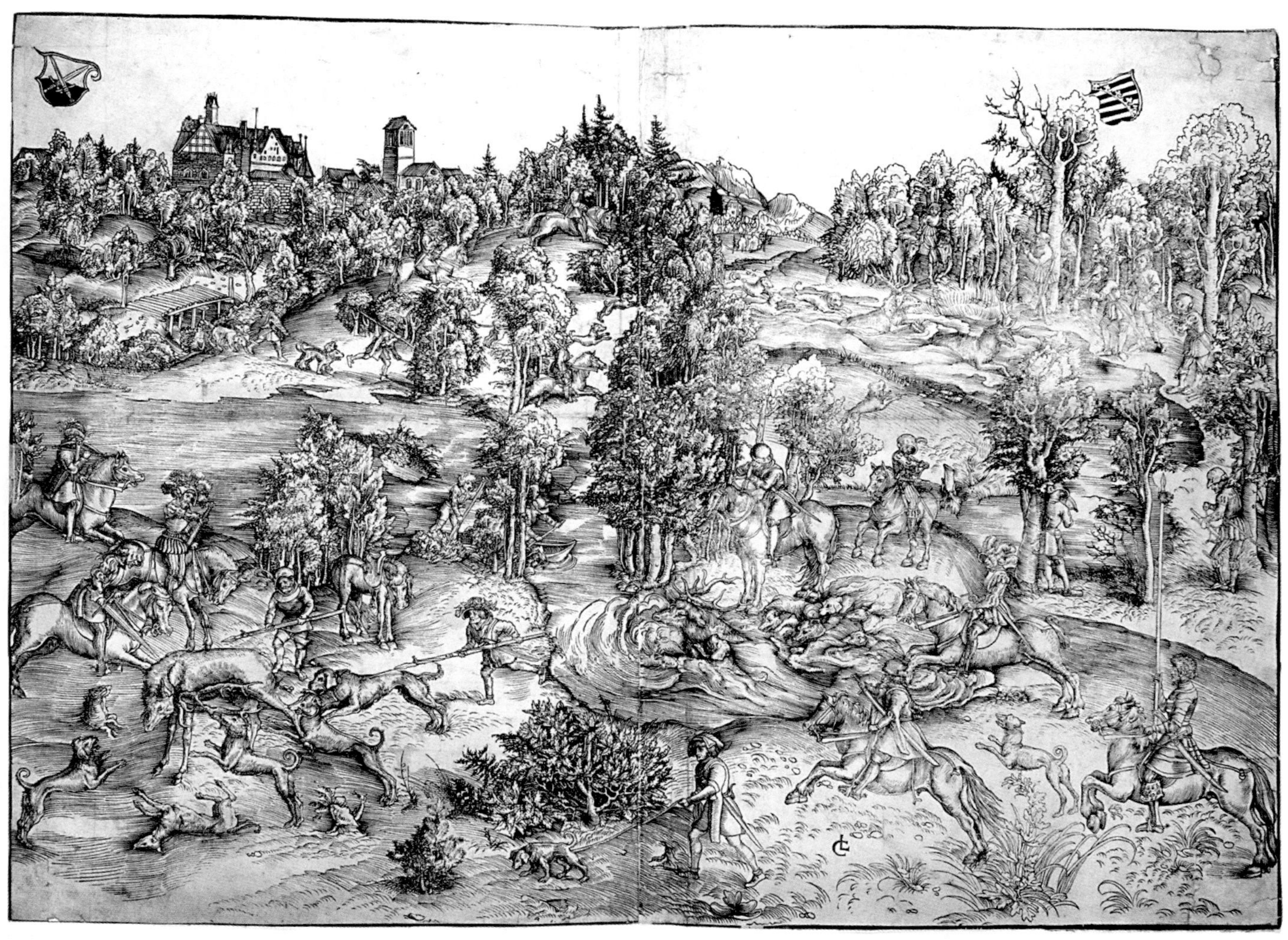

PROVENANCE

Bequeathed by Francis Douce (1757–1834) to the University of Oxford, 1834; transferred from the Bodleian Library to the Ashmolean Museum, 1863

SELECTED LITERATURE

Bartsch 1866, no. 119, p. 292; Van Marle 1931, p. 197; Hollstein 1959, no. 115, p. 92; Francis 1959; Koepplin and Falk 1974, I, no. 138, pp. 194–96, 241–42; Falk 1980, no. 119, p. 412; Andersson and Talbot 1983, no. 120, pp. 222–23; Landau and Parshall 1994, p. 176, fig. 186; Grimm, Erichsen and Brockhoff 1994, no. 143, pp. 321–22; Bartrum 1995, no. 170, pp. 168–69

NOTES

1 Schuchardt 1851–71, I, p. 29.
2 Hollstein 1959, nos. 116–19.
3 See Balis *et al.* 1993.

19, 20 Lucas Cranach the Elder

Frontispiece to *Auff der bocks / zu Leypczick Ant / wort D.M. Luther*

(To the goat of Leipzig. A response by Martin Luther)
designed 1520

Woodcut
Published, Wittenberg, J. Grunenberg, 1521, 8 pp.
Book dimensions: 19.6 × 14.2 cm (page)
Frontispiece dimensions: 16.7 × 12.5 cm (16.4 × 12.3 cm to border)
London, The British Library, inv. 3905.bbb.16

Frontispiece to *Das diese wort Christi, das ist mein leib … Mart. Luther*

(The words of Christ … Martin Luther)
designed 1525

Woodcut
Published, Wittenberg, Michael Lotter, 1527, 80 pp.
Book dimensions: 19.8 × 14.6 cm (page)
Frontispiece dimensions: 19.8 × 14.6 cm (17.1 × 12 cm to border)
London, The British Library, inv. 3905.bbb.67

THESE TWO BOOK FRONTISPIECES of the 1520s provide interesting comparisons with the Courtauld *Adam and Eve* (cat. 1), including their similar narrative organisation (see essay by Stephanie Buck). Like many of the book illustrations produced by Cranach and his workshop, both were re-used on a number of occasions. Cat. 19 was probably designed in 1520 for the book *Consolation in Bad Luck*, left unfinished by the Nuremberg town councillor Peter Stehel, who died in that year, and completed by Georg Spalatin (1484–1545), chancellor to Elector Frederick of Saxony. During the autumn of 1519 Luther was commissioned to write a similar text for the Elector, who was recovering from illness, and Koepplin and Falk have argued that cat. 19 was also intended to be the frontispiece for this publication (it appeared in print in 1522). In 1521 it was used once more for the present book, a publication of Luther's famous disputation with Johannes Eck at Leizpig in June 1519 (Eck is here called the 'goat' of Leipzig). The main factor linking these books is the Wittenberg publisher Johann Grunenberg, whose monogram IG appears prominently under the title, to the right of a depiction of a printing press. It seems that Grunenberg had commissioned the frontispiece, and was free to use it as he chose. It appears as the title page of seven books he published between 1520 and 1525.

There is nothing to match this illustration in Cranach's oeuvre. The tone is apparently light-hearted and comic. A series of vignettes are arranged around the text panel in the centre, most of which relate to the theme of finding consolation in the face of bad luck. These include a beggar, so drunk that he fails to notice the bees circling his head; a chicken thief hurriedly making his escape; an owl under attack by smaller birds; and fights between ill-matched animals, including a bear against an ox and a wolf against a sheep. Previous commentators have preferred to see these images as completely irrelevant to the text they accompany, but one can read some of the animal scenes according to long-established traditions of Christian symbolism. For example, the stork at the bottom right was a widely used symbol of prudence, piety and resurrection, while the frogs it prepares to attack were considered to represent damned and defective humanity. It is notable that on at least one occasion Luther stigmatised his opponents as frogs.[1] Similarly, the stag's fight against the dog could be interpreted as the battle of Christ against the devil,[2] while the sheep (the lamb of God, and symbol of the Eucharist) contends against the deceitful wolf. The animal imagery must have seemed appropriate to Grunenberg – and to Luther (who often made use of it) – for the illustration of the text, the response of 'the bull of Wittenberg' to Leipzig's 'goat'.[3]

CAT. 15
SELECTED LITERATURE
Dodgson 1903–11, II, pp. 324 (nos. 1 and 2), 329 (no. 11), 334 (no. 6); Davies 1913, I, no. 259, pp. 447–49; Benzing 1952, no. 829; Hollstein 1959, no. 44 (Cranach workshop), p. 172; Jahn and Bernhard 1972, p. 422; Koepplin and Falk 1974, I, no. 217, pp. 320–22, 329; Claus 1994, no. 3.4, p. 180, and 3.19, p. 194

CAT. 16
SELECTED LITERATURE
Dodgson 1903–11, II, p. 325, no. 9; Benzing 1952, no. 2239; Hollstein 1959, no. 45 (Cranach workshop), p. 173; Jahn 1955, p. 65; Koepplin and Falk 1974, I, pp. 378–79, 385, no. 257; Schoen 2001, p. 160, note 27

A more direct relationship between text and image is expressed unambiguously in cat. 20. This is one of the most beautiful of Cranach's later book illustrations. It is particularly close to the manuscript illuminations he had made for the Emperor Maximilian's Prayerbook ten years earlier (the male grotesque at the top left is based on an earlier representation of this figure on fol. 58r of the Prayerbook).[4] The precedent is not without significance, for this frontispiece was made to accompany Luther's *German Mass and Order of Service*, first celebrated in Wittenberg at Christmas 1525, and published by Michael Lotter in early 1526. Subsequently, it was only used to accompany other Lutheran tomes. In 1527 Lotter recycled it to introduce Luther's treatise *The Word of Christ*. In the foreground are three stags – the most common animal signifiers of Christ – and a hind stand together peaceably in a quiet landscape, reminiscent of Cranach's visualisations of Paradise (such as cat. 5), and in complete contrast to the normative behaviour of stags with a female deer (recorded by Cranach on the verso of cat. 6).[5] The darkness of the upper register denotes the danger to mankind presented by Original Sin. In the centre a cup or chalice is depicted. This refers to the water and blood which poured from Christ's side on the cross, representing the sacrifice of his body to reclaim mankind from damnation. The threat of sin is shown by the two *all'antica* human grotesques which surround the chalice. They have snake tails, and resemble closely one of the most common iconographic representations of the serpent in Eden, with a human head (for such depictions by Cranach, see cat. 5 and 13). The particularly close connection between text and image, and the unusually high quality of the woodcut, can probably be explained by the great importance of the volume it was first designed for, and Cranach's personal involvement in the sale of this book. CMC

NOTES

1 Friedmann 1980, pp. 217–19.
2 For the Christological symbolism of the stag, see cat. 1 and 5; and for the use of the hound to represent the devil, see fig. 37, where it appears as Eve's familiar.
3 For Luther's fables, see Luther 1995.
4 Reproduced in Rosenberg 1960, pl. 23.
5 The depiction of the animals is also very reminiscent of Cranach's illustrations to Emperor Maximilian's Prayerbook (compare to figs. 12 and 19).

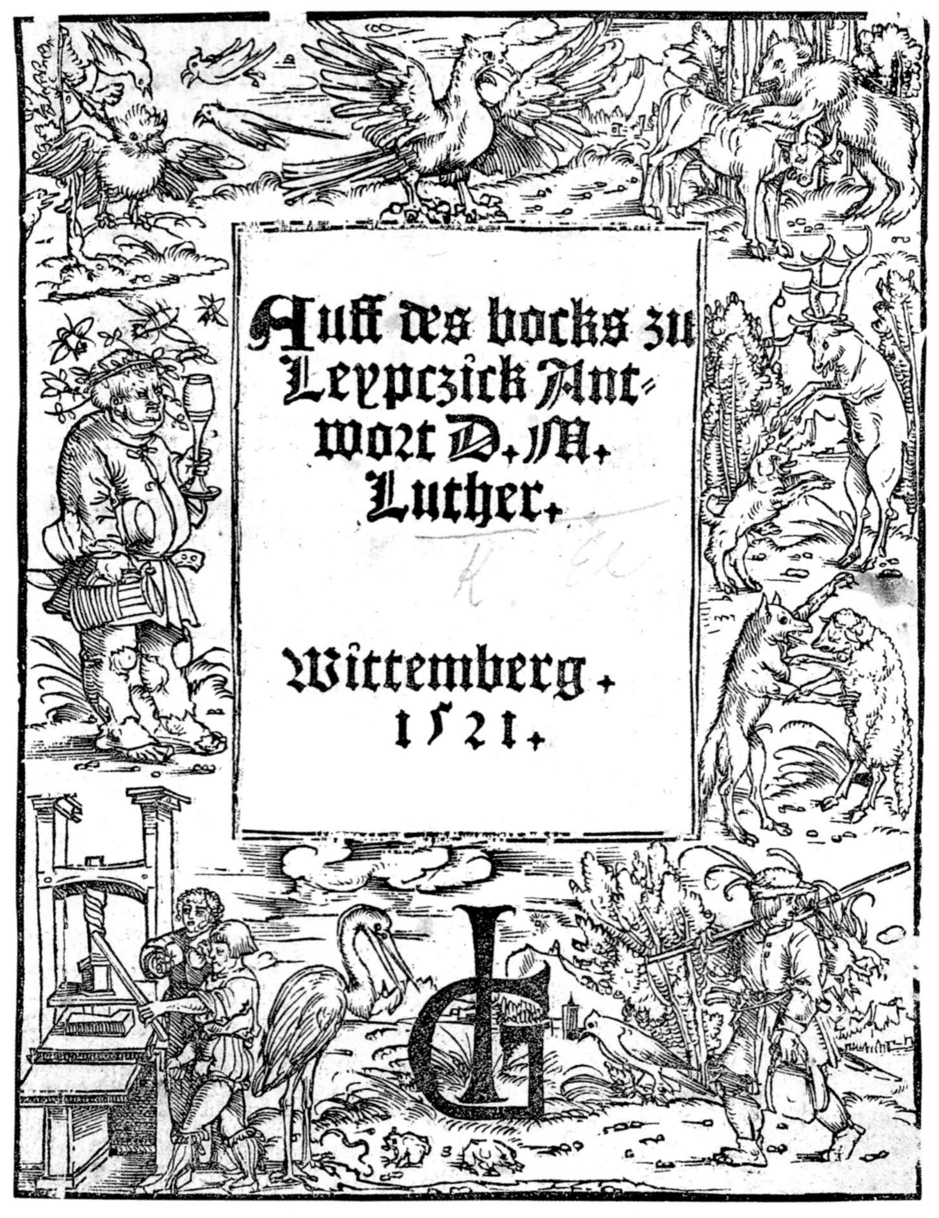
Auff des bocks zu
Leypczick Ant=
wort D. M.
Luther.
Wittemberg.
1521.

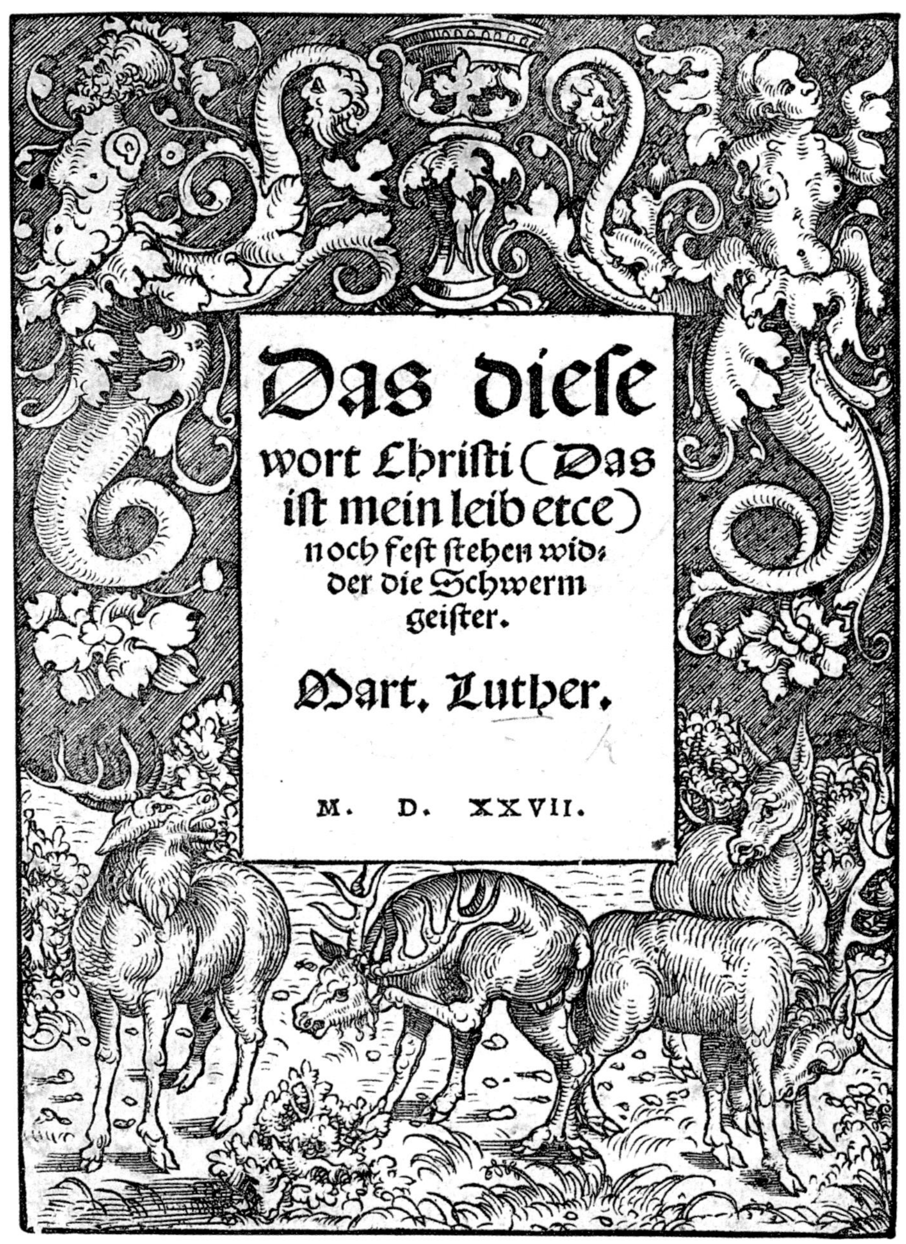

Das diese wort Christi (Das ist mein leib etce) noch fest stehen wider die Schwermgeister.

Mart. Luther.

M. D. XXVII.

21 Albrecht Dürer (1471–1528)

Hercules at the Crossroads, around 1498

Engraving
32.0 × 22.0 cm
Stuck down to mount, so no watermark can be seen.
Oxford, Ashmolean Museum, Department of Western Art, WA 1863.2296

THIS ENIGMATIC ENGRAVING has been subject to various interpretations, and titles. For Adam Bartsch, it represented "the effects of jealousy", while other early commentators called it *The Great Satyr*. However, in August 1520, when Dürer gave an impression of it (along with others of his most beautiful sheets) to João Brandao, the factor of the Portuguese trading community in Antwerp, he described it unambiguously as "the Hercules".[1]

Despite Dürer's certainty, the confusion of other observers is easy to understand. The Greek historian Xenophon's account of Hercules's choice between Virtue and Pleasure was a familiar motif in late medieval and Renaissance art and literature, but Dürer's depiction of it is extremely idiosyncratic. Artists generally showed Hercules asleep at the crossroads, accompanied by visions of female personifications of Virtue and Vice (a very typical example is Raphael's miniature painting in the National Gallery, NG 213). In contrast, Dürer depicts Hercules in more active mode. He appears to be about to bludgeon Pleasure, who reclines lasciviously at the left, accompanied by a notoriously loose-living satyr. However, some commentators have suggested that a sense of indecision – or more positively, moderation – is also implicit in Hercules' pose.[2] He has not yet resolved himself on defence or attack. Rather than preparing to hit Pleasure, is Hercules going to restrain Virtue's assault on her enemy? No definitive answer to this question can be reached, since – as he would do six years later in his *Adam and Eve* – Dürer has chosen to portray the moment between resolution and action, when nothing irreversible has yet happened.

Heavily indebted to Andrea Mantegna and Antonio Pollauiolo, this is perhaps Dürer's most Italianate engraving. It was extremely well-known in the sixteenth century. At least four contemporary print copies exist, by German and Italian artists. Artists also used the *Hercules* as an exemplar of the human form, and as a guide to positioning the male or female figure. Cranach used it as the starting point for his representations of the naked human body on several occasions. Dürer's Hercules, shown from behind, has close parallels in the fighting men in the version of *The Silver Age* now in the Schloßmuseum, Weimar (FR 264). The *contrapposto* of the female personification of virtue informed many of his twisting bodies, both male and female. These include the woman with two children in the National Gallery's *The Silver Age* (fig. 20) and many of his depictions of Eve and Venus (including cat. 1, 2, 14 and 15). Tellingly, Cranach also used Dürer's solution for Virtue's legs to portray Adam, the agent of the key Christian choice between Vice and Virtue, in the Courtauld *Adam and Eve*. CMC

PROVENANCE
Bequeathed by Francis Douce (1757–1834) to the University of Oxford, 1834; transferred from the Bodleian Library to the Ashmolean Museum, 1863

SELECTED LITERATURE
Bartsch 1866, no. 73, pp. 86–87; Meder 1932, no. 63; Panofsky 1955, pp. 73–76, fig. 108; Hollstein 1962, no. 62, pp. 55–56; Strauss 1980, X, commentary, pp. 160–63; Parshall and Landau 1994, p. 314; Schoch, Mende and Scherbaum 2001–04, no. 22 (before state 2a), pp. 76–78; Bartrum 2002, no. 197, p. 245

NOTES
1 Rupprich 1956, p. 154
2 Wind 1938–39; Gollob 1966; Anzelewsky 1983, pp. 66–89.

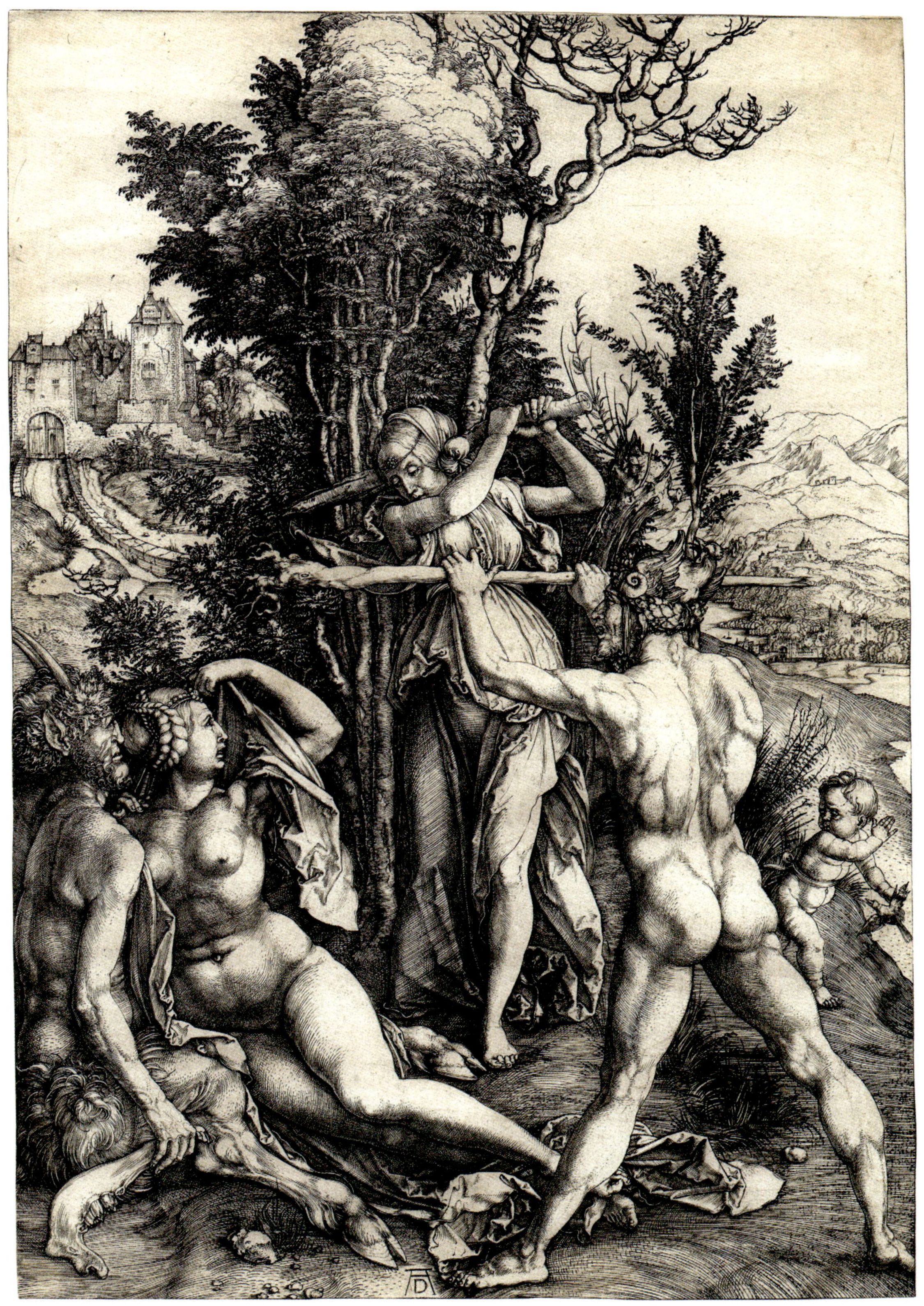

22 Jacopo de' Barbari (active around 1497 – before 1516)
Apollo and Diana, 1502–03

Engraving, 16.0 × 10.0 cm (plate mark); 16.1 × 10.1 cm (sheet)
Signed at the upper left with the caduceus
Watermark: Roue (wheel) (Hind no. 150; Briquet 13270; belonging to a group of watermarks identified by Briquet as chiefly occurring in France)
London, The British Museum, Department of Prints and Drawings, inv. 1895-9-15-89

SAVE HIS PRINTS, relatively little is known for certian about the painter and printmaker Jacopo de' Barbari. Even his nationality is unclear, although he is said to have been born in Bologna, and worked in Venice. He appears to have arrived in Saxony as the Elector Frederick's court painter in 1504, and his name is mentioned regularly in Wittenberg documents of that and the following year. Cranach is often called his successor, but they were summoned to the Saxon court in the same year (Cranach arrived in 1505), so they were, rather – albeit briefly – colleagues and contemporaries. Jacopo appears to have left Wittenberg in the summer of 1506. He subsequently made peripatetic progress round the courts of northern Europe, dying between 1511 and 1516 in the service of Margaret of Austria.

Jacopo's renown lies in his gifts as a printmaker. As David Landau has commented, he was the first Italian artist not trained as a goldsmith who was able to exploit new techniques of engraving with the burin developed in the late fifteenth century. His thirty engravings are remarkable for their refinement and delicacy, and also for their often unusual, sometimes arcane subject-matter. *Apollo and Diana* was one of Jacopo's more influential and typical prints, executed with fine lines and some simple cross-hatching. Although its subject – the sun god and his sister, the goddess of the moon, chastity and hunting – would have been familiar to a sixteenth-century viewer, its unusual mode of representation would not. Apollo stands just off-centre within a circle on a starry half-dome, representing the heavens. Thin striations of light seem to pulse from his body as he prepares to loose an arrow from his bow. To the right, removed from Apollo's heavenly sphere, stands Diana, shown unusually – but aptly for this chaste deity – from behind, accompanied by a stag. A small circle just above her head is the only indication of the moon.

In 1920 Erwin Panofsky demonstrated that Dürer not only knew this print, but made use of it to alter his drawing of *Apollo and Diana* (London, British Museum). Subsequently it also provided the starting point for Dürer's engraving of the same subject. In contrast, Jacopo's impact on Cranach has received less attention, although it was perhaps even more significant: for example, his Apollo was just as probably a source of the idealised 'Apollo Belvedere' male type in Cranach's paintings (including fig. 27) as Dürer's work (cat. 23). An affinity between the two men (which may explain their attraction to the Elector Frederick) can be seen in their mutual interest in printmaking and their parallel skill as recorders of the natural world, demonstrated in Jacopo's *Sparrowhawk* (London, National Gallery) and Cranach's *Two Dead Partridges* (cat. 9).

Jacopo's influence on Cranach seems to have been most pronounced in the 1520s, when Cranach developed new depictions of the early history of man, including cat. 1, 2, 3, 4 (see essay by Susan Foister). Friedlander and Rosenberg noted the connection between Cranach's compositions of *Apollo and Diana* (including cat. 3) and Dürer's engraving.[1] However, Cranach's use of Jacopo's print was equally important, and the figure of Apollo in cat. 3 and his Brussels version of the subject (FR 270) is very closely derived from his engraving of thirty years earlier. Thus both it and Dürer's engraving were Cranach's initial sources for his new conception of Adam and Eve as a narrative scene in mid 1520s, developed in the Courtauld painting (cat. 1) and other works of the same period, including fig. 29. A drawing from the Koenigs collection (fig. 32; see discussion in cat. 1 and 3) represents an intermediary stage between Dürer and Jacopo de' Barbari's interpretations of *Apollo and Diana* and Cranach's *Adam and Eve* (cat. 1), which itself influenced enormously his paintings of *Apollo and Diana*. Thus, Jacopo and Dürer's engravings seem to have been kept in Cranach's shop as tools offering potential solutions to both compositional and iconographic problems. CMC

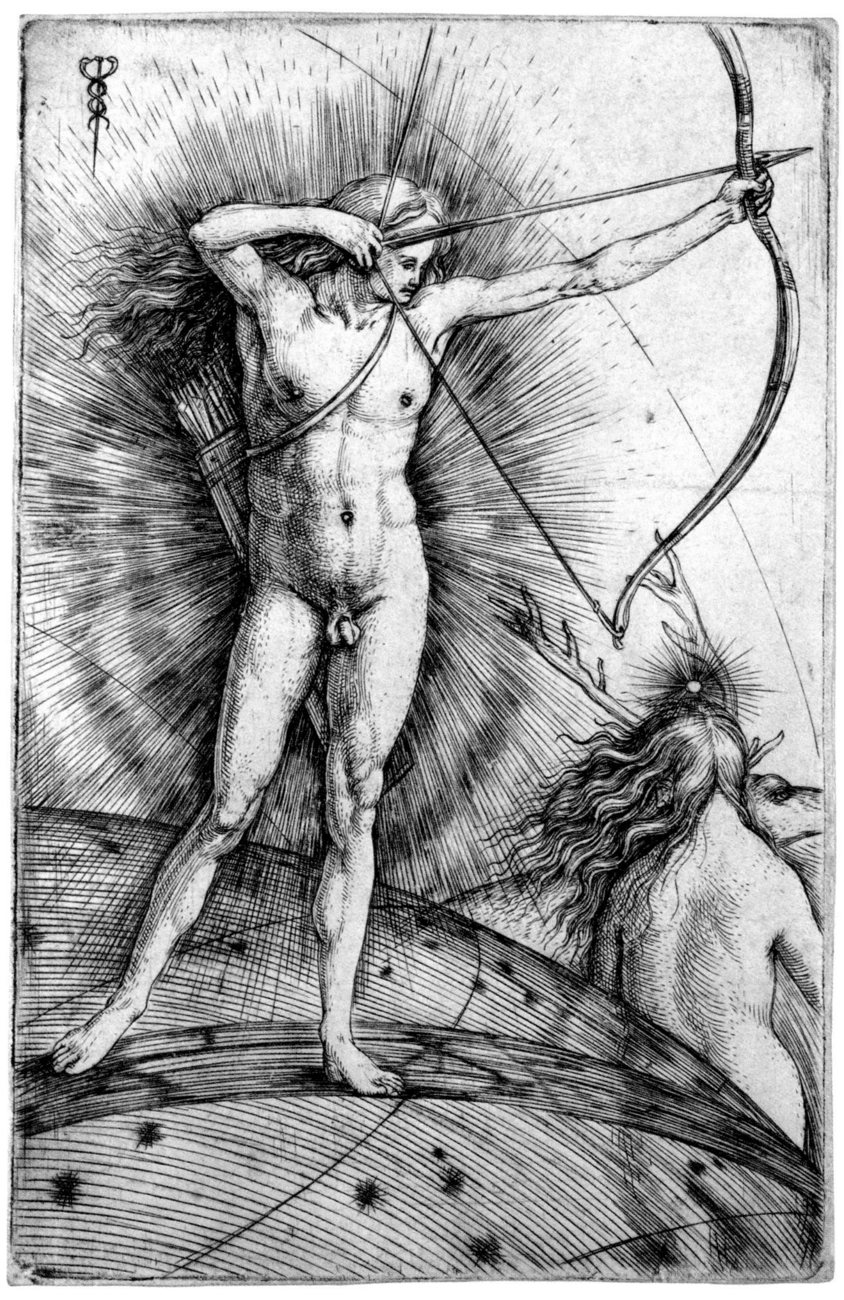

PROVENANCE
Purchased from the Malcolm Collection, 1895

SELECTED LITERATURE

Bartsch 1866, no. 16, p. 593; Kristeller 1896, no. 14; Hind 1910, no. 14, p. 452; Panofsky 1920, pp. 371–73; Hind 1948, pp. 144, 153–54; Servolini 1944, no. 16, pp. 92–94, 191–92; Levenson and Oberhuber 1973, no. 141, pp. 368–69; Levenson 1978, no. 27, pp. 82–83, 124–25, 129, 233–36; Hope and Martineau 1983–84, pp. 1, 306–07 (entry by Landau); Landau and Parshall 1994, p. 77; Zucker 1999, nos. 13, 16 (523), pp. 26–27

NOTE

1 Friedländer and Rosenberg 1978, FR 270–71, pp. 122–23.

23 Albrecht Dürer (1471–1528)

Adam and Eve, 1504

Engraving, 4th state, 25.2 × 19.6 cm (sheet); 24.8 x 19.2 cm (plate mark)
Inscribed in the plate: *ALBERT [VS]\ DVRER/ NORICVS/ FACIEBAT/* [Dürer monogram] *1504* (Albrecht Dürer of Nuremberg made this 1504)
London, The British Museum, Department of Prints and Drawings, 1895-9-15-299

THIS ENGRAVING WAS produced the year before Dürer's second departure for Italy. It is the masterwork of his early maturity and the summation of his meticulous study of a system of human proportion. The importance he attached to it is evident from the exceptionally prominent signature, the number of preparatory studies which survive, both for the main figures of Adam and Eve and the animals which surround them, and the existence of several trial proofs, pulled when Dürer was engraving the plate. The carefully controlled shading, which enhances the engraving's psychological acuity and perception, has made this one of Durer's most admired prints. It was well known shortly after its production, and together with Durer's panels of *Adam and Eve* (fig. 6; 1507) it provided the most important initial models for Cranach's earliest paintings of the subject (figs. 5 and 27).

Adam and Eve stand before the Tree of Knowledge, at the front of the pictorial space. Their beautifully balanced bodies seem at once to move towards and away from each other, echoing their indecision at this fateful moment before the fall. Their eyes look towards each other, but they do not meet: each appears lost in their own thought. Adam gestures towards Eve and the fruit of knowledge she holds, while she observes the serpent placing it delicately with its mouth in her hand.

The world is in equilibrium, but all is about to change. In the top right-hand corner, a mountain goat balances precariously on a mountain crag, mirroring the fact that Adam and Eve are also standing on the edge of a moral precipice. The gracious and controlled movement of the figures enhances the impression (expressed memorably by Heinrich Wölfflin) that Adam and Eve are frozen in time, but not yet in free fall towards an inevitable doom. The classical proportions of Dürer's figures enhance their quasi-divine qualities. Adam is derived – although indirectly – from the idealised *all'antica* masculine bodies of antique statues, such as the *Apollo* Belvedere and the Borghese *Hercules* (for his earlier use of such models, see cat. 21). Eve's body is also inspired by Durer's earlier studies of Vitruvian Man, combined with the type of the Medici *Venus*.

The first couple are surrounded by an apparently odd assortment of animals – a cat and mouse, an elk, a European bison (or bull), a rabbit and a parrot. However, they all carry important symbolic meanings. Erwin Panofsky demonstrated that the first four of these beasts represented the humours (choler, melancholy, phlegm and sanguinity) which governed the body, according to long established medical theory. In Dürer's engraving they are still in harmony, to demonstrate Adam and Eve's state of perfection before the Fall. This is represented graphically by the motif of the normally choleric cat which lies peaceably between Eve and Adam, unaffected by the presence of the nearby mouse.

The general acceptance of Panofsky's very plausible theory has to some extent diminished the importance of the other natural symbols depicted in Dürer's engraving. Adam grasps a branch of the mountain ash, identified during the Middle Ages as the Tree of Life, and which the serpent avoided, according to the influential *Physiologus*. On this branch perches a parrot, a positive symbol of cleverness in contrast to the cunning snake. Cranach was to enhance and expand Dürer's menagerie of Eden to such an extent that his woodcut of 1509 (cat. 12) and later depictions of the Fall of Man (especially cat. 5, and also cat. 1) can seem almost overwhelmed by members of the animal kingdom. Like Dürer, he used studies from life to inform his naturalistic depiction of these beasts, while drawing on long-established allegorical traditions to provide an interpretative framework which would have been immediately familiar to users of his images. CMC

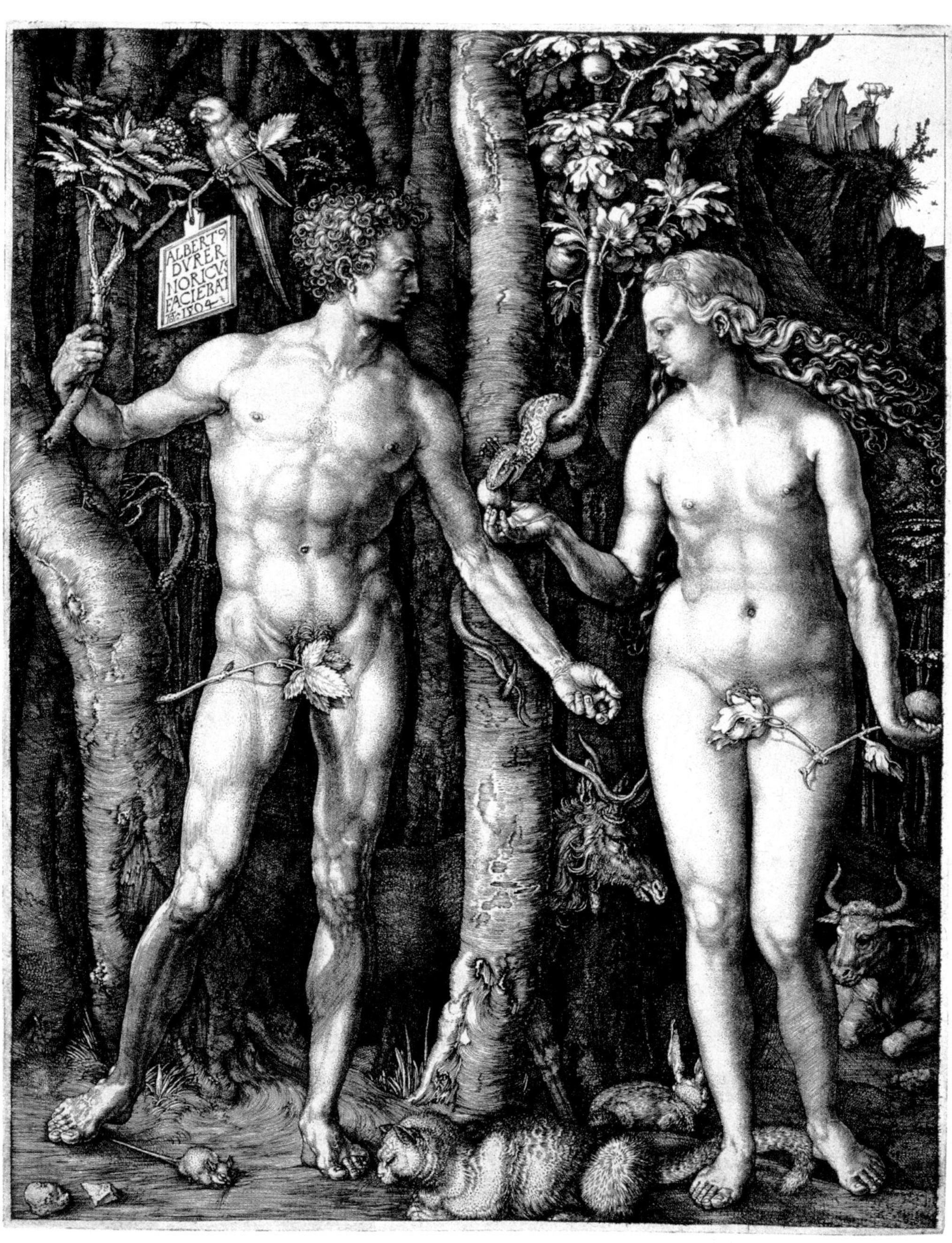

PROVENANCE

W. Edwards (died 1821; Lugt 2616); C. Scarisbruck (1801–1860; Lugt 522, anonymous); J. Malcolm (1805–1893; Lugt 1489), from whom purchased, 1895

SELECTED LITERATURE

Bartsch 1866, no. 1, pp. 30–31; Meder 1932, no. 1, completed plate; Panofsky 1955, no. 108, pp. 84–87; Hollstein 1962, no. 1, pp. 4–5; Strauss 1980, Commentary, no. 1; Jaffé 1993; Landau and Parshall 1994, pp. 311–14; Bartrum 1995, no. 21, pp. 36–37; Schoch, Mende and Scherboum 2001, I, no. 39, pp. 110–13; Schoen 2001, pp. 54–56, 109–12; Bartrum 2002, nos. 86–94, pp. 150–55; Hinz 2006

24, 25 Hans Baldung Grien (1484/5–1545)

The Fall of Man, 1511

Colour woodcut printed from two blocks; the tone block in grey-brown
The outlines of the key block were pricked for transfer.
Some lines have been traced through to the verso in black chalk (?).
The sheet is much damaged, and has been patched in many places.
Trimmed to the edge of the border
Inscribed with the title of the print:
LAPSVS HVMA|NI GENERIS (Fall of the human race);
signed *HGB* and dated *1511* in tablet at bottom left
36.8 × 25.4 cm (to border), 37 × 25.6 cm (sheet)
London, The British Museum, Department of
Prints and Drawings, 1845-8-9-922

Adam and Eve with the Serpent, 1514

Woodcut
Signed *HGB* in tablet at bottom right
22 × 15.3 cm (to border)
London, The British Museum, Department of
Prints and Drawings, 1895-1-22-209

HANS BALDUNG, NICKNAMED GRIEN (Green), was Dürer's most talented pupil. Active as a painter, draughtsman and printmaker, he was one of the more idiosyncratic artists of sixteenth-century Germany. Like Cranach, who also contributed drawings to the Emperor Maximilian's Prayerbook), Baldung had a particular interest in depicting the female form. But while Cranach's women are generally decorous – and decorative – Baldung's representations of women are coloured by his personal fixation with the dangers of female power and sexuality.

The unnerving *Fall of Man* (cat. 24) is dark and filled with foreboding, enhanced by its dark-grey tone. The inscription on the tablet (a device learnt from Dürer: compare to cat. 23) proclaims the fall of the human race. For Baldung, unlike Cranach and Dürer, who show the first couple in a state of Grace, mankind's doom is certain even before Adam and Eve have eaten of the Tree of Knowledge. They have brought it on themselves, unable to control their lustful desires (further symbolised by the two rabbits in the background). This is probably the earliest representation of the Fall as a sexually motivated act. While Dürer and Cranach (compare to cat. 12, 13 and 23 and fig. 6) place Adam and Eve on either side of the tree, Baldung locks them into a lascivious embrace. Baldung's Adam is overcome with longing for his wife, as well as for the fruit of the forbidden tree. He caresses Eve's breasts with one hand, and plucks an apple with his other, unfeasibly long, arm. The couple are of one mind, almost even of one body in their joint intent. A sixteenth-century audience would have been struck by Baldung's representation of Eve's controlling role in this – a further inversion of the natural order. She stands slightly in front of Adam, and dominates the pictorial space. Holding an apple, she looks provocatively out of the print, as if defying the viewer to prevent her and Adam from eating it.

Baldung's slightly later *Adam and Eve with the Serpent* (cat. 25) is also fixated with Eve's evil dominance over Adam. However, it presents a far less unusual interpretation of the Fall. This is probably because it belongs to a series of four woodcuts, contrasting the Fall of Man and the Incarnation of the Virgin Mary, and was intended to be used as a devotional tool. Comparison of the antithetical figures Eve and Mary was a rich vein of late medieval Christianity. While Eve was responsible for the expulsion from Paradise and had doomed mankind, Mary was God's chosen vessel to start the process with which he would redeem humanity. In Baldung's print, Adam and Eve flank the Tree, as is common in representations of the Fall. This takes place in a forest, the usual symbol of primitive paradise in Germanic art (see essay by Susan Foister). The iconography is also absolutely conventional, and emphasises Eve's power over her husband. Adam's passivity is conveyed by his lack of movement and placement in pure profile. He is dwarfed by the powerful and active figure of Eve, who reaches out for an apple and steps forward, as if preparing to offer it to Adam. In keeping with much late medieval belief, Eve is almost identified with the evil serpent, whose body seems to encircle her arm. She becomes the temptress as much as the beast which has tempted her. Although extreme, Baldung's unnuanced representations of female vice reflect a dominant strand of early sixteenth-century culture. Interestingly, this is far less pronounced in Cranach's Eves and Venuses. Even his seductresses maintain a sense of innocence, or at least a desire not to inflict fatal harm.

CMC

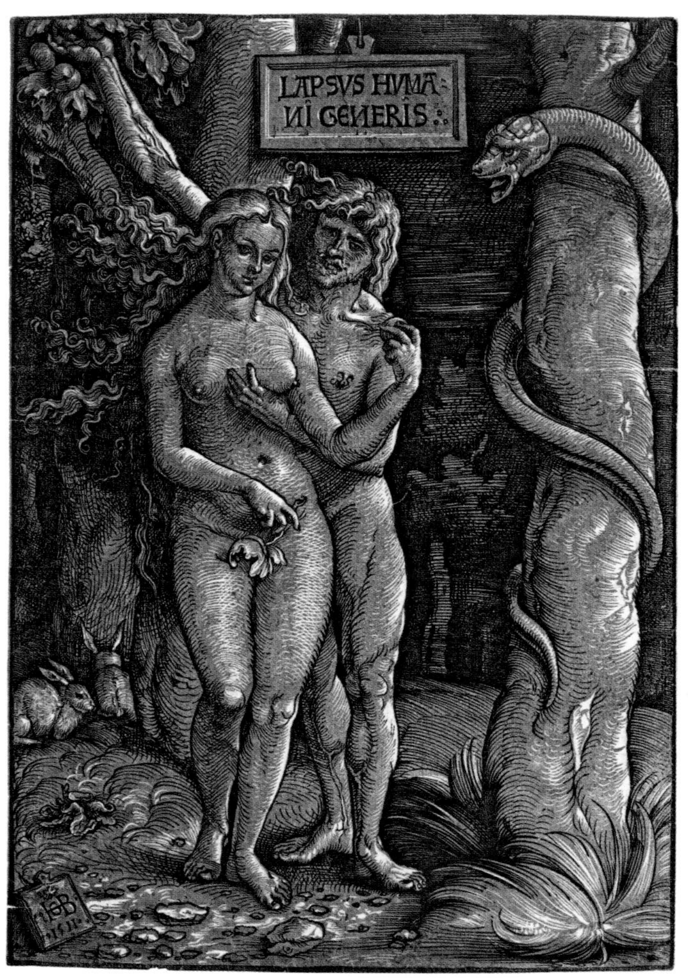

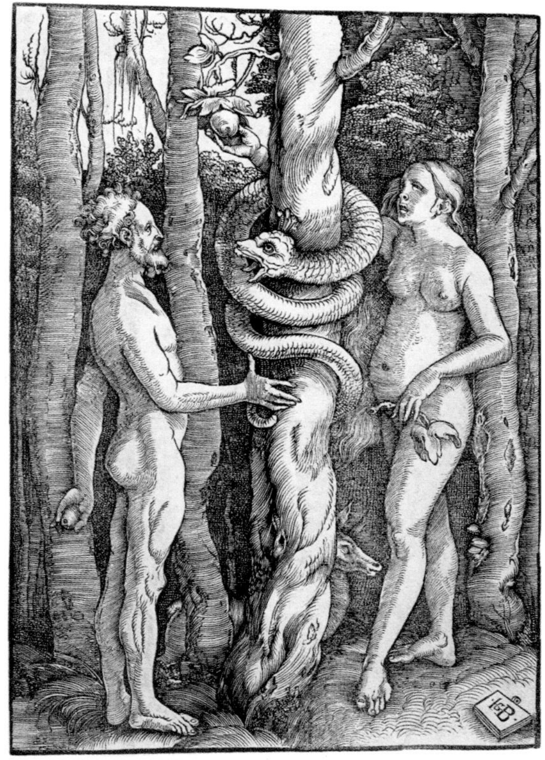

CAT. 24
PROVENANCE
Purchased from Messrs Smith

CAT. 25
PROVENANCE
Presented by William Mitchell, 1895

SELECTED LITERATURE
Bartsch 1866, nos. 3 and 1, pp. 305, 306; Hollstein 1954, no. 3, p. 76, and no. 1, p. 74; Mende 1978, nos. 19 and 33; Marrow *et al.* 1981, pp. 13, 11; Marrow and Shestack 1981, nos. 19 and 38, pp. 120–23; 174-77; Bartrum 1995, no. 58, pp. 71–72 (for cat. 24); Brinckmann 2007, no. 41, pp. 161–63, 214–15

Bibliography

AJMAR AND DENNIS 2006–07: M. Ajmar and F. Dennis, eds., *At Home in Renaissance Italy*, exh. cat., London, Victoria and Albert Museum, 2006–07

ALBERTI 1972: *Leon Battista Alberti, On Painting and On Sculpture. The Latin Texts of De Pictura and De Statua*, edited with translation, introduction and notes by C. Grayson, London, 1972

ANDERSSON AND TALBOT 1983: C. Andersson and C. Talbot, *From a Mighty Fortress: Prints, Drawings and Books in the Age of Luther, 1483–1546*, exh. cat., Detroit, Institute of Arts, 1983

ANZELEWSKY 1971: F. Anzelewsky, *Albrecht Dürer. Das malerische Werk*, Berlin, 1971

ANZELEWSKY 1983: F. Anzelewsky, *Dürer-Studien: Untersuchungen zu den ikonographischen und geistesgeschichtlichen Grundlagen seiner Werke zwischen den beiden Italienreisen*, Berlin, 1983

ANZELEWSKY 1991: F. Anzelewsky, *Albecht Dürer. Das malerische Werk*, Berlin, 1991

ANZELEWSKY 1999: F. Anzelewsky, 'Studien zur Frühzeit Lukas Cranachs d. Ä.', *Städel-Jahrbuch*, vol. 17, 1999, pp. 125–44

ARAGON AND COCTEAU 1957: L. Aragon and J. Cocteau, *Entretiens sur le musée de Dresde*, Paris, 1957

BADSTÜBNER ET AL. 1994: E. Badstübner *et al.*: *Gesetz und Gnade. Cranach, Luther und die Bilder*, exh. cat., Eisenach, Museum der Wartburg, and Torgau, Schloß Hartenfels, 1994

BALIS ET AL. 1993: A. Balis, K. De Jonge, G. Delmarcel and A. Lefébvre, *Les Chasses de Maximilien*, Paris, 1993

BARK 1994: S. Bark, *Auf der Suche nach dem verlorenen Paradies. Das Thema des Sündenfalles in der altdeutschen Kunst (1495–1545)*, Frankfurt am Main, 1994

BARTL AND GÄRTNER 1997: A. Bartl and M. Gärtner, 'Technologische Befunde', in K. Löcher and C. Gries, *Germanisches Nationalmuseum Nürnberg. Die Gemälde des 16. Jahrhunderts*, Stuttgart, 1997, pp. 17–591

BARTRUM 1995: G. Bartrum, *German Renaissance Prints 1490–1550*, exh. cat., London, The British Museum, 1995

BARTRUM 2002: G. Bartrum, *Albrecht Dürer and his Legacy: The Graphic Work of a Renaissance Artist*, exh. cat., London, The British Museum, 2002

BARTSCH 1866: A. Bartsch, *Le peintre graveur*, Leipzig, 1854–70, 21 vols.; vol. 7, Leipzig 1866 (first published Vienna, 1803–21)

BASEL AND BERLIN 1997–98: *Dürer Holbein Grünewald. Meisterzeichnungen der deutschen Renaissance aus Berlin und Basel*, exh. cat., Basel, Öffentliche Kunstsammlung, and Berlin, Kupferstichkabinett der Staatlichen Museen zu Berlin, Preußischer Kulturbesitz, 1997–98

BATH 1992: M. Bath, *The Image of the Stag: Iconographic Themes in Western Art*, Baden-Baden, 1992

BAUCH 1894: G. Bauch, 'Zur Cranachforschung', *Repertorium für Kunstwissenschaft*, vol. 17, 1894, pp. 420–35

BAXANDALL 1980: M. Baxandall, *The Limewood Sculptors of Renaissance Germany*, London and New Haven, 1980

BENZING 1952: J. Benzing, *Buchdrucker-Lexikon des 16. Jahrhunderts (Deutsches Sprachgebiet)*, Frankfurt am Main, 1952

BERLIN 1910: *Zeichnungen alter Meister im Kupferstichkabinett der K. Museen zu Berlin*, II: Deutschland – Niederlande, Berlin 1910

BERLIN 1937: *Cranach Ausstellung. Lucas Cranach d. Ä. und Lucas Cranach d. J. Gemälde, Zeichnungen, Graphik*, exh. cat., Berlin, Deutsches Museum, 1937

BERLIN 1958: *Schätze der Weltkultur von der Sowjetunion gerettet*, exh. cat., Berlin, Staatliche Museen zu Berlin, 1958

BERLIN 1967: *Dürer und seine Zeit. Meisterzeichnungen aus dem Berliner Kupferstichkabinett*, exh. cat., Berlin, Staatliche Museen – Preußischer Kulturbesitz, Kupferstichkabinett, 1967

BERNHEIMER 1953: R. Bernheimer, *Wildmen in the Middle Ages*, Cambridge, 1953

BIERENDE 2002: E. Bierende, ***Lucas Cranach d.Ä. und der deutsche Humanismus. Tafelmalerei im Kontext von Rhetorik, Chroniken und Fürstenspiegeln*** **(Kunstwissenschaftliche Studien 94), Munich and Berlin, 2002**

BIRMINGHAM 1953: *Works of Art from Midland Houses*, exh. cat., Birmingham Museum and Art Gallery, 1953

BISHOP 1937: R. Bishop, *Paintings of the Royal Collection*, London, 1937

BOCK 1921: E. Bock, *Staatliche Museen zu Berlin. Die Zeichnungen Alter Meister im Kupferstichkabinett: Die deutschen Meister. Beschreibendes Verzeichnis sämtlicher Zeichnungen*, M. J. Friedländer, ed., 2 vols., Berlin, 1921

BOMFORD 2002–03: D. Bomford, ed., *Art in the Making: Underdrawings in Renaissance Paintings*, exh. cat., London, National Gallery, 2002–03

BONNET 1992: A.-M. Bonnet, *Der Akt bei Albrecht Dürer*, Munich, 1992

BONNET 1994: A.-M. Bonnet, 'Der Akt im Werk Lucas Cranachs. Bedeutung und Spezifität der "nackten Bilder" innerhalb der deutschen Renaissance-Malerei', in Grimm, Erichsen and Brockhoff 1994, pp. 139–49

BONNET 2001: A.-M. Bonnet, *'Akt' bei Dürer*, Cologne, 2001

BRANDL 1993: R. Brandl, 'The Liesborn Altarpiece: a new reconstruction', *The Burlington Magazine*, vol. 135, 1993, pp. 180–89

BRIQUET: C.M. Briquet: *Les Filigranes. Dictionnaire historique des marques du papier dès leur apparition vers 1282 jusqu'en 1600*, 4 vols., Paris, 1907

BRINKMANN 2007: B. Brinkmann, *Hexenlust und Sündenfall. Die seltsamen Phantasien des Hans Baldung Grien/ Witches' Lust and the Fall of Man. The Strange Fantasies of Hans Baldung Grien*, exh. cat., Frankfurt, Städel Museum, 2007

BUCK 2006: S. Buck, 'Positionen deutscher Zeichenkunst im Gebetbuch Maximilian I.', in I. Lauterbach and M. Stuffmann, eds., *Aspekte deutscher Zeichenkunst*, Munich 2006, pp. 72–84

BUSCH 1973: R. von Busch, *Studien zu deutschen Antikensammlungen des 16. Jahrhunderts*, Tübingen, 1973

CAMPBELL 1985: **S.D. Campbell, ed., *The Malcove Collection. A Catalogue of the Objects in the Lillian Malcove Collection of the University of Toronto*, Toronto, Buffalo and London, 1985**

CAMPBELL 2002: T. P. Campbell, ed., *Tapestry in the Renaissance: Art and Magnificence*, exh. cat., New York, Metropolitan Museum of Art, 2002

CAMPBELL, FOISTER AND ROY 1997: L. Campbell, S. Foister and A. Roy, eds., 'Methods and Materials of Northern European Painting', *The National Gallery Technical Bulletin*, vol. 18, 1997, pp. 6–52

CASTAN 1866: A. Castan., 'Monographie du palais Granvelle à Besançon', in *Mémoires de la sociéte d'émulation du Doubs*, ser. 4, vol. 2, 1866, pp. 73–164

CHARBONNEAU-LASSAY 1940: L. Charbonneau-Lassay, *Le Bestiare du Christ*, Desclée, 1940

CHUDANT 1929: A. Chudant, *Musées de Besançon: Catalogue des peintures et dessins*, Besançon, 1929

CLARK 1977: **K. Clark, *Animals and Men*, London, 1977**

CLARK AND MURRAY 1962: K. Clark (introd.) and P. Murray, *Catalogue of the Lee Collection*, Courtauld Institute Galleries, London, 1962

CLAUS 1994: H. Claus, 'Buchgraphik', in Schuttwolf 1994, vol. 1, pp. 175–201

COHN 1995: M.B. Cohn: 'Retroussage in Cranach's *Penance of St John Chrysostom*', in *Shop Talk: Studies in Honor of Seymour Slive, Presented on his Seventy-fifth Birthday*, Cambridge, MA, 1995, pp. 55–58

COLLINS BAKER 1937: **C.H. Collins Baker, *Catalogue of the Principal Pictures in the Royal Collection at Windsor Castle*, London, 1937**

CROWE AND CALVACASELLE 1877: J.A. Crowe and G.B. Calvacaselle, *The Life and Times of Titian*, 2 vols., London, 1877

CUST 1911: L. Cust, *Notes on Pictures in the Royal Collections*, London, 1911
DAVIES 1913: H. M. Davies, *A catalogue of a collection of early German books in the Library of C. Fairfax Murray*, London, 1913, 2 vols.
DE HAMEL 1986: C. De Hamel, *A History of Illuminated Manuscripts*, Oxford, 1986
DEGEN 1953: K. Degen, 'Die Kreuzigungstafel von Posterstein. Ein wiederaufgefundenes Werk Lucas Cranachs des Älteren', *Zeitschrift für Kunstgeschichte*, vol. 16/2, 1953, pp. 193–202
DEMONTS 1911: L. Demonts, 'Un portrait et un dessin de Lucas Cranach. Acquisitions récentes du Musée du Louvre', *Les Musées de France*, 1911, pp. 18–20
DEMONTS 1937–38: L. Demonts, *Musée du Louvre. Inventaires général des dessins des écoles du Nord, Écoles allemande et suisse*, 2 vols., Paris, 1937–38
DIGBY 1971: G.W. Digby, assisted by W. Hefford, *The Devonshire Hunting Tapestries*, London, 1971
DITTRICH 2004: S. and L. Dittrich, *Lexikon der Tiersymbole. Tiere als Sinnbilder in der Malerei des 14.–17. Jahrhunderts*, Petersberg, 2004
DODGSON 1903–11: C. Dodgson, *Early German and Flemish Woodcuts preserved in the Department of Prints and Drawings in the British Museum*, London, 1903–11, 2 vols.
DODGSON 1933: C. Dodgson, 'Rare Woodcuts in the Ashmolean Museum – I, Dürer and his School', *The Burlington Magazine*, vol. 63, 1933, pp. 23–24
DRESDEN 1937: *Lucas Cranach der Ältere und der Jüngere. Ausstellung von Werken aus dem Besitze der Staatlichen Kunstsammlungen, veranstaltet aus Anlaß der Dresdner Museumswoche von der Staatlichen Gemäldegalerie und dem Staatlichen Kupferstichkabinett*, exh. cat., Dresden, Staatliche Kunstsammlungen, 1937
DRESDEN 1971: *Deutsche Kunst der Dürer-Zeit*, exh. cat., Dresden, Staatliche Kunstsammlungen, 1971
DRESDEN 1992: *Gemäldegalerie Dresden. Alte Meister. Katalog der ausgestellten Werke, anlässlich der Wiedereröffnung der Galerie bearbeitete Auflage*, Leipzig, 1992
DUNKERTON AND SPRING 1998: J. Dunkerton, and M. Spring, 'The Development of Painting on Coloured Surfaces in Sixteenth-century Italy', in A. Roy and P. Smith, eds., *Painting Techniques, History, Materials and Studio Practice* (Contributions to the Dublin IIC Congress, 7–11 September 1998), London, 1998, pp. 120–30
EISLER 1991: C. Eisler, *Dürer's Animals*, Washington DC and London, 1991
ELEN 2004: A.J. Elen, *German Master Drawings from the Koenigs Collection. Return of a Lost Treasure*, exh. cat., Rotterdam, Museum Boijmans Van Beuningen, 2004
ENCYCLOPAEDIA BRITANNICA 1977: *The New Encyclopaedia Britannica*, London, fifteenth edition, 30 vols., 1977
ERASMUS 1979: Desiderius Erasmus, *The Praise of Folly*, translated with an introduction and commentary by C.H. Miller, New Haven and London, 1979
ERICHSEN 1994: J. Erichsen, 'Vorlagen und Werkstattmodelle bei Lucas Cranach', in Grimm, Erichsen and Brockhoff 1994, pp. 180–85
FALK 1980: T. Falk, ed., *The Illustrated Bartsch*, vol. 11, *Sixteenth-Century German Artists: Hans Burgkmair the Elder, Hans Schäufflein, Lucas Cranach the Elder*, New York, 1980
FARR 1987: D. Farr, ed., *100 Masterpieces. Bernardo Daddi to Ben Nicholson. European Paintings and Drawings from the 14th to the 20th Century*, London, 1987
FLECHSIG 1900a: E. Flechsig, *Tafelbilder Lucas Cranachs d. Ä. und seiner Werkstatt*, Leipzig, 1900
FLECHSIG 1900b: E. Flechsig, *Cranachstudien*, Leipzig, 1900
FOISTER 2003: S. Foister, 'Cranachs Mythologien. Quellen und Originaltät', in Schade 2003, pp. 116–29
FRANCIS 1959: H.F. Francis, 'The Stag Hunt by Lucas Cranach the Elder and Lucas Cranach the Younger', *Bulletin of the Cleveland Museum of Art*, vol. 46, 1959, pp. 198–205
FRIEDLÄNDER AND ROSENBERG 1932: M.J. Friedländer and J. Rosenberg, *Die Gemälde von Lucas Cranach*, Berlin, 1932
FRIEDLÄNDER AND ROSENBERG 1978: M.J. Friedländer and J. Rosenberg, *The Paintings of Lucas Cranach*, London, 1978
FRIEDMANN 1980: H. Friedmann, *A Bestiary for St. Jerome*, Washington D.C., 1980
FRYE 1978: R.M. Frye, *Milton's Imagery and the Visual Arts*, Princeton, 1978
GAUS 1971: J.Gaus, 'Die Urhütte. Uber ein Modell der Baukunst und ein Motiv in der Bildenden Kunst', *Wallraf-Richartz Museum Jahrbuch*, vol. 23, 1971, pp. 7–70
GAUTHIER 1901 M.J. Gauthier, 'Le Cardinal de Granvelle et les artistes de son temps', in *Mémoires de la société d'émulation du Doubs*, ser. 7, vol. 6, 1901, pp. 305–51
GEISBERG 1923–29: M. Geisberg, *Der Deutsche Einblattholzschnitt*, Munich, 1923–29, 40 vols.
GIEHLOW 1907: K. Giehlow, *Kaiser Maximilians I. Gebetbuch. Mit Zeichnungen von Albrecht Dürer und anderen Künstlern*, Vienna 1907
GIRSHAUSEN 1937: T.L. Girshausen: *Die Handzeichnungen Lukas Cranachs des Älteren*, Frankfurt am Main, 1937
GLASER 1921: C. Glaser, *Lukas Cranach*, Leipzig, 1921
GLASER 1980: H. Glaser, ed., *Quellen und Studien zur Kunstpolitik der Wittelsbacher vom 16. bis zum 18. Jahrhundert. Mitteilungen des Hauses der Bayerischen Geschichte*, vol. 1, Munich, 1980
GOLDBERG, HEIMBERG AND SCHAWE 1998: G. Goldberg, B. Heimberg, M. Schawe, *Albrecht Dürer. Die Gemälde der Alten Pinakothek*, Munich, 1998
GOLDNER 1988: G. Goldner, L. Hendrix and G. Williams: *European Drawings 1. Catalogue of the Collections, The J. Paul Getty Museum*, Malibu, 1988
GOLLOB 1966: H. Gollob, 'Der Herkules des Wiener Chelidonius von 1515', *Gutenberg-Jahrbuch*, 1966, pp. 284–86
GOW 1988: A.S.F. Gow, *Theocritus*, 2nd edition, 2 vols., Cambridge, 1988
GRATE 1961: P. Grate: 'Analyse d'un tableau', *L'Œil*, Paris, 1961, pp. 30–37, 80
GRIMM, ERICHSEN AND BROCKHOFF 1994: C. Grimm, J. Erichsen and E. Brockhoff, Lucas Cranach. *Ein Maler-Unternehmer aus Franken*, exh. cat., Kronach, Festung Rosenberg, and Leipzig, Museum der bildenden Künste, 1994
HAND AND MANSFIELD 1993: J.O.Hand with the assistance of S.E. Mansfield, *The Collections of the National Gallery of Art Systematic Catalogue. German Paintings of the Fifteenth through Seventeenth Centuries*, Washington DC and Cambridge, 1993
HAMPE 1928: T. Hampe, 'Albrecht Dürer als Künstler und als Mensch. Sein Leben und sein Schaffen', in *Festschrift des Vereins für Geschichte der Stadt Nürnberg*, Nuremberg, 1928, pp. 1–67
HASSIG 1995: D. Hassig, *Medieval Bestiaries. Text, Image, Ideology*, Cambridge and New York, 1995
HEISER 2002: S. Heiser, *Das Frühwerk Lucas Cranach des Älteren. Wien um 1500 – Dresden um 1900*, Berlin, 2002
HELLER 1827: J. Heller, *Das Leben und die Werke Dürers*, 1827
HELLER 1854: J. Heller, *Lucas Cranach's Leben und Werke*, 2 vols., Nuremberg, 1854
HENTSCHEL 1948: W. Hentschel, 'Ein unbekannter Cranachaltar', *Zeitschrift für Kunstwissenschaft*, vol. 2, 1948, pp. 35–42
HESIOD 1954: Hesiod, *Works and Days*, ed. H.G. Evelyn-White, Cambridge, 1954
HEYDENREICH 1998: G. Heydenreich, 'Herstellung, Grundierung und Rahmung der Holzbildträger in den Werkstätten Lucas Cranachs d. Ä.', in Sandner 1998, pp. 181–200
HEYDENREICH 2002: G. Heydenreich, *Painting Materials, Techniques and Workshop Practice of Lucas Cranach the Elder*, University of London, Courtauld Institute of Art, PhD thesis, 2 vols, 2002
HEYDENREICH 2007: G. Heydenreich, *Lucas Cranach the Elder: Painting Materials, Techniques and Workshop Practice*, Amsterdam 2007.
HIEATT 1980: A.K. Hieatt, 'Eve as Reason in a Tradition of Allegorical Interpretation of the Fall', *Journal of the Warburg and Courtauld Institutes*, vol. 43, 1980, pp. 221–26
HIEATT 1983: A.K. Hieatt, 'Hans Baldung Grien's Ottawa "Eve" and its Context, *Art Bulletin*, vol. 65, 1983, pp. 290–304
HIND 1910: A.M. Hind in S. Colvin, ed., *Catalogue of Early Italian Engravings in the British Museum*, London, 1910
HIND 1948: A. M. Hind, *Early Italian Engraving*, London, 1948
HINZ 1994: B. Hinz, '"Sinnwidrig zusammengestellte Fabrikate"? Zur Varianten-Praxis der Cranach-Werkstatt', in Grimm, Erichsen and Brockhoff 1994, pp. 174–79
HINZ 2000: B. Hinz, 'Venus im Norden', in E. Mai, ed., *Faszination Venus, Bilder einer Göttin von Cranach bis Cabanel*, exh. cat., Cologne, Wallraf-Richartz Museum, 2000, pp. 32–49
HINZ 2006: B. Hinz, 'Albrecht Dürer: Adam & Eva – Mann und Weib', in I. Lauterbach and M. Stuffmann, eds., *Aspekte deutscher Zeichenkunst*, Munich, 2006, pp. 39–50
HOLDEN 1974: A. Holden, editor and translator, *Greek Pastoral Poetry*, Harmondsworth, 1974
HOLLSTEIN 1954: F.W.H. Hollstein, *German Engravings, Etchings and Woodcuts, ca. 1400–1700*, vol. 2, *Altzenbach – B. Beham*, Amsterdam, 1954
HOLLSTEIN 1959: K.G. Boon and R.W. Scheller, eds., *F.W.H. Hollstein. German Engravings, Etchings and Woodcuts, ca. 1400–1700*, vol. 6, *Cranach – Drusse*, Amsterdam, 1959

HOLLSTEIN 1962: K.G. Boon and R.W. Scheller, eds., *F.W.H. Hollstein. German Engravings, Etchings and Woodcuts, ca. 1400–1700*, vol. 7, *Albrecht and Hans Dürer*, Amsterdam, 1962

HOPE AND MARTINEAU 1983–84: C. Hope and J. Martineau, eds., *The Glory of Venice*, exh. cat., London, Royal Academy, 1983–84

HOUWEN 1997: L.A.J.R. Houwen, *Animals and the Symbolic in Medieval Art and Literature*, Groeningen, 1997, 20 vols.

JAFFÉ 1993: I. Jaffé, 'The Tell-tale Tail of a Parrot. Dürer's *Adam and Eve*', *Print Collector's Newsletter*, vol. 24, 1993, pp. 52–53

JAHN 1955: J. Jahn, *Lucas Cranach als Graphiker*, Leipzig, 1955

JAHN 1972: J. Jahn, *1472–1553, Lucas Cranach d. Ä.: Das gesamte graphische Werk*, Herrsching, 1972

JAHN AND BERNHARD 1972: J. Jahn and M. Bernhard, *Lucas Cranach d. Ä., Das gesamte graphische Werk. Mit Exempeln aus dem graphischen Werk Lucas Cranach d. J. und der Cranachwerkstatt*, Munich, 1972

JUNIUS 1926: W. Junius, 'Aus der Gefangenschaft des Kurfürsten Johann Friedrich von Sachsen', *Zeitschrift des Vereins für Thüringische Geschichte und Altertumskunde* vol. 34 (26/2), 1926, pp. 226–34

KOCH 1913: F. Koch, ed., *Verzeichnis der Gemäldesammlung des Westfälischen Kunstvereins im Landesmuseum zu Münster*, Münster, 1913

KOEPPLIN 1973: D. Koepplin, *Cranachs Ehebildnis des Johannes Cuspinian von 1502. Seine christlich-humanistische Bedeutung*, diss., Basel, 1973

KOEPPLIN 2003a: D. Koepplin, *Neue Werke von Lukas Cranach und ein altes Bild einer polnischen Schlacht – von Hans Krell*, Basel, 2003

KOEPPLIN 2003b: D. Koepplin, 'Ein Cranach-Prinzip', in Schade 2003, pp. 144–65

KOEPPLIN AND FALK 1974: D. Koepplin and T. Falk, *Lucas Cranach. Gemälde, Zeichnungen, Druckgraphik*, 2 vols., Basel, 1974–76

KOERNER 1993: J.L. Koerner, *The Moment of Self-Portraiture in German Renaissance Art*, Chicago and London, 1993

KOERNER 2004: J.L. Koerner, *The Reform of the Image*, London, 2004

KOLDE 1881: D.T. Kolde, *Friedrich der Weise und die Anfänge der Reformation*, Erlangen, 1881

KOLIND POULSEN 2000: H. Kolind Poulsen, 'Choice and Redemption: On Lucas Cranach the Elder's *Melancholia* in the Statens Museum for Kunst', *Statens Museum for Kunst Journal*, vol. 4, 2000, pp. 40–75

KOLIND POULSEN 2002: H. Kolind Poulsen, *Cranach*, exh. cat., Copenhagen, Statens Museum for Kunst, 2002

KOLIND POULSEN 2003: H. Kolind Poulsen, 'Fläche, Blick und Erinnerung. Cranachs Venus und Cupido als Honigdieb im Licht der Bildtheologie Luthers', in Schade 2003, pp. 130–43

KÖNIG ET AL. 1998: E. König, F. Anzelewsky, B. Brinkmann and F. Steenbock, *Das Berliner Stundenbuch der Maria von Burgund und Kaiser Maximilians. Handschrift 78 B 12 im Kupferstichkabinett der Staatlichen Museen zu Berlin–Preußischer Kulturbesitz*, exh. cat., Berlin, Staatliche Museen zu Berlin – Kupferstichkabinett, 1998

KORENY 1985: F. Koreny, *Albrecht Dürer und die Tier- und Pflanzstudien der Renaissance*, Munich, 1985

KREN AND MCKENDRICK 2003: T. Kren and S. McKendrick, *Illuminating the Renaissance: The Triumph of Flemish Manuscript Painting in Europe*, exh. cat., Los Angeles, The J. Paul Getty Museum, and London, Royal Academy of Arts, 2003

KRISTELLER 1896: P. Kristeller, *Engravings and Woodcuts by Jacopo de' Barbari*, London, 1896

KUNZ 1994: Armin Kunz, 'Gedruckte und andere Heilige: Zur Rolle der Graphik im Werk Cranachs des Älteren', in Tacke 1994, pp. 93–104

LANDAU AND PARSHALL 1994: D. Landau and P. Parshall, *The Renaissance Print 1470–1550*, New Haven and London, 1994

LEBBRAND 1989: J. Lebbrand, *Speculum bestialitatis. Die Tiergestalten der Fastnacht und des Karnevals im Kontext christlicher Allegorese*, Munich, 1989

LEEMAN 1984: F.W.G. Leemann, 'A Textual Source for Cranach's "Venus with the Honey Thief"', *The Burlington Magazine*, vol. 126, 1984, pp. 274–75

LEIDINGER 1922: G. Leidinger, *Albrecht Dürers und Lukas Cranachs Randzeichnungen zum Gebetbuche Kaiser Maximilians I in der Bayerischen Staatsbibliothek zu München*, Munich, 1922

LEVENSON 1978: J.A. Levenson, *Jacopo de' Barbari and Northern Art of the Early Sixteenth Century*, Ann Arbor, 1978

LEVENSON AND OBERHUBER 1973: J.A. Levenson and K. Oberhuber, *Early Italian Engravings from the National Gallery of Art*, exh. cat., Washington DC, National Gallery of Art, 1973

LEVEY 1959: M. Levey, *The German School: The National Gallery Catalogues*, London, 1959

LEVEY 1964: M. Levey, in *The National Gallery Report 1962–64*, London, 1964, pp. 37–38

LEVEY AND WHITE 1961: M. Levey and C. White, 'The German Exhibition at Manchester', *The Burlington Magazine*, vol. 103, 1961, p. 487

LIPPMANN 1895: F. Lippmann, *Lucas Cranach. Sammlung von Nachbildungen seiner vorzüglichsten Holzschnitte und seiner Stiche*, Berlin, 1895

LLOYD 1991: C. Lloyd, *The Queen's Pictures: Royal Collectors through the Centuries*, exh. cat., London, The National Gallery, 1991

LONDON 1946–47: *Catalogue of the Exhibition of the King's Pictures*, exh. cat., London Royal Academy of Arts, 1946–47

LONDON 1977: *Silver Jubilee Exhibition: The Queen's Pictures. The Story of the Royal Collection from Henry VIII to Elizabeth I*, exh. cat., London, The Queen's Gallery, Buckingham Palace, 1977

LONDON 1987: *Picture in Focus: Lucas Cranach's 'Adam and Eve'*, exh. handlist, London, Courtauld Institute Galleries, 1987

LOVEJOY AND BOAS 1935: A.O. Lovejoy and G. Boas, *Primitivism and Related Ideas in Antiquity*, Baltimore, 1935

LÜBBEKE 1991: Isolde Lübbeke, *The Thyssen-Bornemisza Collection. Early German Paintings 1350–1550*, London, 1991

LÜCKE 1998: M. Lücke, 'Die Wittenberger Archivalien zum Leben und Wirken Lucas Cranachs d. Ä.', in Cranach-Stiftung, ed., *Lucas Cranach d. Ä. und die Cranachhöfe in Wittenberg*, Halle, 1998, pp. 11–59

LUCRETIUS 1924: T. Lucretius Carus, *De Rerum Natura*, ed. W.H.D. Rouse, Cambridge, 1924

LUGT: F. Lugt, *Les Marques de collections de dessins et d'estampes*, Amsterdam 1921; *Supplément*, The Hague 1956

LUTHER 1995: *Martin Luthers Fabeln und Sprichwörter*, ed. R. Dithmar, Darmstadt, 1995

MACCULLOCH 2003: D. MacCulloch, *Reformation. Europe's House Divided, 1490–1700*, London, 2003

MANCHESTER 1961: *German Art 1400–1800 from Collections in Great Britain*, exh. cat., Manchester, City Art Gallery, 1961

MARROW AND SHESTACK 1981: J. Marrow and A. Shestack, *Hans Baldung Grien: Prints and Drawings*, Washington DC, National Gallery of Art, and New Haven, Yale University Art Gallery, exh. cat., 1981

MARROW ET AL. 1981: J. Marrow, W.L. Strauss, E. Jacobowitz and S.L. Stephanek, eds., *The Illustrated Bartsch*, vol. 12, *Hans Baldung Grien, Hans Springinklee, Lucas van Leyden*, New York, 1981

MARX 1997: H. Marx, 'Cranach und Dürer. Zur Bildnisfrage bei Cranachs Katharinenaltar von 1506', *Dresdener Kunstblätter*, vol. 41/1, 1997, pp. 11–24

MARX 2005–06: H. Marx , 'Dresden als Cranach-Palast und der "moderne" Cranach', in Marx and Mössinger 2005–06, pp. 89–111

MARX AND MÖSSINGER 2005–06: H. Marx and I. Mössinger, eds., *Cranach. Gëmalde aus Dresden*, Chemnitz, Kunstsammlungen, exh. cat., 2005–06

MATSCHE 1994: F. Matsche, 'Lucas Cranachs mythologische Darstellung', in Grimm, Erichsen and Brockhoff 1994, pp. 78–88

MATSCHE 1996: F. Matsche, 'Humanistische Ethik am Beispiel der mythologischen Darstellungen von Lucas Cranach', in W. Eberhard and A. A. Strnad, eds., *Humanismus und Renaissance in Ostmitteleuropa vor der Reformation*, Cologne, Weimar and Vienna, 1996, pp. 29–69

MCDONALD 2004: M. McDonald, *The Print Collection of Ferdinand Columbus (1488–1539): A Renaissance collector in Seville*, London, 2004

MEDER 1932: J. Meder, *Dürer-Katalog. Ein Handbuch über Albrecht Dürers Stiche, Radierungen, Holzschnitte, deren Zustände, Ausgaben und Wasserzeichen*, Vienna, 1932 (reprinted New York, 1971)

MENDE 1978: H. Mende, *Hans Baldung Grien: Das Graphische Werk: Vollständiger Bildkatalog der Einzelholzschnitte, Buchillustrationen und Kupferstiche*, Unterschneidheim, 1978

MICHAELIS 1989–90: R. Michaelis, 'Studien zum Berliner Weltgerichtsaltar des Lucas Cranach', *Aachener Kunstblätter*, vol. 58, 1989–90, pp. 115–32

MILLAR 1978: O. Millar, *The Queen's Pictures*, London, 1977

MONTOUT 1994: M.H. Montout, *Cranach l'Ancien et le Jeune*, Rheims, 1994

MONTREAL 1953: *Five Centuries of Drawings*, exh. cat., Montreal, Museum of Fine Arts, 1953

MÜLLER 1996: C. Müller, *Kupferstichkabinett der Öffentlichen Kunstsammlung Basel. Beschreibender Katalog der Zeichnungen, Bd. III: Die Zeichnungen des 15. und 16. Jahrhunderts, Teil 2A: Die*

Zeichnungen von Hans Holbein dem Jüngeren und Ambrosius Holbein, Basel, 1996

MÜLLER AND KEMPERDICK 2006: C. Müller and S. Kemperdick, *Hans Holbein the Younger: The Basel Years 1515–1532*, exh. cat., Basel, Kunstmuseum, 2006

MURDOCH 1998: J. Murdoch, ed., *The Courtauld Gallery at Somerset House*, London, 1998

NOBLE 1998: B.-J. Noble, *The Lutheran Paintings of the Cranach Workshop, 1529–1555*, University of Illinois, Evanston, PhD thesis, 2 vols., 1998

OVID 1921: P. Ovidius Naso, *Metamorphoses*, ed. F.J. Miller, Cambridge, 1921

PÄCHT 1986: O. Pächt, *Book Illumination in the Middle Ages. An Introduction*, London, 1986

PANOFSKY 1920: E. Panofsky, 'Dürers Darstellung des Apollo und ihr Verhältnis zu Barbari', *Jahrbuch der Preussischen Kunstsammlungen*, vol. 41, 1920, pp. 359–77

PANOFSKY 1955: E. Panofsky, *The Life and Art of Albrecht Dürer*, Princeton, 1955

PANOFSKY 1969: E. Panofsky, *Problems in Titian, Mostly Iconographic*, New York, 1969

PANOFSKY 1972: E. Panofsky, 'The Early History of Man in Two Cycles of Paintings by Piero di Cosimo', in *Studies in Iconology*, New York, 1972, pp.33–68

PARIS 1936: *L'Aquarelle de 1400 à 1900*, exh. cat., Paris, Musée de l'Orangerie, 1936

PARIS 1965: *Le seizième siècle européen. Peintures et dessins dans les collections publiques françaises*, exh. cat., Paris, Musée du Louvre, 1965

PARIS 1991: *Dessins de Dürer et de la renaissance germanique dans les collections publiques parisiennes*, exh. cat., Paris, Musée du Louvre, Cabinet des dessins, 1991

PAUWELS ET AL. 1965: H. Pauwels, H.R. Hoetink and S. Herzog, *Jan Gossaert dit Mabuse*, exh. cat., Rotterdam, Museum Boijmans Van Beuningen and Bruges, Groeninge Museum, 1965

PÉREZ D'ORS 2005: P. Pérez D'Ors, 'Dos cacerías de Lucas Cranach el Viejo en el Museo del Prado', *Bóletino del Museo del Prado*, vol. 41, 2005, pp. 6–22

PÉREZ D'ORS 2007: P. Pérez D'Ors, 'A Lutheran Idyll: Lucas Cranach the Elder's *Cupid Complaining to Venus*', *Renaissance Studies*, vol. 21, February 2007, pp. 85–98

PÉRIER-D'IETEREN 1994: C. Périer-d'Ieteren, 'La technique de Memling et sa place dans l'evolution de la peinture flamande du XVe siècle', in D. de Vos, ed., *Hans Memling. Essays*, Bruges, 1994, pp. 67–77

PICCARD: G. Piccard, *Die Wasserzeichenkartei Piccard im Hauptstaatsarchiv Stuttgart, hrsg. von der Staatlichen Archivverwaltung Baden-Württemberg, Findbuch I: Die Kronen-Wasserzeichen*, Stuttgart, 1961

PIEPER 1962: P. Pieper, 'Deutsche Kunst 1400–1800. Ausstellung in der City of Manchester Art Gallery', *Kunstchronik*, vol. 15, 1962, pp. 3–4

PLINY THE ELDER 1978: Pliny the Elder, *Naturalis historiae*, Book 35, trans. R. König, Munich, 1978

POSSE 1930: H. Posse, 'Dresdner Cranach-Erwerbungen', *Pantheon*, vol. 3, 1930, pp. 495–500

REYNOLDS 1983: L.D. Reynolds, ed., *Texts and Transmission. A Survey of the Latin Classics*, Oxford 1983

ROBERT 2003: J. Robert, 'Die Wahrheit hinter dem Schleier. Lucas Cranachs heidnische Götter und die humanistische Mythenallegorie', in Schade 2003, pp. 102–15

ROBERTS 2002: J. Roberts, ed., *Royal Treasures*, exh. cat., London, The Queen's Gallery, Buckingham Palace, 2002

ROPER 1989: L. Roper, *The Holy Household: Women and Morals in Reformation Augsburg*, Oxford, 1989

ROSENBERG 1960: J. Rosenberg, *Die Zeichnungen Lucas Cranachs d. Ä*, Berlin, 1960

RUHMER 1963: E. Ruhmer, *Cranach*, London, 1963

RUPPRICH 1956: H. Rupprich, ed., *Dürer. Schriftlicher Nachlaß*, 2 vols., Berlin, 1956

SANDNER 1994: I. Sandner, 'Die Analyse von Unterzeichnungen auf Gemälden mit Hilfe der Infrarotreflektographie am Beispiel von Werken Lucas Cranachs d. Ä.', *Deutsche Gesellschaft für Zerstörungsfreie Prüfung e.V. (Berlin)*, vol. 45, no. 1, 1994, pp. 193–202

SANDNER 1998: I. Sandner, ed., *Unsichtbare Meisterzeichnungen auf dem Malgrund Cranach und seine Zeitgenossen*, exh. cat., Eisenach, Wartburg-Stiftung, 1998

SCHADE 1961–62: W. Schade, 'Zum Werk der Cranach', *Jahrbuch Staatliche Kunstsammlungen Dresden*, 1961–62, pp. 29–49

SCHADE 1963: W. Schade, *Altdeutsche Zeichnungen*, exh. cat., Dresden, Kupferstich-Kabinett, 1963

SCHADE 1972: W. Schade, *Lucas Cranach der Ältere. Zeichnungen*, Leipzig, 1972

SCHADE 1974: W. Schade, *Die Malerfamilie Cranach*, Dresden, 1974

SCHADE 1980: W. Schade (trans. H. Sebba), *Cranach, A Family of Master Painters*, New York, 1980

SCHADE 2003: W. Schade, ed., *Lucas Cranach: Glaube, Mythologie und Moderne*, exh. cat., Hamburg, Bucerius Kunst Forums, 2003

SCHÄFER 1994: B. Schäfer, 'Graphik', in Schuttwolf 1994, I, pp. 95–174

SCHAUERTE 2006: T. Schauerte, ed., *Der Kardinal. Albrecht von Brandenburg, Renaissancefürst und Mäzen*, exh. cat., Halle, Moritzburg, Dom, Residenz, Kühler Brunnen, 2006

SCHEURL 1509: C. Scheurl, *Oratio attingens litterarum praestantiam nec non laudem ecclesiae collegiatae omnium Sanctorum Vittenburgensis, habita in eadem ecclesia decimo sexto kalendas Decembris Anno domini 1508* …, Leipzig, 1509

SCHOCH, MENDE AND SCHERBAUM 2001–04: R. Schoch, M. Mende and A. Scherbaum, *Albrecht Dürer. Das druckgraphische Werke*, 3 vols., Munich, London and New York, 2001–04

SCHOEN 2001: C. Schoen, *Albrecht Dürer. Adam und Eva. Die Gemälde, ihre Geschichte und Rezeption bei Lucas Cranach d. Ä. und Hans Baldung Grien*, Berlin, 2001

SCHOUWINK 1985: W. Schouwink, *Der wilde Eber in Gottes Weinberg*, Sigmaringen, 1985

SCHRÖDER AND STERNATH 2003: K. Schröder and M.L. Sternath, eds., *Albrecht Dürer*, exh. cat., Albertina, Vienna, 2003

SCHUCHARDT 1851–71: C. Schuchardt, *Lucas Cranach d. Ä. Leben und Werke*, 3 vols., Leipzig, 1851–71

SCHUTTWOLF 1994: A. Schuttwolf, ed., *Gotteswort und Menschenbild: Werke von Cranach und seinen Zeitgenossen*, exh. cat., Gotha, Schloßmuseum, 1994, 2 vols.: vol. 1, *Malerei, Plastik, Buchgraphik, Dokumente*

SCHÜTZ 1972: K. Schütz, *Lucas Cranach der Ältere und seine Werkstatt*, exh. cat., Vienna, Kunsthistorisches Museum, 1972

SERVOLINI 1944: L. Servolini, *Jacopo de' Barbari*, Padua, 1944

SEZNEC 1953: J. Seznec, *The Survival of the Pagan Gods*, New York, 1953

SIEVEKING 1987: H. Sieveking, *Das Gebetbuch Kaiser Maximilians. Der Münchner Teil mit den Randzeichnungen von Albrecht Dürer und Lucas Cranach d. Ae. Rekonstruierte Wiedergabe*, Munich, 1987

SILVER 1983: L. Silver, 'Forest Primeval: Albrecht Altdorfer and the German Wilderness Landscape', *Simiolus*, vol. 13, 1983, pp. 4–43

SIMON 1965: E. Simon, 'Die Reliefmedaillons in Hofe des Palazzo Medici zu Florenz, II', *Jahrbuch der Berliner Museen*, vol. 7, 1965, pp. 49–91

SMITH 1985: A. Smith, *The National Gallery Schools of Painting. Early Netherlandish and German Paintings*, London, 1985

SOX 1995: D. Sox, 'Harold Woodbury Parsons, "Marchand amateur"', *Apollo*, vol. 141, 1995, pp. 19–24

STARKEY 1998: D. Starkey, ed., *The Inventory of King Henry VIII*, vol. 1, London 1998

STECHOW 1966: W. Stechow: *Northern Renaissance Art 1400–1600. Sources and Documents*, New York, 1966

STEIGERWALD 1973: F. Steigerwald, *Lucas Cranach. Gemälde – Zeichnungen – Druckgraphik*, exh. cat., Berlin, Staatliche Museen zu Berlin – Preussischer Kulturbesitz, Gemäldegalerie and Kupferstichkabinett, 1973

STOCKHOLM 1988: *Cranach och den tyska renässansen*, exh. cat., Stockholm, Nationalmuseum, 1988

STOGDON 1991–92: N. Stogdon, *German and Netherlandish Woodcuts. Sale Catalogue no. 8*, New York and London, 1991–92

STOICHITA 1997: V.I. Stoichita, *The Self-Aware Image. An Insight into Early Modern Meta-Painting*, translated by A.-M. Glasheen, Cambridge, 1997

STRAUSS 1980: W. Strauss, *The Illustrated Bartsch*, vol. 10. *Sixteenth Century German Artists: Albrecht Dürer*, New York, 1980

STREHLE 2001: J. Strehle, *Lucas Cranach d. Ä in Wittenberg*, Spröda, 2001

STREHLE AND KUNZ 1998: J. Strehle and A. Kunz, *Druckgraphiken Lucas Cranach d. Ä. Im Dienst von Macht und Glauben*, exh. cat., Wittenberg, Luthersalle, 1998

STUTTGART 1993: *Meisterwerke massenhaft. Die Bildhauerwerkstatt des Niklaus Weckmann und die Malerei in Ulm um 1500*, exh. cat., Stuttgart, Württembergisches Landesmuseum, 1993

TACKE 1992: A. Tacke, *Der katholische Cranach*, Mainz 1992

TACKE 1994: A. Tacke, ed., *Cranach. Meisterwerke auf Vorrat. Die Erlanger Handzeichnungen der Universitätsbibliothek*, exh. cat., Erlangen, Universitätsbibliothek, Halle, Moritzburg, and Augsburg, Universitätsbibliothek, Munich, 1994

THÖNE 1939: F. Thöne, *Lukas Cranach des Älteren Meisterzeichnungen*, Burg b. M., 1939

TIMANN 1994: U. Timann, 'Lucas Cranach und der Holzschnitt', in Grimm, Erichsen and Brockhoff 1994, pp. 201–07

TORGAU 2004: *Glaube und Macht. Sachsen im Europa der Reformationszeit*, exh. cat., 2 vols.,Torgau, Sächsische Landesausstellung, Schloss Hartenfels, 2004

VAN DE WETERING 1997: E. van de Wetering, *Rembrandt: The Painter at Work*, Amsterdam, 1997

VAN MANDER 1604: C. van Mander, *Het Schilder-Boeck*, Harlem, 1604

VAN MARLE 1931: R. van Marle, *L'iconographie de l'art profane*, vol. 1, The Hague, 1931

VIRGIL 1934: P. Virgilis Maro, *Aeneid*, ed. H. Rushton Fairclough, Cambridge, 1934

VIRGIL 1935: P. Virgilis Maro, *Eclogues*, ed. H. Rushton Fairclough, Cambridge, 1935

WARNKE 1984: M. Warnke, *Cranachs Luther. Entwürfe für ein Image*, Frankfurt am Main, 1984

WARSAW 1997: *Pod Jedną Koroną Królewskie zbiory sztrki w Dreźnie*, exh. cat., Warsaw, Muzeum Narodowe w Warszawie, 1997

WASHINGTON 1999: *From Schongauer to Holbein. Master Drawings from Basel and Berlin*, exh. cat., Washington DC, National Gallery of Art, 1999

WASHINGTON, NEW YORK AND SAN FRANCISCO: *The Splendor of Dresden: Five Centuries of Art Collecting. An Exhibition from the State Art Collections of Dresden, German Democratic Republic*, exh. cat., Washington DC, National Gallery of Art, New York, The Metropolitan Museum of Art, and San Francisco, California Palace of The Legion of Honor, 1978–79

WATERHOUSE 1953: E.K. Waterhouse, 'Some Notes on the Exhibition of "Works of Art from Midland Houses" at Birmingham', *The Burlington Magazine*, vol. 95, 1953, p. 306

WEIMAR 1972: *Lucas Cranach*, exh. cat., Weimar, Schlossmuseum, 1972

WERNESS 2004: H.B. Werness, *The Continuum Encyclopedia of Animal Symbolism in Art*, New York and London, 2004

WHITE AND PILC 1993: R. White and J. Pilc, 'Analyses of Paint Media', *The National Gallery Technical Bulletin*, vol. 14, 1993, pp. 86–94

WILSON 1999: C.C. Wilson, 'Lucas Cranach the Younger: The 1549 "Adam and Eve" and Related Drawings', *Zeitschrift für Kunstgeschichte*, vol. 62/4, 1999, pp. 534–40

WIND 1938–39: E. Wind, '"Hercules" and "Orpheus". Two mock-heroic designs by Dürer', *Journal of the Warburg and Courtauld Institutes*, vol. 2, 1938–39, pp. 206–18

WOERMANN 1896–98: K. Woermann, *Handzeichnungen alter Meister im Königlichen Kupferstichkabinett zu Dresden*, Munich, 1896–98

WOLTERS 1938: C. Wolters, *Die Bedeutung der Gemäldedurchleuchtung mit Röntgenstrahlen für die Kunstgeschichte*, Frankfurt am Main, 1938

WOOD 1993: C. Wood, *Albrecht Altdorfer and the Origins of Landscape*, London, 1993

ZAMBON 2001: F. Zambon, *L'alfabeto simbolico degli animali*, Milan, 2001

ZERVOS 1950: C. Zervos, *Nus de Lucas Cranach l'Ancien*, Paris, 1950

ZUCKER 1999: M. J. Zucker, *The Illustrated Bartsch*, vol. 24, *Commentary*, *Part 4: Early Italian Masters*, New York, 1999

ZÜLCH 1935: W.K. Zülch, *Frankfurter Künstler 1223–1700*, Frankfurt am Main, 1935

Photographic Credits

CATALOGUE NOS.

2 National Gallery, London
3 The Royal Collection © 2006 Her Majesty the Queen Elizabeth II
4, 10 The J. Paul Getty Museum, Los Angeles
5 Gemäldegalerie Alte Meister, Staatliche Kunstsammlungen Dresden
6 Photo RMN/© Thierry Le Mage
7 © bpk/Kupferstichkabinett, SMB
8, 9, 11 Kupferstichkabinett, Staatliche Kunstsammlungen Dresden
12, 13, 15, 22, 23, 24, 25 © The Trustees of the British Museum, London
14, 16, 17, 18, 21 © The Visitors of the Ashmolean Museum, Oxford
19, 20 © The British Library

FIGURE NOS.

1 © Musée Bonnat, Bayonne – A. Vaquero
2, 4, 13, 25, 30 © The Trustees of the British Museum, London
3, 9, 22, 37 © Kunsthistorisches Museum Wien
5 © Museo Nacional del Prado
6 © Besançon, Musée des Beaux-Arts et d'Archéologie (Photo Charles Choffet)
7 © Albertina, Wien
10, 33, 34 © Courtauld Institute of Art/Tager Stonor Richardson Photography
12, 19 © Munich, Bayerische Staatsbibliothek
14 © The British Library
15, 28 © bpk/Gemäldegalerie, SMB Jörg P. Anders
16 © Hessisches Landesemuseum, Darmstadt
17 © Vienna, Österreichische Nationalbibliothek
18 © The Visitors of the Ashmolean Museum, Oxford
20 National Gallery, London
21, 27 © Blauel/Gnamm
23 © National Gallery London and Rachel Billinge
24, 29 ©LWL-Landesmuseum für Kunst und Kulturgeschichte Münster/Dauerleihgabe des Westfälischen Kunstvereins
26 © bpk/Kupferstichkabinett, SMB
31 © Museum Boijmans Van Beuningen, Rotterdam
32 © Witt Library, Courtauld Institute of Art, London
35 © The State Hermitage Museum, St Petersburg
6 © Stiftung Schloss Friedenstein, Gotha, Schlossmuseum
40 © Museo Thyssen-Bornemisza
41 The J. Paul Getty Museum, Los Angeles

The infrared reflectography carried out on cat. 1 was done using a Hamamatsu UK High Performance 'super infrared' Vidicon Camera C2741-03. The camera was equipped with a Pentax UK C25011 50mm F1.4 MI lens, fitted with C90100 Extension Tubes for correct focal length. An Envin Scientific Limited IR Pass Filter was fitted to the lens. Lighting was provided by Tungsten Halogen Lamps.